The Changing American Family and Public Policy

ANDREW J. CHERLIN
Editor

The Changing American Family and Public Policy

The Changing Domestic Priorities Series

John L. Palmer and Isabel V. Sawhill, Editors

THE URBAN INSTITUTE PRESS
Washington, D.C. 1988

THE URBAN INSTITUTE PRESS
2100 M Street, N.W.
Washington, D.C. 20037

Kathleen A. Lynch
Director
Christopher N. Clary
Publishing Assistant

Editorial Advisory Board

Martha Burt
William Gorham
Stephen B. Hitchner, Jr.
Kathleen A. Lynch
George Peterson
Raymond Struyk
Katherine Swartz

Copyright © 1988. The Urban Institute. All Rights reserved. Except for short quotes, no part of this report may be reproduced or utilized in any form or by any means, electronic or mechanical, including photocopying, recording, or by information storage or retrieval system, without written permission from The Urban Institute Press.

Library of Congress Cataloging in Publication Data
The Changing American Family and Public Policy
Bibliography: p.
1. Family policy—United States. 2. Family—United States.
3. Social change. I. Cherlin, Andrew J., 1948-
HQ536.F3644 1988 306.8'5'0973 88-20484
ISBN 0-87766-422-6
ISBN 0-87766-421-8 (pbk.)

Printed in the United States of America

9 8 7 6 5 4 3 2

Distributed in the United States and Canada by
University Press of America
4720 Boston Way
Lanham, Md. 20706

BOARD OF TRUSTEES
Carla A. Hills
Chairman
Katharine Graham
Vice Chairman
William Gorham
President
Andrew F. Brimmer
Theodore F. Brophy
James E. Burke
John J. Byrne
Albert V. Casey
John M. Deutch
Richard B. Fisher
George J. W. Goodman
Fernando A. Guerra, M.D.
Philip M. Hawley
Michael Kaufman
Robert S. McNamara
David O. Maxwell
Eleanor Holmes Norton
Elliot L. Richardson
William D. Ruckelshaus
David A. Stockman
Anne Wexler
Mortimer B. Zuckerman

LIFE TRUSTEES
Warren E. Buffett
Joseph A. Califano, Jr.
William T. Coleman, Jr.
Anthony Downs
John H. Filer
Joel L. Fleishman
Eugene G. Fubini
Aileen C. Hernandez
Vernon E. Jordan, Jr.
Edward H. Levi
Bayless A. Manning
Stanley Marcus
Arjay Miller
J. Irwin Miller
Franklin D. Murphy
Lois D. Rice
Herbert E. Scarf
Charles L. Schultze
William W. Scranton
Cyrus R. Vance
James Vorenberg

THE URBAN INSTITUTE is a nonprofit policy research and educational organization established in Washington, D.C. in 1968. Its staff investigates the social and economic problems confronting the nation and government policies and programs designed to alleviate such problems. The Institute disseminates significant findings of its research through the publications program of its Press. The Institute has two goals for work in each of its research areas: to help shape thinking about societal problems and efforts to solve them, and to improve government decisions and performance by providing better information and analytic tools.

Through work that ranges from broad conceptual studies to administrative and technical assistance. Institute researchers contribute to the stock of knowledge available to public officials and private individuals and groups concerned with formulating and implementing more efficient and effective government policy.

Conclusions or opinions expressed in Institute publications are those of the authors and do not necessarily reflect the views of other staff members, officers or trustees of the Institute, advisory groups, or any organizations that provide financial support to the Institute.

Advisory Board

Changing Domestic Priorities Project

Bernard E. Anderson, Managing Partner, Urban Affairs Partnership
Richard N. Cooper, Maurits C. Boas Professor of International Economics, Center for International Affairs, Harvard University
Nathan Glazer, Professor of Education and Sociology, Harvard University
Robert H. Haveman, John Bascom Professor of Public Affairs, University of Wisconsin, Madison
Hugh Heclo, Robinson Professor of Public Affairs, George Mason University
Carla A. Hills, Co-Managing Partner, Weil, Gotshal, & Manges
Eleanor Holmes Norton, Professor of Law, Georgetown University
Marvin Kosters, Resident Scholar and Director, Market and Regulation Studies, American Enterprise Institute
Robert D. Reischauer, Senior Fellow, The Brookings Institution
Frank Schiff, Former Vice President and Chief Economist, Committee for Economic Development

THE CHANGING DOMESTIC PRIORITIES SERIES

Titles available in the Changing Domestic Priorities Series

Books

THE REAGAN EXPERIMENT
An Examination of Economic and Social Policies under the Reagan Administration (1982), John L. Palmer and Isabel V. Sawhill, editors

HOUSING ASSISTANCE FOR OLDER AMERICANS
The Reagan Prescription (1982), James P. Zais, Raymond J. Struyk, and Thomas Thibodeau

MEDICAID IN THE REAGAN ERA
Federal Policy and State Choice (1982), Randall R. Bovbjerg and John Holahan

WAGE INFLATION
Prospects for Deceleration (1983), Wayne Vroman

OLDER AMERICANS IN THE REAGAN ERA
Impacts of Federal Policy Changes (1983), James R. Storey

FEDERAL HOUSING POLICY AT PRESIDENT REAGAN'S MIDTERM (1983), Raymond Struyk, Neil Mayer, and John A. Tuccillo

STATE AND LOCAL FISCAL RELATIONS IN THE EARLY 1980s (1983), Steven D. Gold

THE DEFICIT DILEMMA
Budget Policy in the Reagan Era (1983), Gregory B. Mills and John L. Palmer

HOUSING FINANCE
A Changing System in the Reagan Era (1983), John A. Tuccillo with John L. Goodman, Jr.

PUBLIC OPINION DURING THE REAGAN ADMINISTRATION
National Issues, Private Concerns (1983), John L. Goodman, Jr.

RELIEF OR REFORM?
Reagan's Regulatory Dilemma (1984), George C. Eads and Michael Fix

THE REAGAN RECORD
An Assessment of America's Changing Domestic Priorities (1984), John L. Palmer and Isabel V. Sawhill, editors (Ballinger Publishing Co.)

ECONOMIC POLICY IN THE REAGAN YEARS
(1984), Charles F. Stone and Isabel V. Sawhill

URBAN HOUSING IN THE 1980s
Markets and Policies (1984), Margery Austin Turner and Raymond J. Struyk

MAKING TAX CHOICES
(1985), Joseph J. Minarik

AMERICA'S CHILDREN: WHO CARES?
Growing Needs and Declining Assistance in the Reagan Era (1985), Madeleine H. Kimmich

TESTING THE SOCIAL SAFETY NET
The Impact of Changes in Support Programs during the Reagan Administration (1985), Martha R. Burt and Karen J. Pittman

REAGAN AND THE CITIES
(1986), edited by George E. Peterson and Carol W. Lewis

PERSPECTIVES ON THE REAGAN YEARS
(1986), Edited by John L. Palmer

SINGLE MOTHERS AND THEIR CHILDREN
A New American Dilemma (1986), Irwin Garfinkel and Sara S. McLanahan

THE REAGAN BLOCK GRANTS
What Have We Learned? (1986), George E. Peterson, Randall R. Bovbjerg, Barbara A. Davis, Walter G. Davis, Eugene C. Durman, and Theresa A. Gullo

MEDICAID
The Trade-off between Cost Containment and Access to Care (1986), John F. Holahan and Joel W. Cohen

CHALLENGE TO LEADERSHIP
Economic and Social Issues for the Next Decade (1988), Isabel V. Sawhill, Editor

Conference Volumes

THE SOCIAL CONTRACT REVISITED
Aims and Outcomes of President Reagan's Social Welfare Policy (1984), edited by D. Lee Bawden

NATURAL RESOURCES AND THE ENVIRONMENT
The Reagan Approach (1984), Edited by Paul R. Portney

FEDERAL BUDGET POLICY IN THE 1980s
(1984), edited by Gregory B. Mills and John L. Palmer

THE REAGAN REGULATORY STRATEGY
An Assessment (1984), edited by George C. Eads and Michael Fix

THE LEGACY OF REAGANOMICS
Prospects for Long-term Growth (1984), edited by Charles R. Hulten and Isabel V. Sawhill

THE REAGAN PRESIDENCY AND THE GOVERNING OF AMERICA
(1984), edited by Lester M. Salamon and Michael S. Lund

CONTENTS

Tables

Figures

FOREWORD

This book is part of The Urban Institute's Changing Domestic Priorities Series, a collection of volumes that assess the impact and significance of the changes in domestic policy that have occurred under the Reagan administration and analyze the critical economic and social issues facing the nation during the 1980s and beyond.

"Family" policy has come of age. While politicians vie with one another in praise of the family, there is wide disagreement about how government should intervene to help families and, indeed, whether government action has been or can be good or bad for families. The current concern is driven by the dramatic changes in family life in the past quarter century—particularly the increases in divorce and in women working outside the home—and their impact on the nation's children. But although the debate is extensive and frequently heated, little rigorous information has been available to guide it.

This book brings a social science perspective to bear on family change and family policy; identifies the determinants of change; and analyzes the role that government has played and can play in affecting the course of family life. The authors examine the trends from the perspective of children, the perspective of mothers and—the group that has received the least attention—fathers.

Many difficult policy choices affecting the family lie ahead. These choices will be quite specific—on child care, parental leave, child support enforcement, tax policy, welfare reform, and so on. They will be promising only if the participants in the policy debate can understand the fundamental determinants of the changes that have taken place, the difference between trends that can be changed and trends that cannot, and the implications for the well-being of families of the many alternative policies proposed by advocates with different interests and perceptions. This book will help the public, and public policymakers sort out these things wisely.

William Gorham
President

Chapter One

THE CHANGING AMERICAN FAMILY AND PUBLIC POLICY

Andrew J. Cherlin

Everyone, by and large, seems to be in favor of the family these days. Unlike the 1960s and 1970s, when many on the political left criticized the family as a restrictive, oppressive, and even outdated institution, today few observers anywhere in the American political spectrum have a bad word to say about it. As a result, supporting the family ought to be as uncontroversial as supporting hot dogs and apple pie. Yet there is much debate about the family, and it remains a political issue. The controversy stems from widespread concern about the dramatic changes that have transformed the family lives of ordinary Americans over the past few decades: foremost among them the great increase in work outside the home among married women, including mothers of young children, and the sharp rise in divorce. The concern extends to politicians and policymakers, who now issue position papers and draft legislation on family-related matters that a generation ago would have been thought too private for public debate.

In this volume, the contributors bring a social scientific perspective to bear on family change and its implications for public policy. The chapters that follow examine the evidence from government statistics, national surveys, historical materials, comparative studies, and other sources to assess the meaning of what Samuel H. Preston, in a widely cited article, called "the earthquake that shuddered through the American family in the past 20 years."[1] As will be noted later in this chapter, the aspect of family life that probably is of most concern to policymakers is the impact of recent changes on the lives of children. Although this topic has been widely discussed, few comprehensive assessments of the well-being of children exist.

In chapter 2, Nicholas Zill and Carolyn C. Rogers present a thorough analysis of recent trends in children's economic situation, physical health, academic achievement, social behavior and attitudes, and emotional well-being. Some of the themes of their chapter are elaborated on by Frank F. Furstenberg, Jr., and Gretchen Condran, who, in chapter 3, examine whether declines in adolescent well-being can be traced to the family.

But social change has also altered the lives of mothers and fathers in important ways. In chapter 4, Cynthia Fuchs Epstein discusses the consequences for women of the great changes in gender roles at home and in the workplace. Less attention has been paid to the changes in the lives of fathers, an omission that Frank F. Furstenberg, Jr., seeks to remedy in chapter 5. Finally, Mary Jo Bane and Paul A. Jargowsky examine, in chapter 6, the implications of all these changes for public policy, and they explore the role that government has played—and could play in the future—in affecting the course of family life.

To be sure, some of the attention to the family by politicians in the 1980s has been less a debate over issues than a contest over who likes the family more. This struggle over vague symbols reached its nadir during the 1984 presidential campaign. Mario Cuomo, in his much acclaimed keynote address to the Democratic convention in San Francisco, urged the party to defend "the family of America." Walter F. Mondale, in his acceptance speech, told how his parents "taught me the values I've carried ever since." In Dallas, Ronald Reagan boasted to the assembled Republicans, "We didn't set a weathervane on top of the Golden Gate Bridge before we started talking about the American family." Yet both sides shied away from specifics for fear of losing the votes of certain groups—employed women, socially conservative men, or housewives. In a fitting summation, the *New Yorker* published a cartoon depicting a candidate standing behind a podium and saying, "Vote for *me*—a man with over three dozen known family values."

Though this contest continues, the debate over the family has since turned gradually from symbols to substance. This movement was evident in two political documents produced in 1986. In September, the Democratic Policy Commission, under the auspices of the Democratic National Committee, issued a statement of principles, the first of which was "stronger families." Noting the "rise of the two-wage-earner family and the single-parent family," the statement called for parental work leaves for infant care, expanded child care choices, flexible work hours, and similar measures to ease the strain on working parents.[2]

Two months later, a Reagan administration task force sent a report on the family to the president that proclaimed, "We are all pro-family now." The report praised parents who stay home to raise children and called for a large increase in the personal tax exemption for dependents. As will be noted later, the exemption is essentially a child allowance—a program that gives more money to parents with dependent children. Unlike expanded child care benefits, an increased tax exemption would provide more money to all eligible households, whether or not the mother works outside the home.[3]

In the past few years, numerous bills have been introduced in Congress concerning family-related programs, including increased support for child care services, parental leave legislation, tougher child support enforcement, changes in dependent care tax credits, and welfare reforms. Regardless of which of these bills become law, it appears that the debate over the family has finally moved beyond generalities to confront specific, difficult policy choices. And it is likely that this debate will persist into the 1990s.

This volume seeks to provide useful background information for persons who wish to be informed about the issues in the current debate. Throughout the volume, the emphasis is on encouraging a broad understanding of the consequences of social change and their relationship to public policy, rather than on endorsing specific programs or taking sides in the debate. To do the latter requires the analyst to make value judgments that lie outside the proper bounds of social science. Nevertheless, our contributors are not indifferent, and they have been encouraged to step back and examine the implications of their findings and interpretations for public policy.

In this introductory chapter, I briefly review the changes in the American family since the 1950s. Then I discuss what, in my view, these changes have meant for children and parents and what the implications are for public policy. Along the way, I refer frequently to the subsequent chapters in the volume, but any conclusions and interpretations are mine alone.

FAMILY CHANGES

In any consideration of the changes that have occurred since the 1950s, it is important to remember that the 1950s were probably the most unusual decade for family life in this century. For example, it was the only period in the past 150 years when the birthrate rose substantially; in the 1950s young adults married at earlier ages than in any twentieth-century decade before or since; and the increase in divorce was unusually low.[4] Although many people think of the

1950s family as "traditional," the falling birthrates, rising divorce rates, and increasing age at marriage of the 1960s and 1970s were more consistent with long-term historical trends.

Marriage, Childbearing, and Divorce

Since the 1950s there has been a steady, upward movement in age at marriage. In 1960 the median age at marriage for women was 20.3; in 1984 it was 23.0. As a result, 57 percent of women ages 20 to 24 in 1984 had never married, compared with 28 percent in 1960.[5] A similar increase in marriage age has occurred for men. Moreover, there has been a sharp increase in the number of unmarried couples living together—from about a half-million in 1970 to about 2 million in the mid-1980s. These two phenomena—the postponement of formal marriage and the rise in cohabitation—have led some observers to question whether the institution of marriage is weakening. But studies suggest that for most young adults, cohabitation is a stage in a courtship process that still leads to marriage. Moreover, the overwhelming majority of men and women will eventually marry, probably 85 to 90 percent of all women and a higher percentage of all men.[6] Although these percentages are lower than those in the unusual 1950s, they suggest that marriage remains a central aspect of adult life.

What has occurred, nevertheless, is an increasing separation of marriage and childbearing. As Zill and Rogers report in chapter 2, only 4 percent of all births in 1950 were to unmarried mothers, but by 1984 the figure was 21 percent. The level of out-of-wedlock births is particularly high in the black population, among whom nearly 59 percent of all births were to unmarried mothers in 1984. But even among white, non-Hispanics in 1984, 13 percent of all births were to unmarried mothers, up sharply from 2 percent in 1950.

Contrary to popular belief, the rate at which unmarried women bear children has gone down for blacks and has increased modestly for all whites except teenagers since 1970. But the *proportion* of births occurring out of wedlock has increased for two reasons: (1) The rate of childbearing has declined even faster for married women than for unmarried ones; (2) It is more socially acceptable now for a single woman to bear a child without marrying the father.

More generally, women are bearing fewer children than in the 1950s. Women who entered adulthood just after World War II had three children, on average. If current rates do not change, young adult women will average about 1.8. In Western Europe, where current birthrates are even lower, the fear of declining population size has prompted some governments to act to increase the number of births. Here in the United States the issue is just beginning to emerge, but our population will continue to increase into the twenty-first century because of the size of the baby boom cohort and immigration.

In addition, the divorce rate roughly doubled between the early 1960s and the mid-1970s. Since then, however, the divorce rate has been on a plateau—albeit a high-altitude one. At current rates, about half of all first marriages would end in divorce. And because a majority of people who divorce will marry again, perhaps one-third of all persons who entered adulthood in the 1970s will eventually marry, divorce, and remarry.[7] The causes of the rise in divorce are not well understood, but they include the increasing economic independence of women, societywide attitudinal shifts, and possibly the relatively unfavorable labor market position of the large numbers of young men from the baby boom generation.

As a result of these changes, the family life course of adults and children has changed greatly since the 1950s. Instability and diversity have increased for adults and children. In 1985, 23 percent of all families with children under age 18 were maintained by a single parent, usually the mother. Most of the growth of single-parent families is due to the rise in divorce; a second factor is the rise in the proportion of births occurring out of wedlock. If current rates continue, about half of all children will spend some time in a single-parent family before they reach age 16. And of those children whose parents divorce and remarry, about half will experience a second disruption before they reach 16.[8]

Women's Labor Force Participation

A related change in the family since the 1950s is the great rise in the number of married women in the labor force. Unlike the trends in marriage, divorce, and family size, which have followed a roller-coaster pattern of ups and downs, the march of mothers into the labor force has been steady and relentless. Even during the family-oriented 1950s married women were increasingly taking jobs outside the home. By 1986, 61 percent of currently married women with children under age 18 were in the labor force compared with 41 percent in 1970 and 24 percent in 1950. Among currently married women with children under age 6, the labor force participation rate stood at 54 percent in 1986, compared with 30 percent in 1970 and

12 percent in 1950.[9] During the 1950s the sharpest increases occurred among mothers of school-age children; in the 1960s and 1970s mothers of preschoolers had the highest rate of increase; and in the 1980s mothers of very young preschoolers have had the highest increase. By 1986, half of all mothers with children age 1 or younger were in the labor force.[10]

Thus, in the post-World War II years women have moved from a pattern in which paid work was either forgone upon marriage or interrupted until the children were in school to a pattern of nearly continuous paid work. About 76 percent of married female workers with children ages 6 to 17 work full time, and 61 percent of those with children under 6 work full time.[11] The greater prevalence of part-time work among women than among men has implications, to be discussed later, for the kinds of child care programs that might be designed.

What brought about this momentous change in women's lives? Because a similar trend has occurred in every developed country, explanations that focus on factors specific to the United States, such as the policies of particular administrations or peculiar characteristics of American postwar culture, are inherently suspect. What we have seen represents no mere shift in American attitudes. Nor can we ascribe this change to short-term macroeconomic conditions. Married women's labor force participation increased in the 1950s and 1960s even though inflation rates were low and productivity and men's wages were rising steadily.

What has happened is that the "cost" of staying home, in terms of forgone earnings, has increased for mothers. That is, women now face better employment opportunities and enjoy higher wages than in the past. To be sure, women workers still earn less, on average, than men. But the important point is that women can expect to earn more than they used to. The demand for women workers has been fueled by the expansion of the service sector, where many occupations have become typed as women's jobs. Moreover, with lower birthrates and longer life expectancies women can no longer expect that child care responsibilities will occupy most of their adult lives.

This is not to say that attitudinal shifts and financial pressures had no effects. At some point during the past few decades, being an employed mother became socially acceptable, perhaps even expected. At some point, enough couples may have bought houses by pooling two incomes to drive prices beyond the easy reach of single-earner couples. But the movement of married women into the paid labor force is an ineluctable trend that is deeply embedded in the growth and development of the United States and all other industrialized nations. It is a movement that may become even stronger as projected labor force shortages make women an increasingly important component of the supply of workers. And as such, it is difficult to see how this movement, which has continued unabated for decades, can be reversed.

The conclusion that working mothers are not going to return home—that, on the contrary, their attachment to the labor force is likely to grow—has profound implications for public policy. Although there are still some people who mourn the loss of the single-earner, "family wage" system so common in the 1950s and who believe its reinstatement would be beneficial, the evidence suggests that the prospects for reinstatement are slim. There will be no return to the 1950s, barring cataclysmic disruptions such as depressions and world wars. Yet social adjustments to this change—in the hours of work and school, for example—are occurring slowly. Right now societal ambivalence about working women prevents these adjustments from occurring, although most observers agree, whether enthusiastically or grudgingly, that mothers are in the labor market to stay.[12]

CHILDREN, MOTHERS, AND FATHERS

What are the consequences of the changes in divorce and employment for the lives of children and their parents? The question of whether children have been harmed is crucial, because society has an interest in the rearing of the next generation. Our government has long regulated the rearing of children in ways almost no one would question any more, such as the way they must be educated and the extent to which they can work for wages. If changes in the family can be shown to have significantly harmful effects on children, then reasonably broad support for government intervention might develop. Moreover, to some extent, adults freely choose their family situations and can therefore be assumed to benefit from those choices. For example, at least one ex-spouse is presumably happier after a divorce; many, if not most, employed mothers derive satisfaction from their work, and all derive income. Of course, there are important constraints on adults' decisions about work and family roles, but children can be said to have no choices at all, and it is not clear that they fully share the benefits that their parents may gain from a divorce, from a job, or even from additional income. If certain costs are being imposed on children by recent family changes, some public intervention on their behalf might be justified.

Children's Lives

Two important questions about the consequences for children need to be answered: Has the well-being of children declined? And can these declines, if any, be linked to family-related behaviors such as the growth of single-parent families or the employment of mothers? Unfortunately, the evidence on these issues is far from definitive, and reasonable people might make differing interpretations. Nevertheless, the following conclusions seem warranted: In some important respects, children are less well off than two decades ago. But only a portion of the decline in the well-being of children can be attributed to increasing marital instability or out-of-wedlock childbearing, and little or none of the decline can be clearly linked to the increasing number of mothers working outside the home.

With respect to family income, on average, children are better off than they used to be. After adjusting for inflation and changing family size, the mean family incomes of children increased 46 percent between 1962 and 1983. The increase occurred because of rising real incomes prior to 1973 and because of falling birthrates, which resulted in smaller families and hence more income per child. But during the same period, the gap widened between the family incomes of poorer children and of better-off children.[13] It is this growing inequality of income, reflected in the increase since 1973 in the proportion of children in poverty (20 percent in 1985, according to Zill and Rogers in chapter 2), that has generated concern. The rise in marital disruption and in the proportion of out-of-wedlock births worsened the economic position of children by increasing the number of single-parent families, whose incomes grew slowly. At the same time, the growth in the number of working mothers—by increasing the number of two-earner families—helped the economic position of children.

The economic harm to children from parental divorce occurs because fathers generally earn more than mothers, but children remain with their mothers in about 90 percent of divorces. In the first year after divorce the living standard of women drops, on average, 30 percent, whereas the living standard of men actually rises 10 to 15 percent.[14] The drop is sharpest for women and children in families that are relatively well off before divorce. This pattern suggests that middle-class families in which the husband has high earnings and the wife's labor market experience is limited suffer the largest declines. For example, in one national survey, the Panel Study of Income Dynamics (PSID), white children in families with predivorce incomes above the median experienced a 38 percent decline in living standards in the year after the divorce.

Nevertheless, few better-off children plunge below the poverty level as a result of divorce. Yet for children in families that are just getting by, a parental divorce often means a fall into poverty. Among white children in the same study who were in families with predivorce incomes below the median, 14 percent were poor before the divorce, but 41 percent were poor in the year after the divorce. And although this dramatic increase in poverty lasted only a year or two for most, five years later 18 percent of these children were still poor.[15]

In principle, fathers could compensate their ex-wives and children by providing adequate child support payments. But child support payments tend to be low and unreliable. In a 1985 Bureau of the Census survey, only 48 percent of mothers who were supposed to receive child support payments reported receiving the full amount, 26 percent received partial payment, and 26 percent received nothing.[16] In addition, the average amount received is modest (about $2,200 per year), and child support awards are rarely indexed for inflation.

Many divorced women, especially those who are relatively young and less educated, improve their economic position by remarrying. The addition of male income has a substantial effect: five years after the divorce, women in the PSID who had remarried had a standard of living nearly equal to divorced men or intact married couples. Yet even for women who remarry, there is likely to be an interval of a few years when the mother and her children have a lower income, and a few years can be a long time in the life of a child.

The breakup of a marriage also can cause emotional troubles for children. Observers agree that the experience of a parental divorce is initially traumatizing for nearly all children involved. But most children appear to recover eventually and resume normal emotional and cognitive development.[17] National surveys suggest that the long-term effects are moderate for most children, although more severe for children whose parents divorce when they are quite young (see chapters 2 and 3). Only a minority of children appear to suffer long-term negative emotional consequences from divorce.

Does the fact of having an employed mother harm the development of children? Hundreds of studies have succeeded mainly in demonstrating how difficult it is to give a simple answer to this question. The studies suggest that the effects, if any, depend on a host of factors, such as social class, race, the mother's desire to work or not to work, and the age and sex of the child. Moreover, there still are few studies of the effects of various day care arrangements on children. Researchers agree on a few important characteristics by which to judge day care programs; the level of training or experience of the care givers, the number of children per care giver, and the stability of the arrangements. But beyond these factors, themselves not well understood, these is little agreement about what does, and does not, constitute satisfactory child care.

The conclusion of a National Academy of Sciences panel that reviewed the research on maternal employment was that no consistent negative or positive effects on children's well-being could be found. In some specific circumstances, the panel reported, there is evidence of beneficial effects (for example, on poor, minority children and possibly on girls); in other circumstances there is evidence of harmful effects (possibly on boys from middle-class families); and in many circumstances there is no evidence of any substantial effects one way or the other.[18] Overall, the research to date, although far from satisfactory or definitive, does not show pervasive, harmful effects on children. Thus there is little basis for lumping the employment of mothers with other family behavior such as divorce, teenage childbearing, and family violence that nearly always produces short-term, if not long-term, stress for children.

In other measures of children's well-being reported by Zill and Rogers (chapter 2) the trends appear mixed. American children are healthier than ever, but the rate of improvement in health has slowed in recent years. The infant mortality rate (the proportion of children who die before their first birthday) has declined steadily from about 30 per 1,000 births in the late 1940s to about 10 per 1,000 currently. And the death rate for children ages 1 to 14 continued to fall over the past decade to about 34 per 1,000 children. Moreover, parents are better educated: in 1969 there were 3.7 births to women with less than twelve years of schooling for every birth to a college-educated woman; by 1984 the ratio had fallen to 1.3 births to women with less than twelve years of schooling for every birth to college-educated women. Children seem to benefit intellectually from having better-educated parents and from having fewer siblings with whom to divide parental attention.[19]

Still, there have been some disturbing trends in other domains.

As is well known, the average scores of college-bound high school students on the Scholastic Aptitude Test declined substantially between the 1960s and the 1980s. But it is not at all clear that this decline can be linked to family change. According to the leading study, "two-thirds to three-quarters" of the initial decline between 1963 and about 1970 was a compositional effect caused by a more diverse college applicant pool—that is, larger proportions of students were taking the test and thus diluting the quality.[20] After 1970, however, compositional effects accounted for only about one-fourth of the continuing decline. The report speculates that the rest of the fall could stem from a number of factors, including a reduced emphasis on competence in reading and writing and a diminished "seriousness of purpose" in the schools, the effect of television, and changes in the family.

As for trends in the social behavior of children and adolescents, there is no question that a number of indicators worsened between the early 1960s and the mid-1970s, but it is also important to note that most of the trends have leveled or reversed since the mid-1970s. For example, juvenile arrest rates increased 41 percent between 1965 and 1975 but since then have remained stable or declined slightly. Suicide rates among young people between the ages of 15 and 19 more than doubled between 1960 and the late 1970s but have not risen much since. A similar pattern is evident for marijuana use and premarital sexual activity. In general, the indicators of antisocial or potentially self-injurious behavior in chapter 2 show that although levels are higher now than in the early 1960s, nearly all the increases had occurred by the late 1970s.

In any assessment of the causes of these trends, it is important to consider their timing. In a widely quoted 1986 article, demographers Peter Uhlenberg and David Eggebeen described these trends in adolescent well-being and hypothesized that the deterioration was due to the increased participation of mothers in the labor force and to the increase in marital instability.[21] But they presented no direct evidence linking trends in adolescent behavior to mothers' employment or divorce. Zill and Rogers question this link and, in chapter 3, Furstenberg and Condran argue in more detail that this explanation for the trends does not fit the facts.

Consider the labor force participation rates of mothers with children ages 6 to 17. Between 1965 and 1975, while indicators of adolescent well-being were deteriorating, the labor force participation rate for this group of women rose from 42 percent to 52 percent. So far, so good for the Uhlenberg-Eggebeen hypothesis. But between

1975 and 1985, when the rate rose from 52 percent to 67 percent, the indicators remained stable or improved. Moreover, during the quiescent 1950s, the rate rose from 27 percent to 39 percent. It is difficult to see how this steady increase in mothers' employment since World War II could have caused a decline in adolescent well-being only during one 15-year period but not before or since. Thus, the evidence linking an increase in employed mothers to declining adolescent well-being is weak.[22]

Although it is plausible that changes in the family have had adverse effects on the well-being of children, there is little convincing evidence to support this proposition. To be sure, such links are difficult to substantiate. Moreover, the emotional trauma and frequent income losses that occur in the immediate aftermath of a parental divorce must be at least temporarily detrimental to children. And the existence of child care arrangements of low quality, a standard that is hard to define, may be harmful to an unknown number. But with these important caveats, the case against the family has not been proved. It appears that the effects of divorce on children's emotional and cognitive well-being may be less serious than had been feared. And it appears likely that for many children—possibly for most children—having a mother who works outside the home is not detrimental.

Women's Lives

The movement of married women into the labor force and the trends in marriage, divorce, and fertility have certainly altered the lives of American women. The most common status for American women with children under age 18 in the 1980s is to be both married and working outside the home.[23] There were 13.8 million such women in 1985. But housewives have not disappeared: 10.2 million married mothers of children under age 18 who were not working outside the home in 1985.

There were also 6 million women with children under age 18 who were maintaining their own families in 1985. About 1 out of 10 was widowed and 2 out of 10 had never married; but most—about 7 out of 10—were separated or divorced.[24] The increase in marital dissolution since the 1960s means that it is quite common for women to live for a time as separated or divorced single parents. As already noted, many women—especially older, middle-class women—experience a declining standard of living at least temporarily after the dissolution of a marriage. Yet it must also be said that the greater freedom to end an unhappy marriage undoubtedly has been beneficial to some women, such as those whose husbands were physically abusive. For younger mothers with employment experience, a divorce is not necessarily an economic disaster, and it may have psychological benefits that compensate for any economic loss.

Nearly two-thirds of all mothers (including the married and the unmarried ones) with children under age 18 are employed outside the home.[25] The most tangible benefit of work outside the home is, of course, the additional income it provides. For white married couples in 1985, the median income was $25,307 when the wife was a full-time homemaker compared with $36,992 when she was in the labor force. The comparable figures for black couples were $15,129 and $30,502.[26]

Beyond income, employment can also bring greater self-esteem and self-confidence, although it can also bring increased feelings of pressure and anxiety. The rapidly growing research literature suggests that whether the net contribution of employment to women's psychological well-being is positive or negative depends on two factors: whether the woman wants to work outside the home and whether she receives adequate support from her family, her employer, and other institutions.

For example, sociologists who interviewed a national sample of married women in 1978 reported that the least depressed women were of two kinds: those who were employed and preferred to be and those who were not employed and preferred not to be. Wives who were employed but did not want to be were significantly more depressed, and the most depressed of all were those who were not employed but wanted to be.[27] As the preference for employment increases among women,[28] working outside the home would be expected to become a source of improved well-being for more women. But the second factor, support from others, is still problematic. In a 1976 national sample of white, married couples, sociologists compared indicators of mental health among employed wives and nonemployed wives. They found that employed wives whose husbands shared the child care tasks at least equally showed better levels of mental health than nonemployed wives, whereas employed wives who continued to do more of the child care showed worse levels of mental health.[29]

Most studies still find that the husbands of employed women spend only slightly more time on family care than do the husbands of stay-at-home wives. This situation leaves many employed wives (and most single mothers) facing the so-called double burden of work and family responsibilities. Although employed women tend to reduce the time they spend on child care and housework, their total time spent on obligatory activities increases. In a sample of families with children in metropolitan Toronto in 1980, wives who had full-time jobs and children age three or younger spent more than 10 hours a day, on average, on paid work, child care, and housework combined. In contrast, similar wives who were not employed spent about 8½ hours a day on all tasks. The extra effort came out of the leisure time of employed wives: they spent 1½ hours a day, on average, on leisure pursuits, while wives who were not employed averaged more than 2½ hours for leisure. Nor did the husbands of employed women contribute much more than those of nonemployed women. Consistent with other studies, the husbands of women who were employed full-time averaged 57 minutes a day of housework, a minimal increase over the 43 minute average for husbands whose wives did not work outside the home.[30]

Evidence such as this led the author of a recent book to argue that the lack of assistance by husbands, employers, and government has resulted in "a lesser life" for women who combine working and rearing children.[31] But these tensions are not inevitable; rather, as Epstein argues in chapter 4, they reflect the persistence of social norms and social institutions that were established when the majority of mothers stayed home. Most husbands still leave most of the family chores to their wives, and most employers still run their businesses on the assumption that someone is available to deal with family responsibilities—leading to the refrain that what every employed woman needs most is a wife. If the current set of social arrangements were altered—and there are indications that changes are occurring slowly[32]—it might become less stressful for women to combine work and family roles. The large number of mothers, both married and single, who are employed—about 17.5 million in 1985—suggests why combining employment and family responsibilities has become a central family issue of the 1980s. The implications for public policy are discussed later.

Men's Lives

The behavior of American fathers is a paradox. On the one hand, men are feeling freer to involve themselves emotionally in fatherhood. This was strikingly confirmed in 1986 with the publication of *Fatherhood*, a slim volume by entertainer-educator Bill Cosby, that sold more than 2 million copies in hard cover and became the fastest selling general nonfiction book in the history of U.S. publishing. Cosby's book, and the many others like it, serve to legitimate fatherhood as a role in which men can take pride. "Just what *is* a father's role today?" asks Cosby. And after listing some tasks that most fathers cannot do well, like cooking, he continues: "The answer, of course, is that no matter how hopeless or copeless a father may be, his role is simply to *be* there, sharing all the chores with his wife. Let her *have* the babies, but after that, try to share every job around."[33]

As noted earlier, however, few fathers share every job around, even when their wives work outside the home. The amount of work men do in the home has been slow to increase. And the statistics on child support already mentioned suggest that a large number of divorced men are failing to support their children. One national survey found that half the teenagers living with their divorced mothers had not seen their fathers in the past year; only one-sixth saw their fathers as often as once a week on the average.[34] Moreover, more men than women remarry, so that many men migrate from one family to another (see chapter 5).

What we have seen, then, is the emergence of two contrasting visions of fatherhood, what Furstenberg calls in chapter 5 the "good dad–bad dad complex." Fathers feel freer to be involved with their children, and some are; they also feel freer to leave, and many do. The emergence of this dual pattern, writes Furstenberg, may be rooted in the declining division of labor in the home. The separation of the work place from the home, which occurred during industrialization, created a more rigid division of responsibilities. Fathers began to specialize almost exclusively on economic responsibilities, at the expense of their day-to-day contact with their children. But with the contemporary movement of married women into the labor force, the division of labor has become less rigid. Although fathers are encouraged to become equal partners at home, they are no longer the sole source of economic support and thus may feel freer to end their marriages.

To be sure, not all divorces are initiated by men. The improved labor market opportunities for women—especially for women with high education and extensive work experience—have allowed more unhappy wives to leave their husbands.[35] (It is difficult to determine the proportions of divorces that are initiated by men or by women, because ex-spouses often develop contradictory accounts of the events that occurred.) Nevertheless, women are still more constrained by the economic risks of divorce because most husbands have greater earning potential than their wives and because child support payments tend to be modest and irregularly paid.

Fatherhood, in essence, has become more of a voluntary activity.

Fathers can choose to play a greater role or no role at all. In the 1950s, in contrast, strong social pressure forced men to accept the responsibility of supporting their wives and children (although these pressures also discouraged men from doing much child care).[36] Since then, the strictures have weakened, because of an ideology of personal liberation or the rising employment rates and wages of women.

Men are not necessarily better off because of these changes. To be sure, the "good dads" may benefit emotionally from closer ties to their children, and the "bad dads" may escape from financial responsibilities. But a number of studies suggest that the 1950s style of marriages were good for men's health and well-being: married men lived longer, had fewer illnesses, and had a greater sense of well-being than did unmarried men.[37] The question remains as to whether marriage today is as good a deal for men as it was during the heyday of the breadwinner–homemaker marriage. The gains from the easing of the breadwinner burden have probably been more than offset by the increasing pressures to do more around the home and the loss of services and support from busier working wives. Nonetheless, marriage still provides men with an emotional anchor that they need—perhaps increasingly so, according to one study.[38] Yet some men may be able to satisfy these emotional needs from a series of two or three long-term relationships as well as they can from a lifelong marriage.

FAMILY CHANGE: IS THERE A ROLE FOR GOVERNMENT?

How should public policy respond to the changes in the family that have just been reviewed? The disturbing trends in the well-being of children and adolescents appear to be only loosely connected to increasing marital dissolution; yet it is clear that many children experience a sharply lowered standard of living following a parental separation and that most experience at least short-term emotional trauma. Children with adequate child care arrangements appear unlikely to be harmed by having a mother who works outside the home; but many children do not have adequate arrangements. And there is the strain on employed women who must maintain multiple roles without much social or institutional support. These problems—the economic consequences of divorce, the adequacy of child care arrangements, and the strain on employed mothers—are, at the least, worth public attention. Some possible responses are examined in the following pages.

Child Support Enforcement

The lack of compliance with court-ordered child support payments gives strong justification for expanded efforts to compel absent fathers to pay adequate levels of support. Over the past several years a broad consensus has emerged in favor of such efforts. Conservatives tend to see these measures as enforcing traditional family obligations, whereas liberals tend to see them as providing assistance to women and children. The widespread concern about child support enforcement led to the passage of the Child Support Enforcement Amendments of 1984 (42 U.S. Code Section 651), which will probably improve the level of compliance with court-ordered child support payments. The amendments require the states to establish procedures under which child support payments are to be withheld from the wages of the noncustodial parent if the payments are delinquent one month. The legislation also requires the states to establish commissions that will set statewide standards for child support payments.

Moreover, the legislation authorized an experimental system in Wisconsin. Under this program, which began in July 1987, the amount of child support is determined as a simple percentage of the noncustodial parent's gross income: 17 percent for one child, and 25, 29, 31, and 34 percent for two, three, four, and five or more children, respectively. The obligation is automatically withheld from the noncustodial parent's paycheck, as is done with payroll taxes. In four Wisconsin counties, children are to receive either the amount paid by the noncustodial parent or an assured amount set by the state—whichever is larger.[39] Although such an approach is similar to current practice in several European countries,[40] it represents an innovation for the United States.

Child Allowances

Beyond child support enforcement, there are few generally agreed upon proposals concerning family problems. Some believe that greater financial resources should be made available to all parents who are rearing children. To this end, they advocate raising the value of the personal tax exemption for dependent children only.[41] The value of the personal exemption has eroded substantially relative to the rise in real income over the past few decades. The 1986 Reagan administration report endorsed the goal of eventually raising the exemption from its current level of about $2,000 to $4,000 to $5000.[42] This proposal is essentially a variation on the child allowances granted in most other Western countries. Because it would assist all families with children, it would help hard-pressed single-parent families and employed parents who cannot afford the cost of satisfactory child care. But because of its neutrality toward the employment of mothers, it appeals to people who believe that public policy ought to encourage—or at least not discourage—the formation of single-earner, breadwinner–homemaker families.

But child-allowance-like programs have some serious drawbacks. The first is cost. Because benefits are spread so broadly, the program would be expensive. According to an estimate by Espenshade and Minarik, doubling the personal exemption for dependent children from $2,000 to $4,000 would cost about $19 billion per year.[43] At a time of concern over budget deficits, the price tag alone could discourage enactment of such a program. In addition, there is no guarantee that the benefits would accrue to children. We can only assume that parents would spend their additional income in a way that would benefit the family as a whole. Moreover, because a tax exemption is worth more to wealthier families, who are taxed at a higher rate, much of the benefit would accrue to children from middle- and upper-income families.

Child Care

Other proposals would provide support only for child care services provided by nonfamily members. These proposals lack the universality of a child allowance, in that no assistance is provided to parents who care for their own children. But they have the virtue of ensuring that the funds will be spent on the care of children.

■ *CURRENT POLICIES*

The federal government currently funds several child care programs, but, with the exception of the Dependent Care Tax Credit, all are restricted to children from low-income families. According to one estimate, expenditures for child care for low-income families totaled $2.1 billion in 1986, a 50 percent reduction from the amount spent in 1980.[44] Largely as a result of budget cuts in 1981, federal expenditures on care for children from low-income families failed to keep pace with inflation in the 1980s.

In contrast to the declining expenditures on low-income children, the cost of the Dependent Care Tax Credit increased from $956 million in 1980 to $3.4 billion in 1986.[45] The credit allows families to deduct part of their child care expenses from their income taxes, but the percentage that can be deducted is larger for low-income families. Nevertheless, all families can deduct at least 20 percent (up to a maximum of $480 for one child and $960 for two or more children). More than six million families, about half of them with incomes under $25,000, are estimated to have used the credit in 1983.[46] However, low-income families with no tax liability—whose numbers have grown as a result of the 1986 tax reform—receive no benefit from the tax credit.

■ *PROPOSED POLICIES*

Some proposals would seek only to alter the flow of benefits under the Dependent Care Tax Credit. Such proposals would eliminate benefits to upper-income families, thus producing a savings to the Treasury which would then be made available to the states as child care vouchers for low- and moderate-income families.[47] This approach would provide assistance to poor families with no tax burden.

More ambitious proposals would seek to expand the supply of care givers, to improve the quality of care, and to subsidize the cost for low- to middle-income families at a price of several billion dollars in federal and state funds. In one current version, most of the funds would be provided to the states to help families with incomes below a cutoff point to purchase child care. Each state could determine the method of assistance, which could include vouchers for parents or grants for providers. The rest of the funds would be used by the states to pay administrative costs, to train child care workers, to establish information and referral services, and to bring child care centers and family day care homes up to federal standards.[48]

■ *POLICY ISSUES*

In any consideration of the more ambitious proposals, it is important to assess the current supply of child care services available to working parents. It is clear that the supply of day care centers and private nursery schools has increased substantially since the 1970s.[49] These facilities primarily serve children of ages three to five. What is less clear is the supply of so-called family day care homes, in which a person (often a mother with her own children) cares for young children in her home. It is estimated that 60 percent of such homes are unlicensed and unregistered, thus constituting a vast gray market of possibly a million homes. Family day care is heavily used by parents of infants and one-year-olds, the very group of mothers whose labor force participation has increased most rapidly in the past decade. Yet the limited information that exists suggests that the growth in family day care homes has lagged behind the growth in centers and nursery schools. Thus, it seems plausible that the supply of care givers for very young preschool children has not kept pace with the demand. The adequacy of the supply for older preschool children is harder to judge.

There is also general concern about the quality of care provided in existing settings, particularly in family day care homes. Because of the lack of regulation, it is up to the parents to determine whether a potential care giver runs a safe, satisfactory home. Occasional newspaper stories about children who are abused or killed in fires in unsafe, overcrowded homes suggest that finding good care may be difficult. Nevertheless, beyond physical comfort and safety, there is little agreement or evidence, as already noted, about just what constitutes adequate care. Obviously, a higher ratio of care givers to children is preferable to a lower ratio, and a stable arrangement is preferable to a shifting series of settings. Other things being equal, trained, experienced care givers probably provide better care.

Difficult trade-offs exist among availability, quality, and cost. All proposals require that family day care providers register with the state in order to receive payments. And some proposals would move quickly to bring all providers into compliance with existing regulations and eventually to enforce new, and presumably tougher, federal health and safety standards. Yet even the requirement that all providers be registered might in itself raise the price of care. It is suspected that much of the income earned by family day care providers is not reported to the Internal Revenue Service (IRS), an arrangement that holds down the price. Many of the newly registered providers might conclude that it is too risky to hide income from the IRS anymore. And stricter standards would probably raise the price further. In the absence of a substantial infusion of new funds, the supply of care givers might decline. A two-tiered system might evolve, consisting of a higher-priced, regulated market in which vouchers are accepted and a lower-price, unregulated market in which only cash is accepted.

Similarly, it is well known that workers at licensed day care centers are hired at low wages, often the minimum wage. The low wages contribute to frequent staff turnover and to concern about the quality of the care givers. Some proposals would seek to increase salaries for child care givers. This goal would probably benefit children by improving the quality and stability of care. But it would also substantially raise costs in this labor-intensive enterprise, especially if coupled with stricter rules about staff-to-child ratios. The point of this discussion is not that care should be unregulated and wages low, but rather that the trade-offs need to be thought through carefully.

Another issue concerns the settings that should be used to provide child care. Currently a wide range of care situations exist: in a 1982 census survey of employed women with preschool-age children, 43 percent reported that they relied primarily on care by relatives, 22 percent reported that their child was cared for in a family day care home, and only 15 percent reported that their child attended a nursery school or day care center.[50] As already mentioned, many parents of very young children use family day care; so do many parents of school-age children who need after-school or vacation care. Center and nursery school care predominates for children ages three though five.[51] The widespread use of family day care for infants and toddlers appears to reflect, in part, the parents' preferences and, in part, constraints of availability (few centers will accept children under age two) and cost. But group care appears to be widely acceptable for children age three and older.

There has been growing attention to the possibility of using public schools as the site for the care and early education of three- to five-year-olds as well as after-school care for older children. In the early nineteenth century preschools were common in some states: in 1840, 40 percent to 50 percent of all three-year-olds in Massachusetts were enrolled in public or private school.[52] But in this century, there has been little interest in education for three- and four-year-olds until recently. Schools are attractive settings for several reasons. They are established, universal institutions, and their programs would probably be open to all children, regardless of the parents' employment status. They have existing physical plants that are becoming underutilized because of the decline in birthrates. They are the logical location for after-school programs and perhaps summer vacation programs as well. Moveover, most school funds are raised by state and local taxes. Presumably, any new initiatives would continue this mode of funding, thus making smaller demands on the federal budget than would be the case with a national program of vouchers and subsidies to parents and providers.

Nevertheless, school settings might pose some difficulties. The salaries of teachers and school custodians are far higher, on average, than those of day care workers; pressure to raise the salaries of the latter would probably increase. As noted, this pressure might have the salutary effect of raising the quality of care, but it might also raise the price substantially. In addition, a heavy reliance on school-based programs would do nothing to relieve the problems of the supply and quality of infant and toddler care, which may be more serious.

A final issue concerns who should pay the cost of any new child care programs. The use of public funds would result in a transfer from childless adults to those with children. The principle that education is a public good that everyone should pay for has long been accepted. But should people without children be asked to subsidize the care of preschool-age children as well? An argument could be made that the bearing and rearing of children represent a public good, especially in an era of below-replacement birthrates, and that people who delay or forgo childbearing have a social responsibility to assist those who become parents.

A more difficult question is whether a married couple in which one partner has chosen to stay home with the children should subsidize the cost of care for the children of two-earner families. On average, two-earner families have higher incomes and have experienced more favorable income growth during the past several decades than have other families.[53] Thus, it is hard to argue that all such families should receive direct public subsidies for child care. A stronger case can be made for subsidizing two-earner families in the lower portion of the income distribution and single-parent families of modest means as well. It could be argued that their employment is necessary to give their children a decent standard of living and that their children ought not to suffer inadequate care as a result.

The Responsive Workplace

Another set of programs and proposals seeks to alter the conditions of work, through efforts to be undertaken both by government and by corporations, so that the workplace is more responsive to the family obligations of employees. Perhaps the best known of such innovations is flexible working hours, which were permitted for 14 percent of all nonfarm, wage and salary workers in the United States in 1985.[54] (In a metropolitan Toronto study, mothers who were working flexible hours reported feeling substantially less pressed for time.)[55] In addition to offering flexible hours, a small but growing number of firms in this country, probably about 2,000 to 3,000, offered their employees some kind of child care assistance in the mid-1980s. Most of this assistance took the form of information and referral services, small discounts at selected local child care centers, or flexible benefit plans. Under the latter, employees can take part of their fringe benefits in child care assistance; in some version, employees can set aside part of their salary in a fund that can be used to pay for child care in tax-free dollars.

Information services can make it easier for employees to find satisfactory child care, although such services do little to increase the supply of care or to help employees pay for it. The salary reduction and flexible benefit plans provide financial assistance at little cost to the employer; but such plans mainly assist higher-income workers, who can afford temporary reductions in take-home pay and who pay a higher marginal tax rate. Most workplace reforms are limited to large firms; small employers cannot or will not provide them.[56] Overall, reforms initiated by firms can help employees to better integrate their work and family obligations, but expectations about the extent and effects of corporate reform should be modest. Few firms have on-site child care centers, and the reports on those that do are mixed.

In part because corporate initiatives are likely to be modest, some advocates of change in the workplace look to government for action. One program being debated would provide employed parents with leave for infant care, some form of which is provided in most Western nations. Infant care leave might significantly ease the strain on new parents and their newborn children, but its implementation is not without difficulties. The length of the leave specified in recent bills seems to have arisen from political compromise rather than from studies of child development. An advisory panel of child development specialists and policy analysts convened by the Yale Bush Center in Child Development and Social Policy in 1985 recommended a six-month leave, and even their reports leave unclear why this exact length was chosen.[57] Moreover, even if the leave is to be unpaid, the costs of hiring replacements or making do with fewer workers are likely to be passed along in the form of higher prices, especially by small firms that cannot adjust easily to the loss of an employee. Some observers worry that employers will discriminate against women of childbearing age if parental leave is mandated. Others charge that only middle-class, married women will be able to take an unpaid leave. Thus, what looks at first like a straightforward way to help parents care for infants has become a controversial issue.

Unintended Consequences

According to another school of thought, the government should do nothing about family problems because government action only makes social problems worse. The 1986 Reagan administration report warned that "the indirect impact of government activity is often more important than its intended effect."[58] It cited the unanticipated economic consequences for women and children of the movement toward no-fault divorce, and it argued that "the fabric of family life has been frayed by the abrasive experiments of two liberal decades."[59]

What can be said about this argument with respect to the issues presented in this chapter? Should the unanticipated consequences of say, expanded child care or parental leave programs be of concern here? Despite the warnings, it can be argued that fundamental family trends such as changes in divorce, marriage, and birthrates are little affected by government social or economic policies. For example, although no-fault divorce may have decreased wives' bargaining power in divorce settlements, a number of studies in the United States and Western Europe have demonstrated that the introduction of no-fault divorce laws did not increase the rate of divorce over what it otherwise would have been.[60] Rather, it appears that changes in the law ratified existing changes in people's attitudes and behavior.

One can also cite the experiences of such East European nations as Romania and Czechoslovakia, which have attempted to boost their low birthrates by providing substantial economic incentives and, in the case of Romania, outlawing nearly all forms of contraception and abortion. In 1966, the Romanian government banned abortion, restricted access to contraceptives, and instituted a whole range of special benefits and preferences for parents. The birthrate shot up temporarily in 1967, but it has since declined to pre-1967 levels. The Czechoslovak government has provided exceptional financial incentives: in 1981 a family with three children received family allowances that amounted to 53 percent of the average manufacturing wage. But these huge subsidies have only modestly affected the birthrate.[61] It seems reasonable to conclude that any feasible child care program or family allowance in the United States would be unlikely to influence the birthrate very much in either direction.

It is possible that there could be some further labor supply response to increased child care assistance. In two Census Bureau surveys, 13 percent to 17 percent of nonemployed women responded that they would look for work or return to work "if satisfactory child care were available at reasonable cost."[62] But it is hard to know what "satisfactory child care" and "reasonable cost" meant to the respondents. And as has been noted, married women's labor force participation has been increasing steadily and rapidly over the past few decades despite the lack of government child care programs that reach beyond the poor. This rise is rooted in basic changes in our society and hence is unlikely to be modified substantially by government action. Moreover, opinions differ about whether further increases of female workers would be detrimental: feminists and policymakers concerned about economic competitiveness and the size of the gross national product might welcome a faster increase.

Bane and Jargowsky argue in chapter 6 that "family support policies such as day care and parental leave may substantially affect the lives of families and children. They may be well justified in terms of these benefits. The evidence suggests, however, that they should not be expected to bring about much change in family structure or behavior." This conclusion is a double-edged sword. On the one hand, it implies that policymakers need not worry about the unintended consequences of potential programs. On the other hand, it implies that the direct effects on family trends are likely to be smaller than some advocates believe. For example, those who hope that expanded child care programs might help raise the U.S. birthrate will probably be disappointed.[63] Rather, what child care programs might do is provide a better environment for children and some relief to overburdened working mothers.

CONCLUSIONS

The policies discussed in this volume are likely to be debated in the months and years ahead. Perhaps because the pace of change in families has finally slowed, we now seem ready as a society to make the necessary adjustments. As to exactly what these adjustments imply for government policy, reasonable people can and will disagree. However, here are a few general observations that seem broadly applicable to the current debate:

□ The reality is that large and increasing numbers of married women will probably remain at work outside the home. Whether this trend is welcomed as good for women and good for the economy or whether it is acknowledged with regrets about the passing of the breadwinner–homemaker family, its acceptance must be the cornerstone of any realistic family policy

□ The benefits of family-oriented policies should not be overpromised or oversold. These policies are unlikely to solve problems such as antisocial and self-destructive behavior among adolescents, below-replacement birthrates, or the sluggish growth of labor productivity. They are even unlikely to solve fully the problems to which they are directly addressed, such as providing adequate child care and reducing the strain on employed mothers, although they may make substantial progress toward easing these more limited problems.

□ The flip side of observation 2 is that the unanticipated consequences of government programs on the structure of American families are likely to be modest. Trends in marriage, divorce, childbearing, and women's labor force participation respond to long-term economic and cultural shifts and are unlikely to be altered significantly by any feasible programs of the type discussed in this chapter. It is more useful to focus attention instead on the direct, intended consequences of the policies under consideration.

□ Government can provide valuable symbolic leadership. One of the most important aspects of any child care, child allowance, or parental leave legislation would be to send a signal to corporate and community leaders that the needs of children (and of their parents) deserve more attention. Such a symbolic shift by political leaders would help legitimate these needs and would hasten the nongovernmental adjustments that must be made.

This chapter appears in a somewhat altered form as chapter 5, "The Family," in Isabel V. Sawhill, ed., Challenge to Leadership: Economic and Social Issues for the Next Decade *(Washington, D.C.: Urban Institute Press, 1988. My thanks to Laurence E. Lynn, Jr., Isabel Sawhill, and Timothy Smeeding for comments on earlier versions.*

Notes

1. Samuel H. Preston, "Children and the Elderly: Divergent Paths for America's Dependents," *Demography* 21 (1984): 435–57. See also "Children and the Elderly in the United States," *Scientific American* (1984): 44–49.

2. E.J. Dionne, Jr., "Family and Ethics Are Bywords in '86 Races," *New York Times* (September 28, 1986), 1.

3. Gary L. Bauer, "The Family: Preserving America's Future," Report of the Working Group on the Family (Washington, D.C.: U.S. Department of Education, Office of the Under Secretary, November 1986).

4. Andrew J. Cherlin, *Marriage, Divorce, Remarriage* (Cambridge, Mass.: Harvard University Press, 1981).

5. U.S. Bureau of the Census, "Marital Status and Living Arrangements: March

1984," *Current Population Reports*, Series P- 20, no. 399, Washington, D.C. (August 1985); and U.S. Bureau of the Census, *Historical Statistics of the United States, Colonial Times to 1970*, Washington, D.C., 1975.

6. Cherlin, *Marriage, Divorce, Remarriage*; and David E. Bloom and Neil Bennett, "Marriage Patterns in the United States, Discussion Paper No. 1147," (Cambridge, Mass.: Harvard Institute of Economic Research, April 1985).

7. Cherlin, *Marriage, Divorce, Remarriage*.

8. Larry L. Bumpass, "Children and Marital Disruption: A Replication and Update," *Demography* 21 (1984): 71–82.

9. Nancy S. Barrett, "Women and the Economy," in Sara E. Rix, ed., *The American Woman 1987–88: A Report in Depth* (New York: W.W. Norton, 1987), 100–49; and *Economic Report of the President* (Washington, D.C., January 1987).

10. *Economic Report of the President*, 1987.

11. Ibid.

12. For a grudging acceptance, see Allan C. Carlson, "What Happened to the 'Family Wage'?" *Public Interest* 83 (1986): 3–17.

13. Robert Haveman, Barbara L. Wolfe, Ross Finnie, and Edward N. Wolff, "The Well-Being of Children and Disparities among Them over Two Decades: 1962–1983," in John L. Palmer, Timothy M. Smeeding, and Barbara B. Torrey, eds., *The Well-Being of the Aged and Children in the United States: Intertemporal and International Perspectives* (Washington, D.C.: Urban Institute Press, 1988).

14. Greg J. Duncan and Saul D. Hoffman, "Economic Consequences of Marital Instability," in Martin David and Timothy Smeeding, eds., *Horizontal Equity, Uncertainty, and Economic Well-Being* (Chicago: University of Chicago Press, 1985).

15. Ibid.

16. U.S. Bureau of the Census, "Child Support and Alimony: 1985," *Current Population Reports*, Series P-23, no. 152, Washington, D.C., August 1987.

17. Cherlin, *Marriage, Divorce, Remarriage*.

18. Sheila B. Kamerman and Cheryl D. Hayes, eds., *Families that Work: Children in a Changing World* (Washington, D.C.: National Academy Press, 1982).

19. Judith Blake, "Family Size and the Quality of Children," *Demography* 18 (1981): 421–42.

20. Advisory Panel on the Scholastic Aptitude Test Score Decline, "On 38 Further Examinations" (New York: College Entrance Examination Board, 1977).

21. Peter Uhlenberg and David Eggebeen, "The Declining Well-Being of American Adolescents," *Public Interest* 82 (1986): 25–38.

22. Nevertheless, it is true that the period of deterioration in indicators of adolescent well-being, roughly the early 1960s to the mid-1970s, corresponded to the period in which the U.S. divorce rate increased sharply, as already described. But the effect on teenagers should have peaked several years after the rise in divorce because most divorces occur early in marriage. The very large number of young children who experienced parental divorce in the 1960s and early 1970s entered adolescence in the late 1970s and 1980s. Yet the indicators of well- being had leveled off by then.

23. Cherlin, "Women and the family," in Rix, ed., *The American Woman*: 67–99.

24. U.S. Bureau of the Census, "Household and Family Characteristics: March 1985," *Current Population Reports*, Series P-20, no. 411, Washington, D.C., 1986.

25. Cherlin, "Women and the Family."

26. U.S. Bureau of the Census, "Consumer Income," *Current Population Reports*, Series P-60, no. 156, Washington, D.C., 1987.

27. Catherine E. Ross, John Mirowsky, and Joan Huber, "Dividing Work, Sharing Work, and In-Between: Marriage Patterns and Depression," *American Sociological Review* 48 (1983): 809–23.

28. Andrew Cherlin, "Postponing Marriage: The Influence of Young Women's Work Expectation," *Journal of Marriage and the Family* 42 (1980): 355–65.

29. Ronald C. Kessler and James A. McRae, Jr., "The Effect of Wives' Employment on the Mental Health of Married Men and Women," *American Sociological Review* 47 (1982): 216–27.

30. William M. Michelson, *From Sun to Sun: Daily Obligations and Community Structure in the Lives of Employed Women and Their Families* (Totowa, N.J.: Rowman and Allanheld, 1985).

31. Sylvia Ann Hewlett, *A Lesser Life: The Myth of Women's Liberation in America* (New York: William Morrow, 1986).

32. See Cherlin, "Women and the Family."

33. Bill Cosby, *Fatherhood* (New York: Doubleday, 1986), 61.

34. Frank F. Furstenberg, Jr., Christine Winquist Nord, James L. Peterson, and Nicholas Zill, "The Life Course of Children of Divorces, Marital Distruption and Parental Contact," *American Sociological Review* 48 (1983): 656–68.

35. For evidence linking higher earning potential for married women with higher probabilities of divorce, see Andrew Cherlin, "Work Life and Marital Dissolution," in George Levinger and Oliver C. Moles, eds., *Divorce and Separation: Context, Causes and Consequences* (New York: Basic Books, 1979), 151–66: and Heather L. Ross and Isabel V. Sawhill, *Time of Transition: The Growth of Families Headed by Women* (Washington, D.C.: Urban Institute Press, 1975).

36. Barbara Ehrenreich, *The Hearts of Men: American Dreams and the Flight from Commitment* (New York: Anchor Press, 1983).

37. Jessie Bernard, *The Future of Marriage* (New York: World Publishing Co., 1972).

38. Joseph Veroff, Elizabeth Douvan, and Richard A. Kulka, *The Inner American: A Self-Portrait from 1957 to 1976* (New York: Basic Books, 1981), especially 23–24.

39. Irwin Garfinkel and Sara S. McLanahan, *Single Mothers and their Children: A New American Dilemma* (Washington, D.C.: Urban Institute Press, 1986).

40. Mary Ann Glendon, *Abortion and Divorce in Western Law* (Cambridge, Mass.: Harvard University Press, 1987).

41. Carlson, "What Happened to the 'Family'?"; and Allan C. Carlson, "Taxing Families Into Poverty," *Journal of Family and Culture* (1987): 7–15. Recently, Carlson has had some second thoughts; see his commentary, "Facing Realities," *Public Interest* 89 (1987): 33–35.

42. Bauer, "The Family."

43. Thomas J. Espenshade and Joseph J. Minarik, "Demographic Implications of the 1986 U.S. Tax Reform," *Population and Development Review* 13 (1987): 115–27.

44. Alfred J. Kahn and Sheila B. Kamerman, *Child Care: Facing the Hard Choices* (Dover, Mass.: Auburn House, 1987).

45. Ibid.

46. Ibid.

47. See, for example, the Child Care Act of 1987, introduced in the House of Representatives by Nancy Johnson (R-Conn.).

48. For example, legislation has been introduced on behalf of a coalition of nearly seventy national organizations calling itself the Alliance for Better Child Care, which would authorize $2.5 billion in federal expenditures (with a matching 20 percent required of the states) and provide benefits to families with incomes below 115 percent of their state medians.

49. The information in this paragraph comes from Kahn and Kamerman, *Child Care*.

50. An additional 6 percent reported that their child was cared for by a nonrelative in their home, 9 percent reported that the mother cared for the child while working, and 5 percent provided no information. U.S. Bureau of the Census, "Child Care Arrangements for Working Mothers: June 1982," *Current Population Reports*, Series P-23, no. 129, Washington, D.C., November 1983, table A.

51. Kahn and Kamerman, *Child Care*.

52. Susan M. Juster and Maris A. Vinovskis, "Changing Perspectives on the American Family in the Past," *Annual Review of Sociology* 13 (1987): 193–216.

53. Joseph J. Minarik, "Family Incomes," in Isabel V. Sawhill, ed., *Challenge to Leadership: Economic and Social Issues for the Next Decade* (Washington, D.C.: Urban Institute Press, 1988).

54. The information in this paragraph is taken from Sheila B. Kamerman and Alfred J. Kahn, *The Responsive Workplace: Employers and a Changing Labor Force* (New York: Columbia University Press, 1987).

55. Michelson, *From Sun to Sun*.

56. Kamerman and Kahn, *Responsive Workplace*.

57. Advisory Committee on Infant Care Leave, "Statement and Recommendations" (New Haven, Conn.: Yale Bush Center on Child Development and Social Policy, November 26, 1985); and Edward Zigler and Susan Muenchow, "Infant Day Care and Infant Care Leaves: A Policy Vacuum," *American Psychologist* 38 (1983): 91–92.

58. Bauer, "The Family," 7.

59. Ibid.

60. Gerald C. Wright, Jr., and Dorothy N. Stetson, "The Impact of No-Fault Divorce Law Reform on Divorce in American States," *Journal of Marriage and the Family* 40 (1978): 575–80; and Jacques Commaille, Patrick Festy, Pierre Guibentif, Jean Kellerhals, Jean-François Perrin, and Louis Roussel, *Le Divorce en Europe Occidentale* (Paris: Institut National d' Etudes Démographiques, 1983).

61. Michael S. Teitelbaum and Jay M. Winter, *The Fear of Population Decline* (Orlando, Fla.: Academic Press, 1985).

62. Harriet B. Presser and Wendy Baldwin, "Child Care as a Constraint on Employment: Prevalence, Correlates, and Bearing on the Work and Fertility Nexus," *American Journal of Sociology* 85 (1980): 1202–13; and Martin O'Connell and David E. Bloom, *Juggling Jobs and Babies: America's Child Care Challenge* (Washington, D.C.: Population Reference Bureau, Inc., February 1987).

63. See Ben J. Wattenberg, *The Birth Dearth* (New York: Pharos Books, 1987).

Chapter Two

RECENT TRENDS IN THE WELL-BEING OF CHILDREN IN THE UNITED STATES AND THEIR IMPLICATIONS FOR PUBLIC POLICY

Nicholas Zill
Carolyn C. Rogers

During the past 25 to 30 years, the family situations in which American children are reared have changed profoundly. Divorce is more common. More unmarried women are bearing and rearing children. Employment of mothers outside the home has become the norm rather than the exception, for mothers with young children and those with older children. Parents' levels of education have risen, average family size has fallen, and child-rearing philosophies and disciplinary practices have changed. Some of the new realities of American family life seem to be stressful or at least problematic for both children and parents. Some of the changes appear to be beneficial, and others to have both positive and negative aspects as far as children are concerned. Few of our economic, political, or social institutions have fully adapted to the new realities of family life.

Many people are concerned about the effects that these new family circumstances and other social and political changes may be having on the well-being and development of today's children. Indeed, it has become a common experience in recent years to read gloomy appraisals of the condition of children and youth in the United States. For example, in his often-cited presidential address to the Population Association of America, demographer Samuel Preston concluded that "conditions have deteriorated for children and improved dramatically for the elderly."[1] In a widely discussed article in *Public Interest*, Peter Uhlenberg and David Eggebeen argued that "a comparison of youth in 1980 with youth in 1960 reveals that . . . most indicators of well-being show a marked deterioration." (Chapter 3 addresses the Uhlenberg-Eggebeen thesis in detail.)

For many years, Marian Wright Edelman and the Children's Defense Fund have proclaimed a veritable litany of dismal statistics about poor and minority children as part of their successful efforts to persuade Congress and the Reagan administration to increase expenditures on child health and welfare programs.[2] Although its legislative agenda differs from that of the Children's Defense Fund, the administration's Working Group on the Family also painted a negative picture of America's children in its recent report called *The Family: Preserving America's Future.*[3] Numerous other books, articles, and reports sounding similar themes could be listed.[4]

Although changes in the family are most often cited as problematic for children, some commentators attribute the presumed deterioration in children's well-being to broader social problems or faulty government policies. Exactly which policies are seen to be at fault depends on the commentator's political persuasion. Conservatives tend to believe that young people have been corrupted by moral relativism, permissiveness, and the liberal excesses of the recent past, particularly welfare programs, which are viewed as discouraging work, encouraging family breakup, and subsidizing parenthood outside marriage. Liberals, conversely, tend to feel that the problems of children and youth stem from persistent inequities and discrimination in our society, as well as from social programs that have not gone far enough. Still other commentators argue that changes in young people's behavior and well-being over the past three decades may have more to do with the changing size, composition, and distribution of the youthful population than with changes in the family or government policies.[5]

Before we try to resolve which factors are responsible for changes in children's well-being, however, it is essential to determine how indicators of young people's well-being have changed over the past three decades. Doing this turns out to be more complex than is suggested in most of the reports just cited. In fact, child welfare is a multifaceted phenomenon, and not all recent changes in indicators of well-being have been for the worse. Moreover, when trends in well-being are examined in some detail, they tend not to support the explanations of social problems that are commonly offered.

This chapter is an appraisal of trends in children's well-being in the United States since the 1960s. We begin by reviewing changes in the size and composition of the child population over the past three decades, as well as some of the more notable changes in the circumstances of children's family lives. Then we examine recent trends in measures of children's well-being, including indicators of economic well-being, physical health, academic achievement, social behavior and attitudes, and emotional well-being. We evaluate how well the observed trends accord with "family disintegration" hypotheses and other popular theories about recent social change in

America. Finally, we discuss some of the implications of these trends for government policies on children and families.

THE SIZE, COMPOSITION, AND DISTRIBUTION OF THE CHILD POPULATION

To understand the evolving situation of young people in the United States, it is important to know how the overall size of the child population has changed (table 2.1).

Population Size

As of July 1986, there were approximately 63.3 million persons under the age of 18 living in the United States. Largely as a result of the post-World War II baby boom and the subsequent "birth dearth" of the 1970s, there has been a marked fluctuation in the overall size of the child population during the past three decades. The total number of children increased substantially during the 1960s, from just over 64 million in 1960 to nearly 70 million in 1970. Then the number fell during the 1970s, so that by 1980 it was again below 64 million. During the 1980s, the size of the child population has hovered around 63 million.

Although the number of children has fallen since the early 1970s, the size of the overall population has continued to increase. Thus, children now make up a smaller fraction of the total population than they did in the recent past. Children under age 18 made up more than a third of the U.S. population in 1960, whereas they now constitute just over a quarter of the population. Families with children, particularly married couples with children, represent a decreasing proportion of all households.[6] In addition, the proportion of adults in the labor force who have children at home has declined.[7]

Another way of gauging the relative size of the child and adult populations is through the "youth dependency ratio." This is the number of persons under 18 years of age in the population per 100 persons ages 18 to 64 years. This ratio decreased from 60.6 in 1970 to 42.6 in 1986.[8] A lower youth dependency ratio has been interpreted as a good thing for a society because it means that there are more adults available to support, supervise, and socialize the young people in the society. But the interests of children may receive less attention in a democratic, capitalistic society when there are fewer voters

Table 2.1 NUMBER OF CHILDREN, BY AGE, RACE, AND SPANISH ORIGIN (number in millions)

	1960	1970	1980	1985	1990[a]	2000[a]
Total, aged 0–17	64.2	69.6	63.7	63.0	64.3	67.4
Age						
0–5	24.3	21.0	19.6	21.6	23.0	21.3
6–11	21.7	24.6	20.8	19.8	21.8	22.9
12–17	18.2	24.1	23.3	21.6	19.5	23.2
Race and ethnic origin						
White	55.5	59.1	52.5	51.1	51.9	53.5
Nonwhite[b]	8.7	10.6	11.2	11.9	12.4	13.9
Black	n.a.	9.5	9.5	9.6	10.3	11.4
Spanish origin	n.a.	n.a.	n.a.	6.3	7.1	8.7
Children as percentage of total U.S. population	36	34	28	26	26	25

Source: "Preliminary Estimates of the Population of the United States by Age, Sex, and Race: 1970 to 1981," *Current Population Reports.* Series P-25, no. 917, table 1; "Estimates of the Population of the United States by Age, Sex and Race: 1980 to 1985," *Current Population Reports*, Series P-25, no. 985, table 1; "Projections of the Population of the United States: 1983 to 2080." *Current Population Reports*, Series P-25, no. 952, table 6 (middle series); 1970 census volume, "Characteristics of the Population, U.S. Summary," table 52; 1960 census volume, "Characteristics of the Population, U.S. Summary," table 155; and "Projections of the Hispanic Population: 1983 to 2080," P-25, no. 995, table 2 (middle series).
n.a. Not available
a. Projected.
b. "Nonwhite" includes blacks, Indians, Japanese, Chinese, and all other races except white. Blacks constitute the great majority of nonwhites. People of Spanish origin can be of any race.

with children in the electorate and fewer producers and consumers of goods and services for children in the national economy.

The number of young children has started to increase again, and the total number of children is expected to rise to about 67 million by the year 2000. The projected increase reflects the increasing number of adults in their childbearing years, since the average number of children born to each woman has not increased. The proportion of children in the population is expected to remain constant at about 25 percent.

Differential Fertility

Fertility rates (births per 1,000 women ages 15 to 44 years) have fallen since 1970 among virtually all age and race groups, and they are expected to remain low in future years.[9] However, these rates began to decline earlier and fell more steeply among nonminority than among black and Hispanic women, and, within each ethnic group, among better educated than among less well educated women. In the past, higher birth rates among lower socioeconomic and minority groups were offset by higher rates of infant and childhood mortality in these groups. This has been less true recently, however, as a result of dramatic reductions in minority death rates.[10] Thus, in the past several decades, growing numbers of U.S. children have come from the least well-off segments of society.

Although fertility rates have now fallen among minority as well as nonminority women, black and Hispanic rates remain somewhat higher than nonminority rates. In addition, substantial numbers of Hispanics and Caribbean blacks of childbearing ages have immigrated to the United States. Therefore, the child population in the year 2000 will not only be larger, it will also contain a larger proportion of minority youth. Black children, who now constitute 15 percent of the child population, will make up 17 percent of the population in the year 2000, and Hispanic children, now 10 percent of all children, will climb to 13 percent by 2000.[11]

Geographic Concentration of Minority Children

Not only do young people from the least well-off demographic groups make up a growing segment of the overall child population, but also these minority youth are concentrated in the inner cities and close-in suburbs of the major metropolitan areas. In 1986, 46 percent of children under age 18 who lived with one or both parents lived in the suburbs of metropolitan areas, 30 percent lived inside the central cities, and 23 percent lived in nonmetropolitan areas. But, whereas 51 percent of white children lived in suburbs, only 25 percent of black children and 34 percent of Hispanic children were suburban residents. Conversely, 59 percent of black children and 56 percent of Hispanic children lived in central cities, but only 25 percent of white children did so.[12]

Deep ethnic divisions also continue in the types of housing in which American children live. As of 1985, just under 65 percent of all children under the age of 18 lived in housing that was owned by their parents or another household member. However, the proportion in owned housing was nearly 70 percent for white children, but only about 40 percent for both black and Hispanic children. About 2.4 million children, a majority of whom were black or Hispanic, lived in publicly subsidized housing in 1985. Nearly 17 percent of black children, 6 percent of Hispanic children, and 2 percent of white children lived in publicly subsidized housing.[13]

More minority families with children are living in the suburbs of metropolitan areas than was true in the past.[14] The movement to the suburbs of middle-class black and Hispanic families as well as middle-class white families, however, may well have intensified many of the social problems that confront young people who must grow up in inner-city ghettos. These problems include a lack of positive role models and legitimate employment opportunities; pervasive alcohol and drug abuse; extensive corruption and crime; the loss of the "know-how" and activism of middle-class citizens; and a relative absence of neighborhood associations, church groups, and informal support networks.[15]

An illustration of just how extreme a problem population concentration can become is provided by the notorious South Bronx area of New York City. As of the 1980 decennial census, nearly 454,000 people lived in this area, 49 percent of whom were Hispanic, 42 percent black, and 7 percent non-Hispanic whites. Sixty-one percent of the adult population of the South Bronx had not completed high school, and 59 percent of the area's families had incomes below $10,000 per year. There were twice as many single-parent households as two-parent households in the area; 40 percent of the households were on welfare. One out of four babies born in the area was born to a teenage mother. Among those South Bronx residents who were in the labor force, the unemployment rate as of February 1986 was more than 15 percent.[16]

The concentration of social problems in urban communities is rarely matched by a similar concentration of fiscal and problem-solving resources. Hence, many inner-city agencies operate in an atmosphere of continual crisis and function in ways that are less than optimal, if not downright counterproductive. Unfortunate examples of this may be found in the criminal justice system of almost any major U.S. city. To keep from being overwhelmed by the size of their caseloads, these agencies make extensive use of tactics such as plea bargaining, outright dismissal of minor charges, and unsupervised parole. Experience with these agencies, far from discouraging a young person from pursuing a life of crime, may well teach the youngster that it is relatively easy to "beat the system."

Conversely, the concentration of problem youth and families in the inner cities can lead to economies of scale in the delivery of goods and services to these individuals and families. This is in contrast to the situation in rural areas, where the poverty population is often widely dispersed and the task of locating and assisting needy families can be prolonged and relatively costly.[17]

THE CHANGING CIRCUMSTANCES OF CHILDREN'S FAMILY LIVES

Changing Family Living Arrangements

In 1986, some 23 million children—more than one-third of all U.S. children under age 18—were living in some arrangement other than a two-parent family in which both biological parents were present. More than 13 million were living with their mothers only, 76 percent more than in 1970. Nearly 1.6 million were living with their fathers only, double the number in 1970. And approximately 5.5 million were living with one biological parent and one stepparent.[18]

Current estimates are that one-third of today's children will experience their parents' divorce, almost half will spend some time in a single-parent family, and about one-quarter will live with a stepparent by the time they are 16 years of age.[19] For most of human history, substantial numbers of children experienced the loss of one or both parents. In the past, though, the usual cause of family disruption was the death of a parent. Now the reasons are more likely to be separation, divorce, or birth outside marriage.

■ *CHILDREN OF SEPARATION AND DIVORCE*

The family circumstances of U.S. children have been greatly affected by high rates of marital disruption. Although the divorce rate has been rising since at least the middle of the nineteenth century, there was an especially steep and sustained increase in the frequency of divorce during the 1960s and 1970s.[20] Between 1960 and 1975, the number of children whose parents were legally divorced each year more than doubled, going from less than a half-million per year to more than a million per year (figure 2.1).

As of 1986, there were 5.4 million children under age 18 living

Figure 2.1 DIVORCES AND CHILDREN INVOLVED

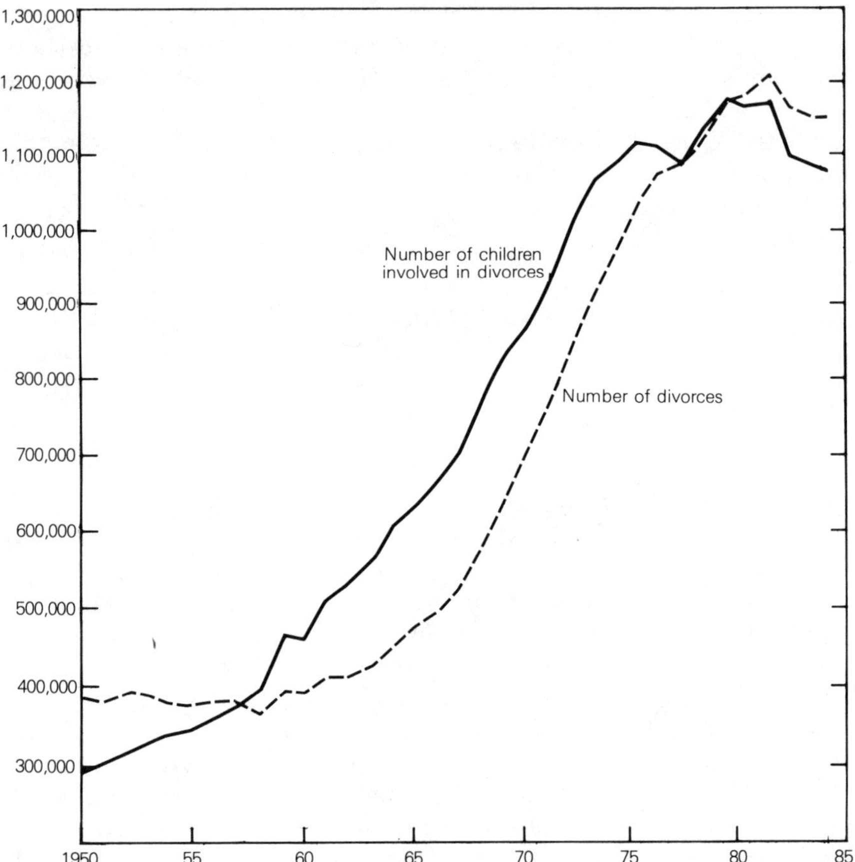

Source: National Center for Health Statistics, "Advance Report of Final Divorce Statistics, 1984," *Monthly Vital Statistics Report* 35, no. 6 (1986), figure 2.

with their mothers only as a result of divorce, more than double the number in 1970 (table 2.2). In addition, there were nearly 3 million children living with separated mothers in 1986, and about 1.1 million more living with their fathers only as a result of divorce or separation. As figure 2.1 and table 2.2 show, the growth in the numbers of children living with divorced and separated mothers or fathers has slackened in the 1980s. Nevertheless, as of 1984, there were still more than a million children whose parents became divorced in a given year.

Table 2.2 CHILDREN LIVING WITH ONE PARENT ONLY

	Number of children under age 18				
	1970	1982	1985	1986	Percentage change 1970–86
Child lives with mother who is			Number in millions		
Divorced	2.3	5.1	5.3	5.4	+135
Separated	2.3	3.1	3.0	2.9	+ 26
Never married	0.5	2.8	3.5	3.6	+620
Widowed	1.4	1.1	0.9	0.9	− 36
Total children living with mother only[a]	7.5	12.5	13.1	13.2	+ 76
Child lives with father who is			Number in thousands		
Divorced	177	658	750	796	+350
Separated	152	255	329	289	+ 90
Never married	30	114	260	318	+960
Widowed	254	144	162	145	− 43
Total children living with father only[a]	748	1,189	1,554	1,579	+111

Source: U.S. Bureau of the Census, *Current Population Reports*, Series P-20, no. 410, "Marital Status and Living Arrangements: March 1985" and earlier reports; and unpublished data from the Current Population Survey, U.S. Bureau of the Census.

a. Includes children in "married, spouse absent" families, not separately shown.

■ *CHILDREN BORN TO AND REARED BY UNMARRIED WOMEN*

Childbearing and child rearing by unmarried women have increased substantially in the second half of the twentieth century (table 2.3). In 1950, only 4 percent of all births were to unmarried mothers, whereas in 1985, births to unmarried mothers accounted for an estimated 22 percent of all births. About 60 percent of all black births, 28 percent of Hispanic births, and 14.5 percent of white births in 1985 were to unmarried mothers. More children are also being reared outside marriage. Thus, as of 1986, 3.6 million children–nearly 6 percent of all children under age 18–were living with mothers who had never married (table 2.2). One-quarter of all black children and 2 percent of all white children were living with never-

Table 2.3 BIRTHS TO UNMARRIED WOMEN (thousand)

	1950	1960	1970	1975	1980[a]	1985[a]
Total number	142	224	399	448	666	828
Number to women under age 20	59	92	200	223	272	280
Percentage of total births to women under age 20	42	41	50	50	41	34
Nonmarital birthrate[b]						
Total	14.1	21.6	26.4	24.5	29.4	32.8
White	6.1	9.2	13.9	12.4	17.6	21.8
Nonwhite	71.2	98.3	89.9	79.0	77.2	73.2
Black	n.a.	n.a.	95.5	84.2	82.9	78.8
Hispanic	n.a.	n.a.	n.a.	n.a.	52.0	n.a.
Non-Hispanic	n.a.	n.a.	n.a.	n.a.	27.7	n.a.
As percentage of all births						
Total	4.0	5.3	10.7	14.2	18.4	22.0
White	1.7	2.3	5.7	7.3	10.0	14.5
Nonwhite	16.8	21.6	34.9	44.2	48.5	51.4
Black	n.a.	n.a.	37.6	48.8	55.3	60.1
Hispanic	n.a.	n.a.	n.a.	n.a.	23.6	29.5
Non-Hispanic	n.a.	n.a.	n.a.	n.a.	18.5	21.6

Source: National Center for Health Statistics, *Vital Statistics of the United States*, Annual Natality Volumes for 1950, 1960, 1970, and 1975; "Advance Report of Final Natality Statistics, 1980," *Monthly Vital Statistics Report*, 31, no. 8, Supplement, tables 2 and 15; and "Advance Report of Final Natality Statistics, 1985," *Monthly Vital Statistics Report* 36, no. 4, Supplement, tables 2 and 18; "Births of Hispanic Parentage, 1980," *Monthly Vital Statistics Report* 32, no. 6, Supplement, September 23, 1983, tables 7 and 11; "Births of Hispanic Parentage, 1983–1984," *Monthly Vital Statistics Report*, forthcoming Spring 1987 (based on 23 reporting states and the District of Columbia).

n.a. Not available.

a. Since 1980, these numbers have been produced by a new method. This change has increased estimates of childbearing to unmarried women, particularly among older women. Since younger women account for the majority of all births to unmarried women, the overall effect of the new method has been small, increasing the estimated number of births to unmarried women in 1980 by 3.5 percent. (National Center for Health Statistics, "Advance Report of Final Natality Statistics," *Monthly Vital Statistics Report*, 1980, 31, no. 8, Supplement.)

b. Births per 1,000 unmarried women ages 15 through 44.

married mothers.[21] The number of these children continued to grow in the 1980s, but, as shown in table 2.2, recent indications are that the rate of growth has started to decline.

Social and Economic Characteristics of Different Types of Families

Children growing up in mother-only households often face multiple burdens: their mothers may have little education, low income, and high unemployment; in addition, many of these children lack contact with or support from their absent fathers, depend on government assistance, and face ethnic discrimination. This cluster of disadvantages is especially characteristic of children living with mothers who have never married. Although children with divorced mothers are also disadvantaged, they are more apt to have mothers who are comparatively well educated, work full-time, and receive at least some assistance from the absent father.

Table 2.4 presents a social and economic profile of children living in two-parent and single-parent families as of March 1985.

Even though never-married mothers tend to spend more hours at home with their children than divorced mothers do, children living with divorced mothers are more likely to participate in a variety of family activities, to have an intellectually stimulating home environment, and to do better in school than children living with never-married mothers. Never-married mothers with young children are prone to depression and to feelings of having time on their hands that they do not know how to fill.[22] These differences seem to have more to do with the personal competence and educational background of the mother, and her social and career opportunities, than with her marital situation.

Children living with their fathers only are less economically disadvantaged than children living in mother-only families, but they are quite disadvantaged relative to children living in two-parent families. That is, their fathers tend to have lower incomes, lower education levels, and higher unemployment rates than fathers in two-parent families. Children in father-only families tend to be older, are more likely to be male, and are less likely to be black or Hispanic than children in mother-only families.[23]

As shown in table 2.4, children in single-parent families are more likely than those in two-parent families to live in a household that includes a grandparent or other adult relative. For about one-quarter of those in father-only families and one-tenth of those in mother-only families, the household contains an adult who is not related

Table 2.4 SOCIAL AND ECONOMIC PROFILE OF CHILDREN IN TWO-PARENT AND SINGLE-PARENT FAMILIES, MARCH 1985

	Type of family							
			Mother-only families					
	Two-parent families		All mother-only families	Divorced mother	Never-married mother	Separated mother	Widowed mother	All father-only families
Number of children under age 18 living in each type of family	46,149,000		13,081,000	5,280,000	3,496,000	2,962,000	939,000	1,554,000
Family characteristics								
Parent education level (percentage)	*Father*	*Mother*						
Parent has less than a high school education	19	18	36	23	47	46	38	24
Parent finished 4+ years of college	25	17	7	10	2	5	8	17
Parent employment status (percentage)								
Not in labor force	5	42	39	25	54	45	42	11
Employed full-time	86	35	40	55	26	33	35	72
Unemployment rate[a]	5.4	6.7	16.1	10.6	26.6	20.5	13.5	11.7
Family income (dollars)								
Mean income in 1984	33,182		10,694	13,281	6,225	9,407[b]	17,407	22,164

Assistance from absent parent							
Percentage child support	c	25	42	9	20	c	3
Public assistance							
Percentage receiving Aid to Families with Dependent Children	4	39	27	59	46	16	8
Percentage living in public housing	2	18	12	30	17	7	3
Mother's age							
Percentage of mothers less than 25 years old	8	16	6	40	12	3	d
Ethnic composition							
Percentage of black children in group	8	37	20	67	35	25	18
Percentage of Hispanic children in group	9	12	8	11	21	12	9
Other adults in household (percentage)							
Adult relative other than parent(s) lives in household	16	28	23	35	25	40	22
Adult nonrelative lives in household	1	10	12	10	7	9	25

Source: Analysis by Child Trends, Inc., of public use data from the Census Bureau's March 1985 Current Population Survey, plus figures from U.S. Bureau of the Census, *Current Population Reports*, Series P-20, no. 410, "Marital Status and Living Arrangements: March 1985."

Note: Percentages and other statistics are child-based.

a. Percentage of those in labor force who were unemployed.

b. Mean income shown is for "married, spouse absent" families, a slightly larger group than the "separated."

c. Some of the children in the "two-parent" and "widowed" families were children from previous marriages, and a small fraction of the mothers in these families received child support payments from their former spouses. Because of the special circumstances involved, these percentages are not shown.

d. No mother in household.

to the child, such as a live-in girlfriend, boyfriend, or housekeeper. About 20 percent of children in mother-only families have a half-brother or half-sister living with them. The majority of children living with a biological parent and a stepparent have half- or step-siblings living with them.[24]

Patterns of Parenthood After Divorce

Following a separation or divorce, the usual pattern has been for the child to live with the mother and for the mother to have sole legal custody of the child.

■ *CONTACT WITH NONCUSTODIAL PARENTS*

National survey data from the early 1980s show that within a few years of divorce, the majority of noncustodial fathers have no regular contact with their children and provide little or no financial support. In the National Survey of Children, for example, 52 percent of all adolescents (ages 12 through 16) who were living with separated, divorced, or remarried mothers had not seen their fathers at all in more than a year. Only 16 percent saw the fathers as often as once a week.[25]

Regular contact is more likely when the separation occurred within the previous two years, when the noncustodial father lives less than an hour's drive from the child, and when neither parent has remarried. College-educated fathers are more likely to maintain contact than less educated fathers, and nonminority fathers are more likely to do so than black fathers. Regular contact is also more likely when the mother is the noncustodial parent. There is a positive relationship between frequency of contact with the child and provision of child support.[26]

■ *COOPERATION AND CONFLICT AFTER DIVORCE*

Even when noncustodial parents do maintain regular contact with their children, the survey data show that truly cooperative child rearing by divorced parents is rare. Much more common is "parallel parenting," wherein the noncustodial parent maintains a continuing relationship with the child while having little to do with the residential parent. The data show that, in most instances, divorce does serve to reduce the level of conflict between the parents. But the price paid for the reduction in conflict is the withdrawal of the noncustodial parent from the responsibilities of child rearing and child support or, at the least, a lack of coordination between the child-rearing efforts of the two parents.[27]

■ *THE TREND TOWARD JOINT CUSTODY*

In an effort to assure that children will have frequent and continuing contact with both parents following divorce and that both parents will continue to fulfill their parental responsibilities, a number of states have passed laws authorizing or even encouraging joint custody arrangements. Under these arrangements, both members of a divorcing couple maintain their legal power to make decisions about the child (joint legal custody) and the child may even be required to divide his or her time evenly between the two parents' domiciles (joint physical custody). It remains to be seen whether these laws will produce their intended results and whether negative side effects of joint custody, such as possible prolongation of postdivorce conflict, will be found.

Early data from one ongoing study of more than a thousand divorcing couples with minor children in California, the state that has been in the forefront of the joint custody movement, show that joint legal custody has become the norm in that state. Seventy-nine percent of the families with completed custody arrangements had joint legal custody of their children. Joint physical custody remains relatively uncommon, however, occurring in only 19 percent of the families. Even in contemporary California, the majority of children (69 percent) follow the traditional pattern and live with their mothers after divorce.[28]

Children Who Live with Neither Parent

Although the plight of children in single-parent families has attracted much attention, research indicates that young children who become separated from both of their parents through death or family discord are at even greater developmental risk.[29] The latter group includes children living in institutions or group homes, living with foster families, or being reared by grandparents or other relatives. One positive social trend that has not received much notice is the decline in the number of children who must grow up in such circumstances.

Census Bureau estimates are that about 1.6 million children—2.5 percent of the child population—were living with neither parent in 1986. Most of them—84 percent—were living with relatives other than their parents. The comparable figures for 1960 were 2.2 million children—3.4 percent of the child population—of whom 71 percent lived with relatives.[30] The total number of children in state and local foster care systems around the country declined from about 500,000 in the mid-1970s to about 260,000 in 1983. Although foster care numbers have leveled off or increased slightly in recent years—the total stood at about 290,000 in 1986—they remain well below the levels recorded in the 1970s.[31] Social Security estimates of the number of children under age 18 who were full orphans (both of their parents had died) fell from 82,000 in 1960 to 33,000 in 1985.[32]

Despite their declining numbers, children who cannot live with either parent continue to represent a high-risk group that deserves special policy attention. Minority children and older youngsters are overrepresented here, especially among those for whom it is difficult to find permanent substitute homes.[33] Changing family life-styles and conflicting social policies are making it more difficult to meet the needs of these children. The increase in female employment outside the home, for example, means that there are fewer families that can readily take on a foster child. Programs to reduce the incidence of child abuse, which often require that youngsters be taken away from abusive or neglectful parents, can work at cross-purposes with efforts to keep families together. There is no shortage of childless, middle-class couples looking for children to adopt, but these couples usually much prefer infants to older children, and children of similar social and ethnic background to lower-class, minority children. Even when a white, middle-class couple is prepared to adopt a minority child, they may be discouraged from doing so by social workers who are ideologically opposed to cross-racial adoption.

The Growth of Maternal Employment

Another aspect of children's lives that has changed profoundly is the likelihood of having a mother who works for pay outside the home (figure 2.2). As of 1986, half of all children under age 6, and more than 60 percent of those between the ages of 6 and 17, had mothers who were working full- or part-time or were looking for work. These proportions have increased dramatically since 1970, but with only slight increases between 1985 and 1986. Two recent developments of significance are the employment of mothers full-time and the employment of mothers with very young children.

It is still the case that a majority of mothers with a child under 18 are not working full-time at a given point in time. However, the proportion who are working full-time increased from 29 percent in

Figure 2.2 CIVILIAN LABOR FORCE PARTICIPATION RATES OF MARRIED WOMEN WITH CHILDREN UNDER AGE 18

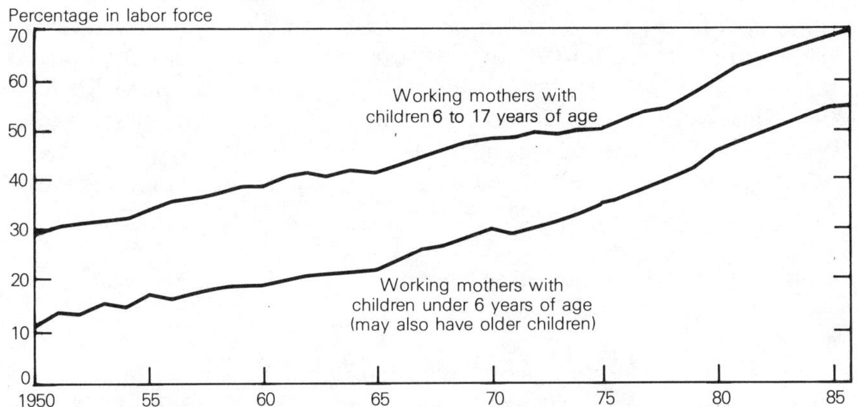

Source: "Time of Change: 1983 Handbook on Women Workers," Bulletin 298; Howard Hayghe, "Rise in Mothers' Labor Force Activity Includes Those with Infants," table 3; unpublished data from the Bureau of Labor Statistics.

1975 to 41 percent in 1986, with the greatest growth occurring among those whose youngest child was under 3 years of age. For these women, the proportion working full-time increased from 19 to 30 percent.[34] Fully half of married mothers with infants under 2 years of age were in the labor force in 1986, compared with less than a quarter in 1970.[35] Single mothers of young children are less likely to be in the labor force than married mothers of young children, but single mothers are more likely to be in the labor force when their children are older. Mothers with young children are more likely to be unemployed than those with older children.[36]

Child Care Arrangements

As maternal employment has grown, so has the need for substitute care for the children of working mothers. For the most part, however, child care in the United States remains a matter of catch-as-catch-can, with most of the burden for finding, arranging, maintaining, and rearranging care falling on the employed mothers themselves. Although trend data on child care arrangements are inadequate, data on the number of children enrolled in preschool programs illustrate the growth in substitute care. The number of children enrolled in public and private nursery schools and kindergartens grew from 4.3 million in 1970 to 6.3 million in 1986, and is projected to rise to more than 7 million in the early 1990s.[37] Among children under age five whose mothers work full time, the most common type of care arrangement has shifted from care in the child's own home to care in the home of another or in a group care center. Among children under age five with mothers who work part-time, care in the child's own home remains the most common arrangement, although between 1965 and 1982 the proportion cared for in the home of another doubled and the proportion cared for in a group care center tripled.[38]

Reduced Family Size, Increased Parent Education

Some of the recent changes in American families seem to bode well for children. Two positive developments are a reduction in the proportion of families that have large numbers of children to care for and an increase in the average educational level of parents. The proportion of all families (including those without children) with four or more children in the home declined from 10 percent in 1970 to 3 percent in 1986. Among blacks and Hispanics, the corresponding decline was from 18 percent in 1970 to 6 or 7 percent in 1986.[39]

The proportion of elementary-school-age children whose parents had at least 12 years of education rose from 62 percent in 1970 to 78 percent in 1985. For black elementary schoolchildren, this proportion went from 36 percent in 1970 to 67 percent in 1985.[40] The educational gains of black women over the last decade have been particularly striking. Thus, even though an inner-city black child of today is more likely to live in a single-parent family than a comparable child of 10 or 20 years ago, the child's mother is more likely to have finished high school or attended college than was the case in the 1960s or 1970s. Table 2.5 presents trend data on the educational attainment of black and white women who bore children between 1969 and 1985. Although increases in black educational attainment have been dramatic, black parents continue to lag behind white parents in average education. For every black child born in 1985 to a mother who had completed college, there were more than four black children born to mothers who had not finished high school. The comparable ratio among white children was about one-to-one. Hispanic parents, many of whom received their educations in other countries, are even further behind. In 1985, only 41 percent of Hispanic schoolchildren had parents who had completed high school.[41]

Table 2.5 LIVE BIRTHS BY MOTHER'S EDUCATIONAL ATTAINMENT

	Number of births to college-educated women[a]			Percentage of women with 12 or more years of school[b]			Ratio of births to college-educated women to births to women with 0 to 11 years of school[c]		
Year	All races	White	Black	All races	White	Black	All races	White	Black
1969	186,314	172,148	9,062	68	72	47	1:3.7	1:3.0	1:18.8
1970	208,510	192,244	10,450	69	73	49	1:3.6	1:2.8	1:17.9
1975	253,255	226,150	16,971	71	75	55	1:2.5	1:2.0	1:10.2
1980	396,594	349,475	31,096	76	79	64	1:1.7	1:1.3	1:5.8
1981	416,542	367,279	32,628	77	80	65	1:1.5	1:1.2	1:5.4
1982	434,361	383,578	33,642	78	81	65	1:1.5	1:1.1	1:5.1
1983	443,485	392,595	33,330	78	81	66	1:1.4	1:1.1	1:5.0
1984	462,685	409,632	34,865	79	82	67	1:1.3	1:1.0	1:4.7
1985	478,863	423,706	36,259	79	82	68	1:1.2	1:0.9	1:4.5

Source: National Center for Health Statistics, *Vital Statistics of the United States*, Annual Natality Volumes for 1969, 1970, 1975, and 1980; "Advance Report: Final Natality Statistics" for 1981, 1982, 1983, 1984, and 1985, *Monthly Vital Statistics Report*.

a. "College-educated" is defined as 16 or more years of school.

b. Excludes "not stated" category.

c. The number of states reporting data on the mother's educational attainment varies by year. In 1969, 36 states were included; in 1970, 38 states; in 1975, 42 states and the District of Columbia; and for 1980 through 1985, 47 states and the District of Columbia.

TRENDS IN INDICATORS OF CHILDREN'S ECONOMIC WELL-BEING

Trends in Family Income and Poverty

Average family income in the United States grew vigorously during the 1960s and early 1970s. But in terms of real purchasing power, the past decade and a half have been a period of economic stagnation or decline for most American families with children. When corrected for inflation, the median family income for U.S. children under age 18 changed only slightly during most of the 1970s, declined between 1979 and 1983, and has recovered modestly since 1984. Dramatically lower inflation and interest rates have been important positive developments during the 1980s. And today's smaller family size means more income per capita at a given family income level.

Nevertheless, the median income for families with children in 1985, $26,720, remained well below the 1973 high mark of $30,501 (in 1985 dollars).[42]

■ *INCOME DIFFERENCES BY TYPE OF FAMILY AND ETHNIC GROUP*

In 1985, children in two-parent families, who had a median family income of $31,451, enjoyed roughly three times the income of children in mother-only families, whose median income was $9,472. The median family income of white children, $28,988, was half again as much as that of Hispanic children, $17,027, and nearly twice that of black children, $14,879. In constant dollar terms, Hispanic children in two-parent families and black children in mother-only families have experienced especially large declines in income since 1979.[43]

■ *CHILDHOOD POVERTY*

Children are more likely than people in other age groups to be living in poverty. In 1986, 20 percent of children under age 18 were below the official poverty line. In contrast, 14 percent of persons of all ages, and less than 13 percent of those age 65 or older, were below the poverty line.[44] The proportion of children who were poor declined sharply in the 1960s, reaching a low of about 14 percent in 1969 (figure 2.3). Increases in the rate of childhood poverty in the 1970s and 1980s coincided with periods of recession in the national economy. Poverty rates have declined somewhat since 1983. Black children and Hispanic children are especially likely to be living in poverty, with 1986 poverty rates of 43 percent and 37 percent, respectively. Another reason why childhood poverty rates have remained high is the increase in the proportion of children living in mother-only families. The poverty rate for these children has ranged between 51 percent and 56 percent since 1970.

Welfare and Noncash Benefits

Although poverty persists, the character of poverty is affected by the availability of Aid to Families with Dependent Children (AFDC) and noncash benefits. In constant dollar terms, total government expenditures on welfare programs more than tripled between 1965 and 1980, but have leveled off in the 1980s.[45]

■ *WELFARE PAYMENTS*

The proportion of children receiving AFDC has stabilized at roughly 11 percent after rising in the 1960s and early 1970s. In 1985, about

Figure 2.3 POVERTY AMONG CHILDREN UNDER AGE 18

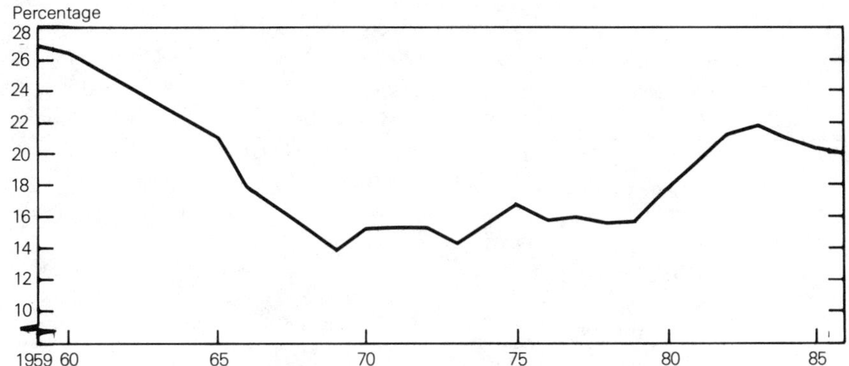

Source: Congressional Budget Office; Bureau of the Census, "Money Income and Poverty Status of Families and Persons in the United States: 1986," *Current Population Reports*, Series P-60, no. 157 (1987).

Note: Rates are for related children under 18, including biological, step-, and adopted children of the householder, and any other children related to the householder by blood, marriage, or adoption. The poverty level is based on money income and does not reflect receipt of noncash benefits such as food stamps. Poverty levels are revised each year to reflect changes in the Consumer Price Index.

47 percent of children whose families were below the official poverty line received AFDC payments.[46] Average monthly AFDC payments vary widely among the states, and benefit levels have generally not kept up with inflation. In constant 1985 dollars, the average per family payment to AFDC recipients declined by 33 percent between 1970 and 1985 (table 2.6).

The fact that AFDC benefits are not regularly adjusted to reflect inflation is one reason why poverty rates for children have been relatively high in recent years. In contrast, Social Security payments to the elderly are indexed for inflation, and poverty rates for the elderly have gone down.[47] The composition of the welfare caseload reflects changing family patterns. Between 1975 and 1984, the proportion of children receiving AFDC who were born outside marriage rose from 31 to 46 percent, while the proportion whose parents were separated or divorced fell from 48 to 38 percent.[48]

■ *NONCASH BENEFITS*

Compared with the early 1960s, today's indigent families with children have a better chance of obtaining food, housing, and medical care. This is because of the introduction in the mid-1960s and 1970s of noncash benefit programs such as food stamps, public housing,

Table 2.6 AID TO FAMILIES WITH DEPENDENT CHILDREN

Year	Total payments (thousand dollars)	Monthly average AFDC payment (current dollars)		Monthly average AFDC payment (1985 dollars)	
		Family	Recipient	Family	Recipient
1950	551,653	71.33	17.64	318.77	78.83
1955	617,841	84.17	23.26	338.11	93.44
1960	1,000,784	105.75	27.75	384.08	100.79
1965	1,660,186	133.20	31.96	454.21	108.98
1970	4,852,964	183.13	47.77	507.27	132.32
1975	9,210,995	219.44	67.65	438.66	135.23
1980	12,475,245	280.03	96.49	365.58	125.97
1985	15,195,835	342.15	116.65	342.15	116.65

Source: U.S. Social Security Administration. *Social Security Bulletin, Annual Statistical Supplement, 1986.*

and Medicaid. Indeed, during the past three decades, the primary type of welfare assistance has shifted from cash to noncash benefits. In 1965, only 24 percent of federal means-tested benefits were in the form of noncash assistance, whereas the 1985 figure was 65 percent.[49]

As of 1985, 30 percent of all children under 18—about one-quarter of all households with children—received one or more of the four main means-tested, noncash benefits. About 23 percent of all children received free or reduced-price school lunches, 17 percent got food stamps, 13 percent were covered by Medicaid, and 6 percent lived in publicly subsidized rental housing.[50] The proportions of households receiving these benefits have changed little in recent years, despite fluctuations in the childhood poverty rate and Reagan administration efforts to cut back the federal role in welfare programs.[51]

Eight out of 10 children in families below the official poverty line participated in at least one of these noncash programs in 1985. More than 6 out of 10 received food stamps, and a similar fraction received subsidized school lunches. About half were covered by Medicaid. One in 5 lived in subsidized housing. Only 1 in 10 took part in all four of the benefit programs, however. Because the poverty index is rarely used to determine eligibility for noncash programs, there are children in families at or above the official poverty line who also receive noncash benefits. In 1985, 42 percent of children in families whose incomes were between the poverty level and double the poverty level received one or more of the noncash benefits, as did 5 percent of those in families whose incomes were double the poverty level or more.[52]

Child Support

Only about 37 percent of the women living with minor children from an absent father receive child support from the fathers.[53] Recent legislative changes, such as the Child Support Enforcement Amendments of 1984, have led to increased federal and state government efforts to facilitate child support awards and to enforce the collection of support payments. The number and total amount of child support collections recorded by the Department of Health and Human Services have increased substantially since the passage of these laws.[54] Nevertheless, Census Bureau surveys indicate that the nationwide proportion of women who were awarded child support increased only slightly between 1978 and 1985, and the proportion of awardees receiving payments in a given year did not change.[55]

The women who are least likely to receive child support are those who need it the most: namely, minority women, women who have little education, and women who have never married or are informally separated, as opposed to being legally divorced. Even when a women receives all the support payments to which she is entitled, the amounts received are typically small. The mean amount of child support received by all women who received some payment in 1985 was $2,215. Average amounts received declined between 1983 and 1985 after adjusting for inflation.[56] Unless average awards, as well as collection rates, are substantially increased, a woman with children from an absent father must go to work full-time or remarry in order to escape poverty and welfare dependency, rather than relying on significant financial help from the absent father.

TRENDS IN INDICATORS OF PHYSICAL HEALTH

Many members of the public believe that the physical health status of U.S. children has deteriorated in recent years. In fact, as gauged by most conventional health indicators, the physical health of American children has never been better. Despite the progress that has been made, however, evidence also suggests we could be doing better in preventing and treating health problems in children.

Figure 2.4 INFANT[a] MORTALITY

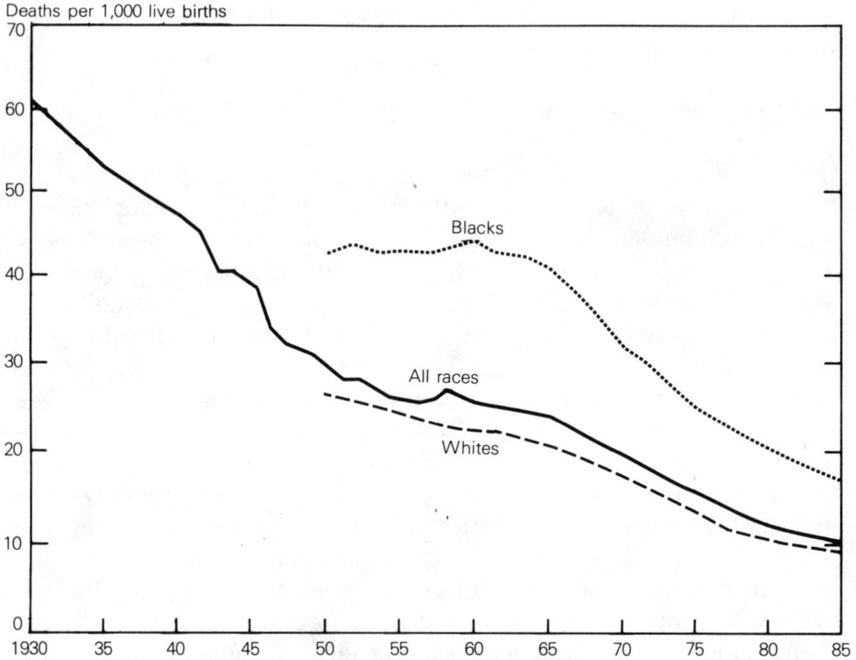

Source: National Center for Health Statistics, "Annual Summary of Births, Marriages, Divorces, and Deaths: United States, 1985," *Monthly Vital Statistics Report* 34, no. 13 (1986), figure 5; "Advance Report of Final Mortality Statistics, 1984," *Monthly Vital Statistics Report* 35, no. 6 (1986), figure 5.
Note: Data are available separately for whites and blacks only for the years 1950 through 1985.
a. Under one year of age.

Trends in Death and Disease

■ *MORTALITY TRENDS*

One widely used indicator of health conditions in a society is the infant mortality rate—the proportion of babies who die within the first year of life. The U.S. infant mortality rate in the mid-1980s—less than 11 infant deaths per 1,000 live births—was less than half of what it was in 1960 and only about one-third of what it was as recently as 1950 (figure 2.4). Death rates for preschool and school-age children have also declined substantially. The death rate in 1985 for children between the ages of 1 and 4 was less than half of what it was in 1960. And the death rate for children between the ages of

Table 2.7 DEATH RATES FOR PERSONS UNDER 25 YEARS OF AGE

	Age of child			
Year	1–4 Years	5–14 Years	15–19 Years	20–24 Years
1960	109.1	46.4	88.3	120.4
1970	84.5	41.3	110.3	148.0
1980	63.9	30.6	97.9	132.7
1981	60.2	29.4	90.7	122.5
1982	57.6	28.3	86.0	114.6
1983	55.9	26.9	81.6	108.8
1984	51.9	26.7	81.0	110.7
1985	51.4	26.3	81.2	108.9

Source: National Center for Health Statistics, "Annual Summary of Births, Marriages, Divorces, and Deaths: United States, 1985," *Monthly Vital Statistics Report*, 34, no. 13 (1986).
Note: Death rate = deaths per 100,000 population in specified age group.

5 and 14 was less than 60 percent of the 1960 rate (table 2.7) Although mortality rates provide only a partial picture of children's health status, these dramatic declines attest to real improvements in the physical health of our young people.

■ *COMMUNICABLE DISEASES AND HEALTH RATINGS*

Many communicable diseases that were once common to childhood, such as diphtheria, polio, and measles, have been eradicated or greatly reduced in frequency.[57] By the time U.S. children enter school, almost 100 percent of them have been immunized against measles, mumps, rubella, diphtheria, and polio.[58] Although virtually all children still have bouts of acute illness or minor injuries from time to time, most grow up physically healthy. Eight out of 10 children are described by their parents as being in "very good" or "excellent" health, and all but about 3 percent are rated in at least "good" health (table 2.8).

Continuing Disparities

■ *INTERNATIONAL COMPARISONS OF INFANT MORTALITY*

Despite the signs of progress just summarized, when the U.S. infant mortality rate is compared with that of other industrialized countries, the United States ranks only seventeenth, behind countries like

Table 2.8 PARENT RATINGS OF CHILDREN'S HEALTH STATUS, 1985 (percentage)

	Excellent	Very good	Good	Fair or poor
Preschool children[a]				
White	57.2	26.3	14.8	1.8
Black	42.4	24.8	28.6	4.2
Total	54.7	25.8	17.2	2.3
Family income				
Under $10,000	41.7	27.3	26.8	4.2
$10,000–$19,999	50.3	29.4	18.0	2.4
$20,000–$34,999	58.3	25.1	14.7	1.8
$35,000 +	65.5	24.3	8.6	1.6
School-aged children[b]				
White	54.4	26.5	16.9	2.3
Black	39.4	26.7	29.0	4.9
Total	52.0	26.5	18.9	2.7
Family income				
Under $10,000	36.3	24.6	32.2	6.9
$10,000–$19,999	44.6	28.9	23.5	3.0
$20,000–$34,999	53.9	28.2	16.0	1.9
$35,000+	64.5	24.6	9.7	1.1

Source: National Center for Health Statistics, "Current Estimates From the National Health Interview Survey: United States, 1985," *Vital and Health Statistics*, Series 10, no. 160, table 70.

a. Preschool age refers to children under 5 years of age.

b. School-age refers to children ages 5 through 17.

Japan, the Scandinavian countries, France, Australia, and Britain.[59] This rank is unchanged from 1980 and contrasts sharply with our rank in per capita gross national product, which is second only to Switzerland.[60] Even if the lower infant mortality rate for white infants is used in the comparison, the United States still comes out relatively low in the standings, with a rank of twelfth.[61] Studies have shown that the problem is not with our technological capabilities for keeping low-birth-weight and other high-risk babies alive. In that respect, the United States ranks at or near the top. Rather, the problem is in the relatively high proportion of low-birth-weight and other high-risk cases with which our medical system must deal.[62]

PRENATAL CARE

One way to help ensure a healthy infant is for the expectant mother to obtain prenatal care early in her pregnancy. Yet for 1 out of every 20 babies born in the United States, and for 1 out of every 10 black or Hispanic babies, the mother has obtained prenatal care either late in the pregnancy or not at all. These proportions have remained essentially unchanged during the 1980s. Pregnant women who are at a higher risk of not obtaining timely prenatal care include young teenagers, school dropouts, unmarried women, and black women. These groups are also at greater risk of producing babies of low birth weight and babies who die during the first year of life.[63] Federal health agencies and a number of private foundations have recently instituted programs to try to get more women in these risk groups to avail themselves of medical care and preventive counseling early in their pregnancies.

SOCIOECONOMIC AND ETHNIC DISPARITIES IN HEALTH STATUS AND HEALTH CARE

A number of child health indicators—mortality rates, health ratings, and some (but not all) measures of illness and injury—show substantial disparities in the health status of children from different segments of American society. Although there are some health problems, such as allergies and teenage motor vehicle fatalities, which are more prevalent among higher socioeconomic groups, most poor children are less healthy than children from more affluent families; children whose parents have little education are less healthy than those whose parents are well educated; and black and Hispanic children are less healthy, on average, than nonminority children.[64] Data on children's use of physician and dental services also show socioeconomic and ethnic disparities, with children from poor and minority families receiving less frequent care than those from middle-class, nonminority families[65]—despite the fact that children from poor families are more likely to need medical or dental care. Although trend studies have shown that access to medical care improved for poor and minority families during the late 1960s and 1970s, patterns of care use have shown little change in recent years.[66]

HEALTH INSURANCE COVERAGE

The extent to which children are covered by some form of health insurance varies across income classes, with only about two-thirds of children from families below the poverty line having such coverage, as opposed to nearly 90 percent of the children in families with incomes of twice the poverty level and above. Health insurance coverage also varies by family type, with more than 85 percent of those from two-parent families being covered, whereas less than 70 percent of those in mother-only families have such coverage. Ironically, children with divorced mothers are less likely to be covered than those with never-married mothers, because the latter are more likely to be eligible for coverage under the Medicaid program.[67]

Accidental Injury and Violence

Accidental injury and violence inflicted on children and youth are major public health problems in the United States.

■ *ACCIDENTAL INJURIES*

Injury is the leading cause of death to children after the first few months of life. The annual toll of childhood injury also includes nearly 10 million emergency room visits and at least one night in the hospital for 1 in every 130 children.[68] Motor vehicle accidents in particular represent a large fraction of childhood deaths and serious but nonfatal injuries. Nearly 7,400 teenagers died in automobile accidents in 1984. This represented more than twice the number of teen deaths due to homicide and suicide combined.[69] Drowning, burns, choking and other forms of suffocation, falls, and poisoning are other causes of death and nonlethal injury that are common in childhood.[70]

As the declining death rates presented earlier suggest, progress has been made in combating many forms of unintentional injury to children and youth. For example, as described in chapter 3, motor vehicle death rates among teenagers, which rose during the 1970s, have dropped more than 20 percent during the 1980s.[71] Studies have shown that improvements in child safety can be attributed at least in part to the beneficial effects of government regulations, such as the federally mandated 55-mile-per-hour speed limit, state laws requiring infant restraint and child seat belt use in motor vehicles, local ordinances obliging homeowners and landlords to install smoke detectors, and federal packaging standards calling for "child-proof" caps on certain drugs and household chemicals.[72] Further progress against these and other sources of childhood injury could and should be achieved. Surveys and observational studies have shown, for instance, that seat belt use among school-age children is far from universal. And, as of 1985, each year more than 60,000 children under age five were reported to have accidentally swallowed prescription medicines.[73]

■ *VIOLENT INJURY AND DEATH*

The total volume of childhood injuries and deaths that are the result of attacks by parents, relatives, acquaintances, or strangers—or are self-inflicted—is less than the number attributable to unintentional causes. However, incidents of violence toward children and adolescents tend to generate more public attention and concern than do occurrences of accidental injury or death. As is true for other age groups, homicide rates for children and youth in the United States are far higher than those in other industrialized countries.[74] (These are discussed in chapter 3.) Nonlethal violent injuries of young people are presumably more common in the United States as well, though adequate comparative statistics are lacking. During the late 1960s and 1970s, there were dramatic increases in the prevalence of many forms of violence, including murders of children and youth and teenage suicide. In the 1980s, homicide rates have declined and suicide rates have leveled off. Nevertheless, both forms of violent death remain two to three times more common among young people than they were in the early 1960s.[75] (Teen suicide trends are discussed later in this chapter. Chapter 3 discusses trends in violent death rates among adults as well as adolescents.)

Homicide rates are higher in adolescence than in childhood, but among children, the rates are higher for infants and preschoolers than for school-age children. Homicide rates are two to three times higher for males than for females, and four to five times higher among black youth than among white youth. Suicide is very rare before adolescence and is more common among older than among younger adolescents. Suicide rates are three to five times higher among adolescent males than among females, although females attempt suicide more often than males do. Unlike homicide, suicide is more common among white than among black teens, with the rates for white adolescents being two to three times higher than those for black adolescents.[76]

■ *CHILD ABUSE*

In the past decade, the problem of abuse and neglect of children by parents and other caretakers has received considerable research and media attention and has been the subject of state and federal legislation. Types of abuse that formerly received little public notice, such as sexual abuse, have been brought out into the open. There is, however, little hard evidence that public and private efforts to combat abuse have notably reduced the frequency of child maltreatment. The total number of reports of cases of abuse and neglect made to agencies around the country rose sharply between 1976 and 1984, from nearly 700,000 to 1.7 million per year.[77] Of course, part or all of this increase could be due to better reporting rather than to actual increases in rates of abuse and neglect.

Statistics on deaths among infants and young children due to homicide and undetermined injury are probably more reliable as indicators of change over time in child abuse, at least with respect to the more extreme forms of abuse. In 1984, there were approximately 8 deaths per 100,000 infants due to undetermined injury or homicide, and 3 such deaths per 100,000 children between the ages of one and four. These rates of violent death have tended to fluctuate within a fairly narrow range since 1970, with no sustained trend upward or downward[78]

The Changing Child Health Picture

As many of the traditional diseases of childhood have been conquered or their effects ameliorated, public health experts have shifted their attention to other types of child health problems, such as the prevention of accidental injury. There is also increasing emphasis on steps that can be taken in childhood to help prevent chronic conditions, such as heart disease and cancer, that are major causes of death and disability in adulthood. Thus, data have been collected on the dietary and exercise patterns and physical fitness levels of school-age children in the United States, and concern has been expressed over the sedentary, TV-bound lifestyles of many young people.

Pediatricians and child health researchers are also paying more attention to conditions such as allergies and asthma, eating disorders, learning difficulties, and emotional and behavioral problems. These conditions, which have a substantial psychological component and do not fit easily into the infectious disease paradigm with which medicine is used to dealing, have been collectively labeled the "new morbidity of childhood."[79] Of course, although many of the older diseases have been conquered or controlled, some new types of infectious disease, such as acquired immunce deficiency syndrome

(AIDS) and the chronic fatigue syndrome, have emerged to plague young people as well as their elders.

Finally, the very success of modern medicine in controlling disease and keeping high-risk individuals alive may be creating new kinds of social and health problems. For example, data from the National Health Interview Survey indicate that the proportion of children with activity-limiting health conditions has increased since 1960.[80] The evidence for the increase has been challenged on methodological grounds, but some observers believe it to be real. They attribute the increase to the progress that has been made in keeping infants who have extremely low birth weights or birth defects or both alive in neonatal intensive care units. Although the infants survive, some of them become children with physical or mental deficiencies, and this occurs at a higher rate than is the case with normal infants. Other observers argue that improved neonatal technology, together with the use of amniocentesis and other forms of genetic screening, are actually reducing the proportion of handicapped children in the population.[81]

Less debatable is the fact that the life expectancy for young people with Down's syndrome, cerebral palsy, cystic fibrosis, and other severely handicapping conditions has increased dramatically in the past several decades. This is due to better medical management of specific acute illnesses, like pneumonia, to which disabled persons are susceptible, and to policy changes that have made it less likely that people with severe handicaps will be relegated to the back wards of large institutions. However, the the longer life spans that handicapped persons can expect create a series of challenges for our social system: how to train these people for productive work, how to provide them with a reasonable quality of life, how to reduce the strain on the families in which they live, and how to pay the often considerable costs of supporting them for many years in group homes or institutions.[82]

TRENDS IN INDICATORS OF ACADEMIC ACHIEVEMENT

An assessment of how the academic achievement of U.S. students has changed in the past three decades depends on which students are focused on. Much attention has been paid to trends in the average scores on the Scholastic Aptitude Tests (SATs) taken by college-bound high school seniors. For this group—that is, the most able students—the picture has been one of long-term deterioration and, more recently, partial recovery. The picture is different, however, if one focuses on minority students or nonminority students from families with little education. The data indicate that these students have made gains since the 1960s, although their performance is still markedly inferior to that of middle-class, nonminority students.

Enrollment and Graduation Trends

American children start school earlier and stay in school longer than they did in the past. The proportion of children who were enrolled in school by the time they were 3 to 4 years old nearly doubled between 1970 and 1985, going from less than 21 percent to just under 39 percent. And the proportion of adolescents who were still enrolled between the ages of 14 and 17 has been around 95 percent in recent years. Data from the October Education Supplement to the Census Bureau's Current Population Survey indicate that about 85 percent of today's young adults have either graduated from high school or completed the requirements for a GED (general equivalency diploma).[83]

Although the validity of various measures of high school completion and dropout has been disputed, trend data from the Current Population Survey indicate that there has been some progress in reducing the dropout rate in recent years. For 1983, the Census Bureau found the cumulative proportion of students who had dropped out of school in grades 10, 11, and 12 to be 14.9 percent, significantly lower than the 17.8 percent dropout proportion that was found for 1973. For black males, the cumulative dropout proportion declined from about 32 percent in 1973 to about 20 percent in 1983, whereas for white males it went from 17 percent to 15 percent.[84]

Data from the longitudinal *High School and Beyond* study are generally consistent with the dropout rates found in the Current Population Survey. These data show that disproportionate numbers of high school dropouts are from families with low socioeconomic status, non-Asian minority backgrounds, and little interest in their children's school work.[85] Actual dropout rates may be somewhat higher than those found in the Current Population Survey and the *High School and Beyond* studies because some students drop out of school before grade 10. In addition, dropout rates for minority students are believed to be considerably higher in the inner cities of the largest metropolitan areas (New York, Los Angeles, Chicago, Detroit, etc.) than in other parts of the country.

Declines in High Achievement

Although American young people may now spend more of their early years, adolescence, and young adulthood in school than was the case in the past, there is widespread concern over just what today's children are learning while they are in school. A number of large-scale testing programs found evidence during the late 1960s and 1970s of deterioration in student knowledge and proficiency in many of the more advanced topics and skill areas. The programs that showed these declines included those involving the standardized testing of student achievement in local areas; the nationwide testing of candidates for college admission; and the assessment of the knowledge, skills, and attitudes of young people at several different ages from national probability samples.[86] The programs differed somewhat with respect to the magnitude and timing of the declines, but there was little to encourage skepticism about the actual occurrence of the declines. In the subsections that follow, we summarize the relevant evidence from two of the major testing programs: the SAT program of the College Entrance Examination Board and the National Assessment of Educational Progress (NAEP).

■ *DECLINES IN SCORES ON COLLEGE-ENTRANCE EXAMINATIONS*

The average test scores of college-bound high school seniors on the SAT dropped appreciably between the early 1960s and the early 1980s (figure 2.5). Mean scores on the mathematics portion of the test fell 36 points, or about three-tenths of a standard deviation, and mean scores on the verbal portion fell 54 points, or about half a standard deviation over that period. In 1982, average SAT scores went up slightly for the first time since 1963. Further increases have occurred since 1982, although the total recovery on each portion has amounted to 10 points or less, or not quite one-tenth of a standard deviation. Thus, average scores remain considerably below those of 25 years ago.

Because SAT averages are based on the scores of self-selected samples of high school seniors, the possibility exists that part or all of the decline in scores could be due to changes over time in the size and composition of the group that takes the test. Analyses done by the Educational Testing Service suggest that the decline in SAT scores that occurred between the mid-1960s and 1971 could be

Figure 2.5 TRENDS IN SAT EXAMINATION SCORES

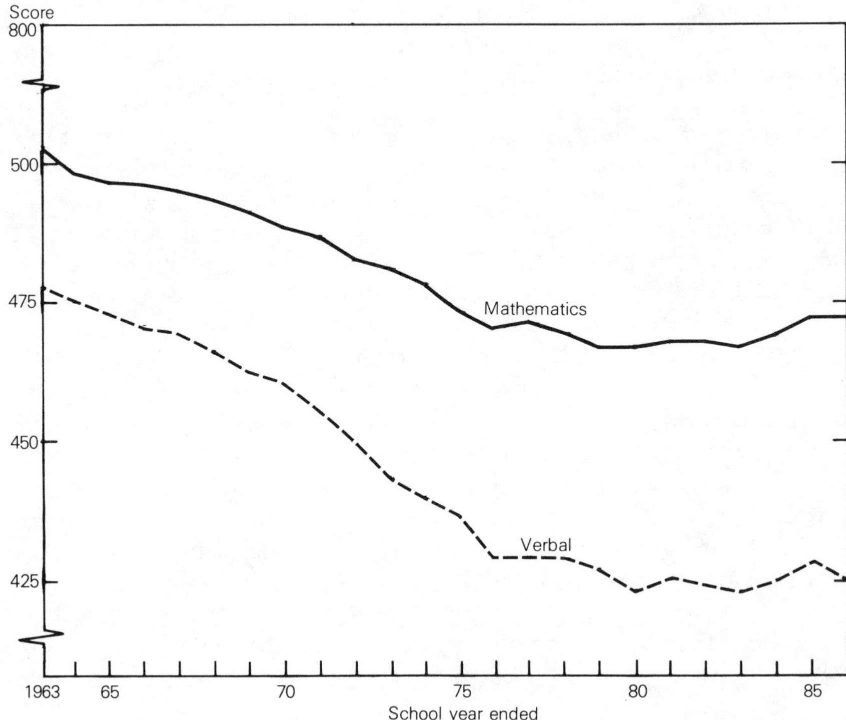

Source: College Entrance Examination Board, *Profiles, College-Bound Seniors, 1981–85*, *News from the College Board*, 14 October 1982; and Gilbert R. Austin and Herbert Garber, eds., *The Rise and Fall of National Test Scores* (New York: Academic Press, 1982).
Note: SAT scores range between 200 and 800.

partly due to compositional changes. The compositional changes were partly offset by "scale drift"—that is, the SATs became gradually easier during this period because of inadvertent errors in the process of equating tests from one year to the next. The continuing decline in scores after 1971 was probably not caused by changes in self-selection, and self-selection does not seem to account for the recent upturn in SAT scores because the proportion of seniors taking the test has actually been increasing lately.[87]

The downward trend did not simply involve an increase in the number of students with low scores. There were also marked drops in the number of students who achieved exceptionally high SAT scores. Between 1966–67 and 1979–80, for example, the total number of students scoring 700 or higher on the mathematical portion of the SAT fell from 55,500 to 38,900. This drop occurred even though the tests were easier and the total pool of students taking the tests was slightly larger in 1979–80. During the same period, the number scoring 700 or higher on the verbal portion of the test fell from 33,200 to 12,300.[88]

■ *FINDINGS OF THE NATIONAL ASSESSMENT OF EDUCATIONAL PROGRESS*

The NAEP is a federally sponsored program begun in 1969 that periodically tests national probability samples of 9-, 13-, and 17-year-olds on a variety of subjects, and sometimes assesses samples of young adults as well. This program also has found evidence of declines in high-level academic skills and knowledge. The NAEP has not found a deterioration in fundamental reading, writing, and arithmetic skills; overall student performance in these basic areas either remained constant or improved slightly over the 1970s and early 1980s. But there have been declines in aspects of mathematical and verbal achievement that go beyond the basics.[89]

In mathematics, for example, NAEP results indicate that most American children do reasonably well at the mechanics of adding, subtracting, multiplying, and dividing. But students do not do well on exercises measuring their understanding of mathematical concepts or their ability to apply computational skills to the solution of practical problems. For example, only 60 percent of 17-year-olds still in school in 1973 could solve simple word problems involving the calculation of percentages, and only 12 percent could calculate the unit cost of electricity, given a simplified utility bill. Performance on both conceptual and word problem exercises declined during the 1970s, so that, by 1978, only 50 percent of 17-year-olds could calculate percentages appropriately and only 5 percent could solve the electricity bill problem.[90]

In assessments of reading skills, exercises measuring literal comprehension—the ability to identify a fact, incident, or idea given in a reading passage—showed improvement among 9- and 13-year-olds during the 1970s, and stable performance among 17-year-olds. But exercises measuring inferential comprehension—the ability to infer from a passage an idea or concept that is not explicitly stated—showed a decline.[91]

As was the case with the SATs, not only did average students perform less well on the more challenging NAEP tasks, but also the most able students did less well. In the reading assessments, for instance, the average scores of students scoring in the top fourth of the achievement distribution went down significantly from the beginning to the end of the 1970s. The declines were evident at both age 13 and age 17, and in several different kinds of exercises, but they were particularly pronounced in exercises measuring the most advanced reading skills and inferential comprehension. Similarly, in the assessments of writing skills, there was a downward trend in the number of better essays written by 13-year-olds and 17-year-olds in a descriptive writing task.[92]

The NAEP has shown that recent cohorts of students lack essential knowledge in several subject areas outside of the "basic skills" triad.[93] Although an understanding of science and technology is increasingly important for rational decision making and day-to-day functioning in our society, students of all ages seem to be learning less about science than their counterparts did in the past. Today's students also know less about the U.S. political system and how it functions. Other subjects in which the current crop of students have been found to be poorly informed include history, literature, art, and music. Findings such as these have prompted several authors to express concern about the "cultural literacy" of today's young people; that is, their mastery of that body of widely shared names, dates, facts, and concepts that makes civilized discourse possible.[94]

Gains in Minority Achievement

The same large-scale testing programs that provided evidence of declines in high academic achievement have produced data showing that the academic achievement of black and Hispanic students in the United States has notably improved over the past 25 years. These ethnic minorities and other disadvantaged groups have shown gains in reading, writing, and mathematical skills that have brought the groups closer but still not up to the performance of children in the nation as a whole.[95]

■ *PERFORMANCE OF MINORITY STUDENTS ON THE NAEP*

Four NAEP tests of reading skills were conducted between 1970–71 and 1983–84. Black 9-year-olds showed considerable improvement in reading performance during the 1970s, followed by a leveling off of performance in the 1980s (figure 2.6). Between 1971 and 1984, the proportion of black children who showed that they had acquired basic reading skills by age 9 rose from 22 percent to nearly 40

Figure 2.6 READING PROFICIENCY TRENDS

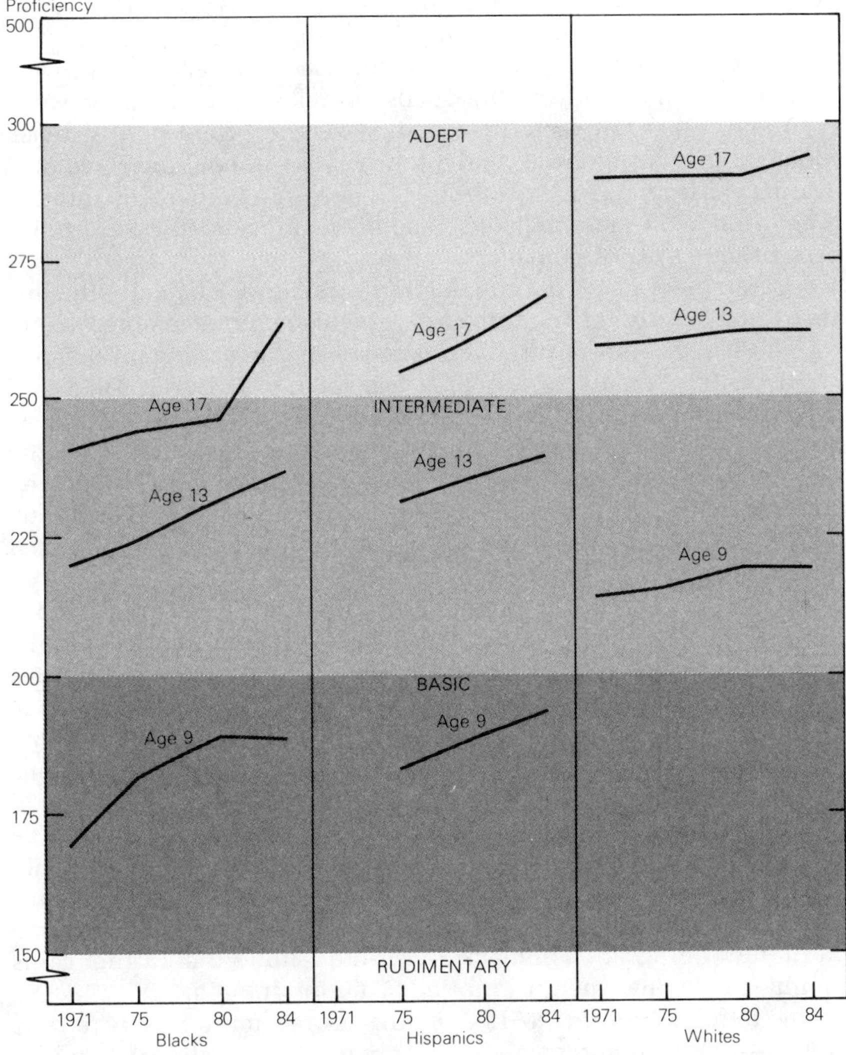

Source: National Assessment of Educational Progress (NAEP), *The Reading Report Card, Progress Toward Excellence in Our Schools: Trends in Reading Over Four National Assessments, 1971–1984*, Educational Testing Service, Report No. 15–R–01 (Princeton, N.J.: Educational Testing Service, 1985).

Note: The means represent weighted general reading proficiency scores on a scale of 0 to 500. NAEP test results are based on national probability samples of students at the specified age levels. Reading tests were conducted in 1971, 1975, 1980, and 1984 for 9- and 17-year-olds, and in 1970, 1974, 1979, and 1983 for 13-year olds.

percent, and the proportion who failed to show even the most rudimentary of reading skills fell from 30 percent to about 16 percent. Black 13-year-olds showed steady improvement in reading performance across the four assessments, and black 17-year-olds showed little improvement during the 1970s but substantial gains between 1980 and 1984. Between 1971 and 1984, the proportion of black adolescents who showed that they had acquired "intermediate" reading skills by age 17 rose from 41 percent to 66 percent, and the proportion who demonstrated "adept" reading skills rose from 7 percent to nearly 16 percent.[96]

Separate assessment data on the reading skills of Hispanic students are available only for the three assessments conducted since 1974–75. These data show steady improvement in the reading proficiency of Hispanic students in all three age groups. Between 1975 and 1984, the proportion of Hispanic children who demonstrated basic reading skills by age 9 rose from 34 percent to 44 percent. Over the same period, the proportion of Hispanic adolescents who showed "intermediate" reading skills by age 17 rose from 57 percent to 69 percent, while the proportion testing at the "adept" level increased from 13 percent to 20 percent.

Despite the gains made by black and Hispanic pupils, their average reading levels remain well below those of nonminority pupils. Among the 9-year-olds tested in 1984, for example, the proportions who had mastered basic reading skills were 39 percent for black children, 44 percent for Hispanic children, and 71 percent for white non-Hispanic children. And among the 17-year-olds, the proportions reading at the "adept" level in 1984 were 16 percent for blacks, 20 percent for Hispanics, and 45 percent for white non-Hispanics. The average black and Hispanic 17-year-olds were reading at a level only slightly above that of average white 13-year-olds. Despite gains, parity has obviously not been achieved. Moreover, the recent leveling off in the reading skills of black 9-year-olds shows that further gains in minority achievement cannot be taken for granted.

The trend found in NAEP reading scores for minority ethnic groups—significant progress, but not enough to close the gap between them and the majority—has also been found in other assessment areas, such as writing and mathematics. And similar trends have been observed with respect to other groups whose achievement has traditionally been below average: namely, pupils who live in the South, pupils living in disadvantaged urban communities or rural areas, and pupils whose parents have less than a high school education. Students from all these groups have made greater strides

Figure 2.7 SAT-VERBAL MEANS, BY ETHNIC GROUP

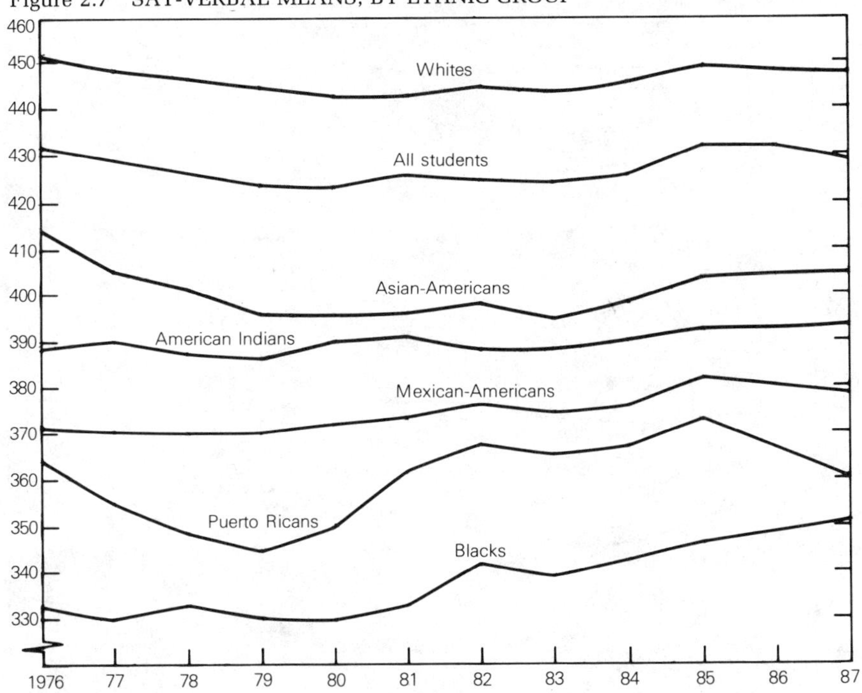

Source: See figure 2.5.

in reading and other academic skills than have their counterparts from more advantaged geographic areas or family backgrounds, but the advances have not been sufficient to eliminate achievement differences.[97]

■ *TRENDS IN THE PERFORMANCE OF MINORITY STUDENTS ON COLLEGE ADMISSIONS TESTS*

Over the past decade, there have been increases in the average scores achieved by black, Mexican-American, and Puerto Rican students who have taken one of the standardized college admission test batteries, the SAT or the American College Testing (ACT) examinations. On the SAT, for example, the mean scores of black students rose by about 20 points on both the verbal and the mathematical sections of the test between 1976 and 1987 (figures 2.7 and 2.8). These increases reduced the black-white gap in SAT means by about 19 percent. The test scores of Mexican-American and Puerto Rican

Figure 2.8 SAT-MATHEMATICAL MEANS, BY ETHNIC GROUP

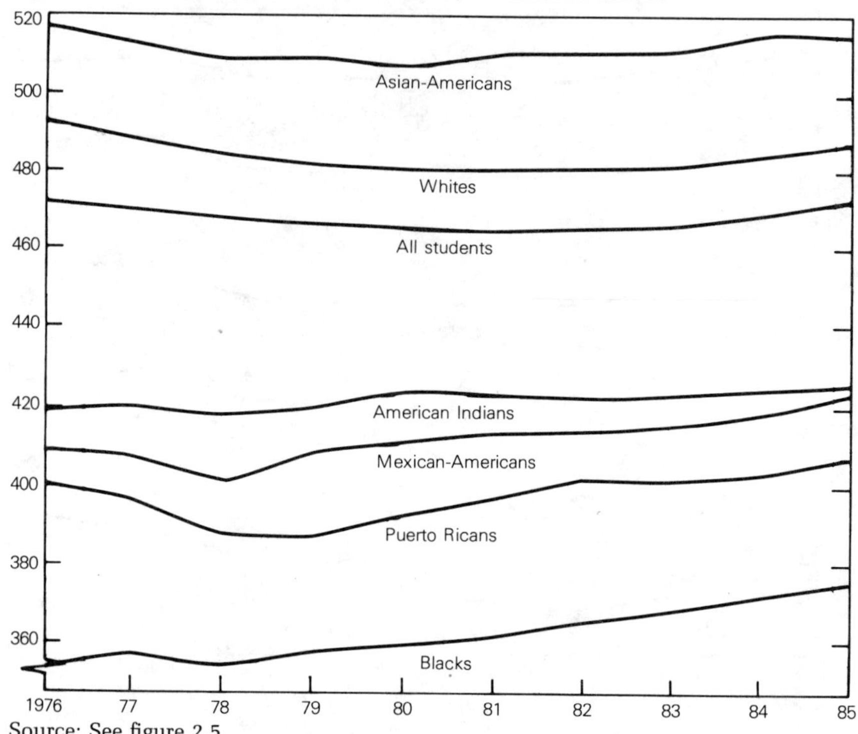

Source: See figure 2.5.

students, which were somewhat higher than the black scores to begin with, also rose, but more modestly, during this period.

The increases in black and Hispanic scores seem to reflect better preparation for college, and not merely changes in the pool of minority students who take the test. There was a decline in the number of black students taking the SAT each year in the early 1980s, but lately there has been an upsurge in black test takers. The conclusion that minority preparation has improved is also supported by the NAEP findings just summarized.

As with the NAEP results, however, the good news must be tempered by some harsh facts about continuing performance disparities. To begin with, those black and Hispanic students who take the SATs are a smaller and more select subset of their ethnic groups than is the case with white non-Hispanic students. Second, the gains that have been made appear quite modest when compared with the large differences across ethnic groups that remain. There is, for instance, still more than a 100-point gap between black and white mean scores on the math portion of the SAT and almost a 100-point difference in the verbal means. Each of these differences amounts to nearly a full standard deviation in magnitude.

The significance of a gap this large may be better appreciated after examining figures on the comparative proportions of black and white students who achieve SAT scores high enough to qualify them for acceptance by the most selective colleges. In 1985, for example, 19 percent of all white students (and 30 percent of Asian-Americans) who took the SAT achieved scores of 600 or more on the mathematical section of the test. In the same year, less than 3 percent of black test takers did this well. And whereas 9 percent of the whites and Asians got scores of 600 or more on the verbal section, only about 1.5 percent of the black candidates scored as high as this on the verbal test.[98] With performance levels as disparate as these, it is hardly surprising that colleges use different standards in evaluating their minority and nonminority candidates. Nor is it a wonder that there should be controversy and resentment among nonminority and Asian students over whether such reverse discrimination is fair.

Finally, we should not simply assume that it is only a matter of time before ethnic gaps in academic achievement disappear. It is conceivable that minority performance on the SATs could level off in the near future, in the way that the reading scores of black 9-year-olds on the NAEP have done. Nor can we take it for granted that black and Hispanic students would automatically do just as well as non-Hispanic whites or Asians if they all went to the same kinds of schools and received the same kinds of educational experiences. Many of the black students who take the SAT *do* go to excellent high schools and have gone to good schools throughout their academic careers. Yet even in these schools, ethnic differences in achievement remain.

TRENDS IN INDICATORS OF SOCIAL BEHAVIOR AND ATTITUDES

In the past three decades, the social behavior and attitudes of young people in the United States have changed profoundly. Some of the changes in teen behavior have been a source of great concern to older generations of Americans. Theft and violence, use of illicit drugs, and early sexual activity outside marriage are all more common among today's teenagers than they were among the teens of 20 to 30 years ago. In the past decade, however, most of the indicators of undesirable behavior among teenagers and young adults have reached a plateau or declined somewhat, rather than showing continued deterioration or dramatic improvement. In addition, some trends in young people's social behavior, such as some of the changes that have occurred in marriage and childbearing, seem to have positive implications for the future. In this section, we review recent trends in youthful crime, drug and alcohol use, fertility-related behavior and attitudes, attitudes about women's and men's roles in the family and the workplace, and goals and values.

Juvenile Crime

Indicators of delinquent and criminal activity by young people in the United States include FBI statistics on juvenile arrests, data from crime victimization surveys, and vital statistics on teenage homicide. All these measures have significant limitations as indicators of the underlying juvenile crime rate. Nevertheless, over the past quarter-century, these imperfect indicators have told a reasonably consistent story about where the juvenile crime rate was going. From the mid-1960s to the mid-1970s, the rate was going up. Since about 1975, however, juvenile crime has remained at about the same level or declined, depending on which form of crime one looks at.

■ *JUVENILE ARREST TRENDS*

In 1985, there were 102 arrests of persons between the ages of 13 and 17 for every 1,000 teens in the population. Thirty-two percent of these arrests were for crimes that are included in the FBI Property Crime Index: namely, arson, auto theft, burglary, and larceny. Four percent of the arrests were for crimes that are included in the FBI Violent Crime Index: namely, aggravated assault, murder, rape, robbery, and nonnegligent manslaughter. The remainder of the arrests were for nonindex crimes, such as vandalism, liquor-law or drug-abuse violations, disorderly conduct, and simple assault. Teens in the 13-to-17 age range have the highest rates of arrest for property crimes, whereas arrest rates for violent crimes are higher in the late teens and early twenties.

Between 1965 and 1975, the total teen arrest rate increased by 41 percent, from 74 to 104 per 1,000. Arrests for property index crimes increased from 25 to 36 per 1,000 (43 percent), while arrests for violence index crimes doubled, from 2 to more than 4 per 1,000.

Since 1975, the teen arrest rate for property index crimes has declined by about 10 percent, while the rate for violence index crimes has remained stable. Because there are fewer teenagers nowadays, the recent stability in youthful arrest rates has meant that teens play a smaller role in overall crime than they did in the past. For example, young people under age 18 accounted for 23 percent of all violence index crime arrests in 1975, but for 17 percent in 1985. And whereas youthful arrests accounted for 48 percent of all property index crime arrests in 1975, that proportion was down to 34 percent in 1985.[99]

■ *TRENDS IN TEEN VICTIMIZATION*

The likelihood that a juvenile crime will result in a recorded arrest depends on a number of factors, such as the propensity of victims to report crime to the police and the routine procedures of police departments for dealing with juvenile suspects. Changes in these factors over time could alter the relationship between the number of arrests and the number of crimes committed by juveniles. Fortunately, independent estimates of the volume of juvenile crime have been available since 1973 from the National Crime Survey (NCS). This program is a federally sponsored monitoring effort in which samples of the U.S. population are asked to report on their recent victimization experiences, including crime incidents that were not reported to the police. Data from this program on trends in the victimization experiences of the teenage population indicate changes in the volume of juvenile crime, because most of the offenses committed against young people are perpetrated by other young people.[100]

The NCS has found victimization experiences to be quite prevalent among teenagers (ages 12 through 19), at least for the kinds of crime measured in the survey. These include crimes of violence (assault, rape, and robbery) and crimes of theft (purse snatching, pickpocketing, and a type of crime that is especially prevalent among teenagers, larceny without contact). During the 1980s, teenage victimization rates for these crimes have generally been about twice as high as those for adults, with annual victimization rates of about 60 per 1,000 for crimes of violence and 124 per 1,000 for crimes of theft. These rates mean that U.S. teenagers experienced a total of about 1.8 million violent crimes and 3.7 million crimes of theft per year.

Despite the relatively high levels of teen victimization, the victimization rates since 1973 for adults as well as teenagers have tended to decline or remain stable, depending on the type of crime involved (figure 2.9). Incidents of personal larceny against teenagers dropped by about 25 percent between 1973 and 1985, whereas the overall rate of violent crime victimization remained essentially stable. Rates for individual categories of violent crime did change somewhat, with reports in two of the more serious categories—aggravated assault and robbery—declining, and incidents of the least serious type of violent crime—simple assault—rising in frequency. Thus, changes in teen victimization rates are consistent with the picture obtained from juvenile arrest rates.

■ *TEEN HOMICIDE TRENDS*

Changes in teenage homicide rates during the past three decades are also consistent with the pattern obtained from arrest statistics. Again, homicide rates are relevant here because most murders of teenagers are committed by other teenagers or young adults. As reported earlier, teen homicide rates rose dramatically during the late 1960s and early 1970s (as did rates for other age groups) but have declined somewhat in the 1980s. (For black teens, the decline began earlier, in the mid-1970s.)[101]

■ *JUVENILES IN CUSTODY*

Despite the recent stability of teen arrest rates and the smaller role that young people play in the total crime picture, the number of juveniles in custody has increased slightly in the past few years. This is probably due to tougher public policies about keeping offenders of all ages incarcerated for the duration of their sentences. There were almost 50,000 young people in custody in public juvenile correctional facilities in 1985, a 3 percent increase over the number incarcerated in 1979. The rate at which juveniles were incarcerated increased by nearly 11 percent between 1979 and 1985, from 16.7 to 18.5 per 1,000.[102]

■ *CHARACTERISTICS OF TEEN OFFENDERS: SEX DIFFERENCES*

Males make up the the vast majority of young people arrested or incarcerated for criminal offenses. Males accounted for 78 percent of all arrests of persons under age 18 in 1985. The male-to-female ratio for juveniles arrested for violence index crimes in 1985 was more than 8:1, while the ratio for property index crimes was nearly 4:1. More than 85 percent of the juveniles in custody in 1985 were

Figure 2.9 VICTIMIZATION

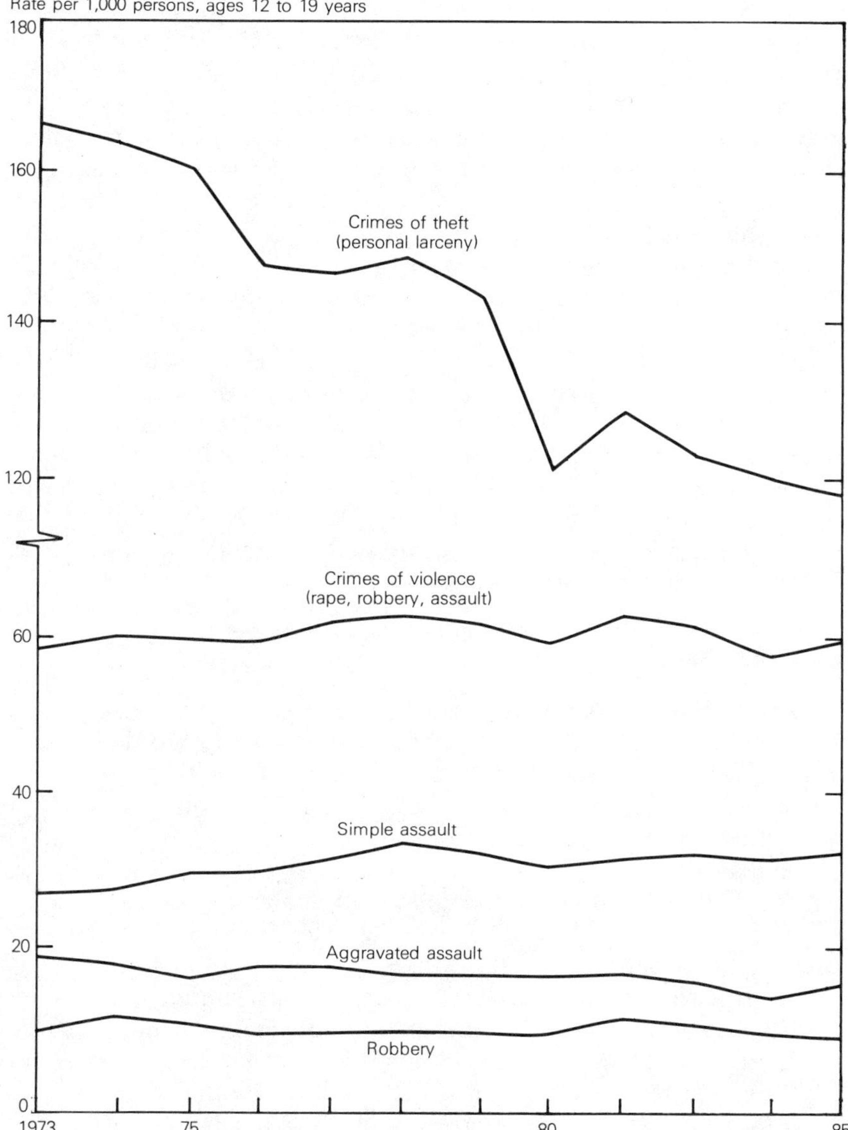

Source: U.S. Department of Justice, Bureau of Justice Statistics, *Teenage Victims: A National Crime Survey Report* (November 1986), figure 1; unpublished data from the Bureau of Justice Statistics.

male. However, the number of females in jails and prisons in the United States has been increasing faster than the number of males.[103]

Data on sex differences in the NCS tell a similar story. When respondents in the crime survey report incidents that involve personal contact with the perpetrators, the respondents are asked to provide information about characteristics of the offender or offenders, including sex, race, approximate age, and whether the person was previously known to the respondent. This is one of the ways we know that most crimes against teenagers are committed by other teenagers. The characterizations of offenders provided in the NCS may be inaccurate, of course, as they are based on the judgment and memory of the victims. Nonetheless, we can be reasonably confident of the NCS finding that for most types of crime, especially violent crimes, both the victims and the perpetrators of the crime are more likely to be male than female. During the early 1980s, for example, male teenagers were about three times as likely as female teenagers to be the victims of robbery, and 96 percent of the robberies committed against male victims were carried out by other males. Three-quarters of the robberies committed against female teens were carried out by male perpetrators as well.[104]

RACE DIFFERENCES

Data from the NCS show that black teenagers are more likely than white teens to be victims of violent crimes, but slightly less likely to be victims of crimes of theft that do not involve violence or the threat of violence. Race differences are especially pronounced for the crime of robbery, where, during the early 1980s, black teen victimization rates were two to three times higher than those for whites. Teenagers, like adults, are likely to be victimized by persons of the same race as themselves, but black teens are overrepresented among perpetrators of violent crimes, particularly the more serious crimes like robbery that are likely to lead to arrest and prosecution. During the early 1980s, for example, more than 40 percent of robbery incidents against white teen victims, and more than 85 percent of those against black teen victims, involved black offenders.[105]

Minority youths also are overrepresented among juveniles arrested or held in correctional facilities. Since 1975, the rate of arrest of black youths under age 18 for property index crimes has been about twice the rate for white youths, and the rate for violence index crimes has been more than six times the white rate. These ratios are actually somewhat lower than those that obtained 15 to 20 years ago. In the late 1960s and early 1970s, three times as many black as white youths were arrested for property crimes, and more than 11 times as many were arrested for violent crimes. In 1985, about 37 percent of the young people held in juvenile correctional facilities were black and about 13 percent were Hispanic. Thus, approximately half of the juveniles in custody were from ethnic minorities.[106]

The fact that victimization data as well as arrest and incarceration statistics show sex and race disparities indicates that there are real group differences in the frequency of criminal behavior, and not just differences in the way suspects of different sexes and races are treated by police departments and courts. Of course, differences of the latter kind may well exist, too.

Drug and Alcohol Use

Of the many changes in young people's social behavior that have taken place over the past quarter-century, none has received more public attention or generated more concern and condemnation than the increased use of marijuana and other illicit drugs. The reasons for the concern have to do with negative health and motivational effects of the drugs, and with the possibility that regular use might lead to addiction. Depending on the circumstances of use, youthful drug users may be at greater risk of serious injury in automobile accidents, fights, or other untoward incidents. Drug use may also be a factor in early sexual intercourse and pregnancy.

Because drugs must often be obtained from shady sources and because young people who use drugs are engaged in illegal acts, there is the further concern that teenage drug use can lead to disrespect for the law or deeper involvement in criminal activities. Drug addicts and drug traffickers have played major roles in the epidemic of violent and property crime that has plagued urban America for the past three decades. However, some would argue that the criminalization of drug use has itself helped to create and perpetuate these criminal elements.

■ *THE RISE IN MARIJUANA USE*

Survey data show that between 1972 and 1977 the proportion of U.S. young people ages 12 through 17 who reported that they had used marijuana within the previous 30 days rose from 7 percent to 17 percent, an increase of nearly 150 percent. In 1979, at the peak of the epidemic in adolescent marijuana use, more than half of all high school seniors reported that they had used the drug within the past year, and more than a third, within the past month. By 1982, nearly two-thirds of all young adults (ages 18 through 25) reported that they had tried marijuana at some point in their development.[107]

The rise in teen marijuana use probably began in the 1960s, although survey data to document the early stages of the trend are not available. Both household and school-based surveys done in the 1980s show that marijuana use has declined from the peak levels of the the late 1970s but has not returned to the lower levels recorded in the early 1970s. For example, the proportion of young persons ages 12 through 17 who used marijuana within the past month fell from 17 percent in 1979 to 12 percent in 1985, which was the same as the 1974 level.[108]

■ *USE OF OTHER DRUGS*

The use by teenagers of other illicit drugs—such as cocaine, amphetamines, and other stimulants; LSD and other hallucinogens; inhalants; barbiturates; and even heroin—also became more prevalent during the 1960s and 1970s, although the pattern of increase differed from one type of drug to another. None of the other drugs attained the popularity of marijuana, and most were much less prevalent. Use of nearly all drugs has declined from peak levels reached in the late 1970s or early 1980s. Cocaine is an exception, as its use has continued to increase, at least until the mid-1980s. Between 1977 and 1985, the proportion of high school seniors who reported using cocaine during the previous month more than doubled, from 3 to 7 percent, although most of the increase occurred before 1980.[109]

■ *ALCOHOL REMAINS NUMBER ONE*

Throughout this period, even when teen marijuana use was at its peak, neither marijuana nor any of the other illicit drugs came close to rivaling alcohol as the most common intoxicant used by adolescents. In 1979, for example, the proportion of young people ages 12 through 17 who reported using alcohol in the previous 30 days was 37 percent, more than twice the proportion who had used marijuana during the same interval. In addition, the proportion of high school seniors who reported use of alcohol within the month was 72 percent, double the number using marijuana at that time.[110] Of course, many young people used both substances regularly.

Survey data indicate that the regular use of alcohol by teenagers has fluctuated since the early 1970s, peaking in 1979 at the same time that marijuana use was peaking, and declining somewhat since then. Nevertheless, as of 1985, two-thirds of all high school seniors were current users of alcohol, compared with one-quarter who were current users of marijuana. Because youthful drinking is so widespread, it is likely that the negative personal and societal effects of teenage alcohol abuse far exceed the effects attributable to teenage drug abuse. The last statement is not meant to minimize the dangers of drug use, but rather to emphasize that teen drinking must be included in any consideration of the hazards and social costs of youthful substance abuse.

Fertility-Related Behavior and Attitudes

■ *EARLY SEXUAL ACTIVITY*

Another recent trend in teen behavior that has dismayed many members of the older generation is the tendency for young people to have sex outside marriage, and to do so at earlier ages, with fewer qualms and greater frequency than their parents did when they were adolescents. Survey data show that between 1971 and 1979, the proportion of never-married females aged 15 to 19 who reported that they had ever engaged in sexual intercourse rose from 28 percent to 46 percent. This increase approached 65 percent in less than a decade.[111]

The rise in teen sexual activity probably began in the 1960s or before, but earlier survey data are not available to document the start of the trend. Surveys done in the early 1980s indicate that the growth in teen sexual activity has slowed or even reversed in recent years. In a 1982 survey, for example, the proportion of female teenagers who had ever had intercourse was found to be 42 percent.[112] Despite this recent leveling off, sexual activity remains more common than it was in the past.

■ *NEGATIVE CONSEQUENCES OF TEEN SEX*

The negative social and economic consequences of having a child while a teenager have been amply demonstrated by research. But many adults object to teen sex even if no pregnancy results from the activity. For some, sex outside marriage violates religious or ethical precepts. Others believe that young teenagers are not emotionally ready for a sexual relationship, or that a premature relationship may limit a young person's social development and academic achievement. Although negative psychological consequences of early sexual experience have not yet been demonstrated by research, it has been found that precocious intercourse correlates with a variety of adolescent misbehaviors, including conduct problems at home or in school, drug use, and delinquency.[113]

Another negative aspect of early sex is that it exposes the youngsters to the risk of sexually transmitted diseases. Various forms of venereal disease have become more prevalent among young people, presumably because of the greater frequency of nonmarital sexual activity. Because of the strong feelings about the impropriety of teen sex and the related issue of abortion, proposals to set up sex education courses, school-based birth control clinics, or other programs to provide teenagers with contraceptive information and services usually stir up controversy. Recently, however, concern about the most lethal of the sexually transmitted diseases, AIDS, has been great enough to overcome the opposition and lead to the initiation of a variety of educational and assistance programs. Concern over AIDS may also be working to reduce the frequency of sexual activity among young people, or at least to lower the number of different sex partners each person has.

■ *CONTRACEPTION AND PREGNANCY*

The surge in teen sexual activity is often attributed to the advent of the Pill and other birth control techniques that are more reliable and convenient than earlier contraceptive methods. These techniques made it easier for young people to have sex without fear of pregnancy, or so the argument goes. Although advances in contraceptive technology have undoubtedly played a role in changing sexual behavior, many teens do not use contraceptives when they begin to be sexually active. Even in 1982, half of all young women between the ages of 15 and 19 reported that they had used no contraceptives when they first had sex, and the majority of those who did practice birth control used "old-fashioned" methods: namely, condoms or withdrawal.[114]

In general, teens who initiate sexual activity at younger ages are less likely to use contraception and more likely to become pregnant during the two years after they begin having sex. Thus, the increase in teen sexual activity has brought with it an increase in adolescent pregnancy. As of 1981, the proportion of women who had experienced a first pregnancy by age 20 was nearly 44 percent.[115]

■ *ABORTION AND CHILDBIRTH*

Pregnancies to younger women are more apt to be unwanted and to end in abortion than those to more mature women. In the mid-

1980s, more that 1 female teenager (ages 15 through 19) in every 10 became pregnant each year, 1 in 20 had a live birth, and 1 in 25 had an abortion; the remainder lost the child through miscarriage or stillbirth. Among female teens who had ever had sex, nearly 1 in 4 became pregnant; 1 in 9 gave birth, and 1 in 11 had an abortion.[116]

The proportion of sexually experienced teens who become pregnant each year has declined slightly since 1970, apparently as a result of improved contraceptive practice. The proportion of those giving birth has declined by nearly 50 percent, reflecting in part the lower pregnancy rate but mostly the increased use of abortion to end teen pregnancies. Because there were also fewer teenagers in the population, the number of births to teenagers each year dropped by more than a quarter between 1970 and 1985. Despite these changes, nearly a half-million babies were born to mothers between the ages of 15 and 19 in 1985 and nearly 400,000 abortions were obtained by young women in the same age range in 1983 (the most recent year for which figures are available).[117]

■ *THE WEAKENED LINK BETWEEN PREGNANCY AND MARRIAGE*

Another change that has occurred in the fertility-related behavior of adolescents is a weakening of the link between pregnancy and marriage. In the past, when a unmarried young woman became pregnant, family and community pressures—and sometimes the young couple's own desires—were likely to lead to a marriage before (or shortly after) the birth of the child. Now, if the pregnant young woman does not decide to have an abortion, she is twice as likely to remain unmarried as to get married by the time the birth occurs. Of first-born babies born to mothers between the ages of 15 and 19 in the early 1960s, 46 percent were conceived outside marriage. But in the case of 51 percent of these nonmarital conceptions, the mother was married by the time the birth occurred. By contrast, in 1980–81, 72 percent of all first births to teen mothers were conceived outside marriage, and only 32 percent of these nonmarital conceptions resulted in the mother's being married by the time of the baby's birth.[118]

As a result of the decreased tendency to legitimize nonmarital pregnancies through marriage and the marked reduction in the number of births to teens who were already married, the proportion of teen births outside marriage almost doubled between 1970 and 1985, from 30 percent to 59 percent. In 1985, 45 percent of the births to white teen mothers and 90 percent of those to black teen mothers occurred outside marriage. Because teen mothers are not marrying, there is a much greater risk that they will have to rely on welfare to support their child. Three-quarters of teen mothers who were not married when their first child was born received Aid to Families with Dependent Children (AFDC) within four years of the birth, as opposed to the one-quarter of married teen mothers who did so.[119] Of course, the employability and prospective earnings of the child's father have something to do with a couple's decision to marry or not to marry in the first place.

■ *POSITIVE MARITAL AND REPRODUCTIVE TRENDS*

Some of the changes in marriage and childbearing patterns seem to have positive implications for the well-being of current and future generations of children. One is the trend toward marriage at later ages. Between 1970 and 1985, the proportion of young men who were still single at age 25 nearly doubled, from 27 percent to 52 percent. For women, the comparable proportion went from 14 percent to 34 percent. On the average, marriages that begin later are more likely to endure than marriages begun when the partners are in their teens or early twenties.[120]

Another positive development is the trend among both whites and blacks toward smaller family sizes and more widely spaced births. Smaller family sizes mean that each child in the family gets a larger share of the human and material resources available to the family. Perhaps because of this, children from small families tend to do somewhat better in school than those from large families, other factors being equal. One of the most remarkable aspects of the trend toward smaller families is the growing use of voluntary sterilization by women and men who have attained their desired family size and wish to avoid further pregnancies. By 1982, surgical sterilization had become the most popular method of birth control used in the United States.[121]

Although the fertility rates of black women are still higher than those of white women, two children now constitute the most common family size for both blacks and whites, and the pregnancy spacing patterns of both races are similar. Black women begin having babies earlier and continue to have a higher proportion of unwanted births than white women. Nearly 24 percent of all black births are unwanted at conception; the comparable figure for whites is 8 percent. Overall, there was a slight decline in the proportion of unwanted births during the 1970s; in 1982, just over 10 percent of all births were unwanted at conception.[122]

The experience of other developed countries and the family plans that American young people have reported in recent surveys suggest that the trends toward later marriages and smaller, more carefully planned families are likely to continue in the future.

Attitudes about Women's and Men's Roles

The past quarter century has seen remarkable changes not only in young people's patterns of sexual behavior, marriage, and childbearing but also in their attitudes about women's and men's roles in the workplace and in the family. Today's young people have obviously been influenced by the feminist movement and the entrance of women into the labor force in increasing numbers. Surveys of young people show shifts in youthful opinions toward greater acceptance of maternal employment and a more equal division of labor within the family.

Among today's high school seniors, for example, endorsement of the principle of equal pay for equal work is nearly universal. On the other hand, there is still considerable opposition to the notion that mothers should work while their children are infants or preschoolers. But as more and more mothers of young children have stayed in the labor force, youthful attitudes have grown more accepting of the practice. Thus, between 1975 and 1986, the proportion of female high school seniors who agreed with the statement, "A preschool child is likely to suffer if the mother works," dropped from 59 percent to 35 percent. Over the same period, the proportion of male seniors who endorsed the statement fell from 74 percent to 58 percent.[123] This is still a majority, of course, but a considerably diminished one.

Samples of high school seniors have also been asked whether they agree or disagree with the following statement about family roles: "It is usually better for everyone involved if the man is the achiever outside the home and the woman takes care of the home and family." Among male students in the high school class of 1977, nearly three-quarters agreed with the statement. By the time seniors in the class of 1986 were surveyed, however, the proportion of males endorsing the proposition had fallen to 46 percent. As might be expected, female high school seniors have tended to disagree with the statement. Less than half of the female students in the class of 1977 agreed with it, and only about one-fifth of the females in the class of 1986 endorsed it.[124]

Although attitudes have shifted toward the desirability of males assuming a more nearly equal share of household and childrearing tasks, it is not clear that the behavior of husbands and fathers has followed suit. More than three-quarters of male high school seniors and 81 percent of female seniors in 1986 agreed with this statement: "Most fathers should spend more time with their children than they do now." However, survey data indicate that even in families where both parents work full-time, women continue to perform the bulk of the child care and housework. And it appears that today's parents still do not expect their sons to pitch in and help around the house the way they expect their daughters to. Reports on the daily activity patterns of male and female children show girls learning domestic skills at earlier ages and doing more household chores than boys do.[125]

All in all, however, the tide of youthful public opinion certainly seems to be running against those who would return the American family to the patterns of the past, where husbands were the sole breadwinners and wives were primarily homemakers.

Goals and Values

■ *FAMILY VALUES ENDURE*

Despite the changes that have occurred in fertility-related behavior and sex-role attitudes, young people do not seem to be turning away from family life as such. Surveys of high school and college students show that getting married and rearing a family still figure prominently among the life goals of most students. For example, more than 80 percent of students in both the high school class of 1972 and the class of 1980 said it was "very important" that they find the right person to marry and have a happy family life. Two years out of high school, the 1980 seniors had grown even more committed to family values.[126]

Surveys of college freshmen in 1970 and 1985 found that the same high proportions, about 70 percent in each sample, chose the terms "very important" or "essential" to characterize their feelings about the goal of rearing a family. Similarly, 68 percent of female high school seniors in 1986 expressed agreement with this statement: "Being a mother and raising children is one of the most fulfilling experiences a woman can have." Only 14 percent of the female seniors disagreed with the statement, while the remaining 18 percent said they felt neutral about it.[127]

■ *INCREASED MATERIALISM*

Not all the news contained in surveys of young people's goals and values is reassuring, however. The surveys indicate that more recent classes of students have become more focused on material success, less concerned about social justice, and less reflective about the meaning and purpose of life. For example, the proportion of high school seniors who said it was very important to them to have "lots of money" jumped from 18 percent in the class of 1972 to 31 percent in the class of 1980. Over the same interval, the proportion who said "working to correct social and economic inequalities" was very important dropped by 50 percent, going from 27 percent to 13 percent of all seniors. Among college freshmen, the proportion who deemed it very important or essential to be "very well off financially" climbed from 41 percent in 1968 to 71 percent in 1985. By contrast, the goal of "developing a meaningful philosophy of life" has plummeted in popularity, dropping from 83 percent to 43 percent endorsement between 1968 and 1985.[128]

■ *DECREASED RELIGIOUS INVOLVEMENT*

There is also evidence that young people have become less religious in recent years. The proportion of high school seniors who reported that they attended religious services once a week or more increased during the late 1970s, but then declined from 43 percent in 1980 to 34 percent in 1986. Nearly half of the class of 1986 said they rarely or never attended church. The proportion of seniors who described religion as being very important in their lives also declined, although less sharply, going from 32 percent in 1980 to 26 percent in 1986. Despite the decline, a 59 percent majority of the 1986 seniors characterized religion as being at least "pretty important" in their lives.[129]

■ *CONTINUING CONCERN FOR THE LESS FORTUNATE*

The indications that young people have become more concerned with material success and less involved with spiritual and humanitarian values must be tempered by evidence that students are at least ambivalent about the competitiveness and materialism in U.S. culture, and supportive of efforts to help those in need. Thus, 79 percent of high school seniors in 1986 agreed with this statement: "People are too much concerned with material things these days." And 62 percent endorsed this statement: "In the United States, we put too much emphasis on making profits and not enough on human well-being." Healthy majorities of the 1986 seniors expressed sympathy for the problems of minority groups and people in trouble and said they would support "a good plan to make a better life for the poor, even if it cost me money." Similarly, nearly two-thirds of recent classes of college freshmen considered it very important or essential to help others who were in difficulty.[130]

TRENDS IN INDICATORS OF EMOTIONAL WELL-BEING

Are there indications that the emotional well-being of children and adolescents has deteriorated over the past three decades and, if so, is increased family stress at least partly responsible for the deterioration? Although available measures of young people's mental health leave something to be desired, several lines of evidence point to the conclusion that the answer to both these questions is yes. Indications of deterioration over time in children's mental health include a rising adolescent suicide rate, greater use of psychological services by children and youth, a higher proportion of children who are said to have had seriously disturbing experiences, and increases in the proportion of students receiving or needing special educational assistance because of chronic emotional problems.

A connection between family disruption and psychological problems in individual children has been found in both cross-sectional and longitudinal studies. However, studies of divorcing families show that although most children who must live through their parents' divorce find the experience stressful, only a minority show long-term behavioral effects of the disruption. Most of the young people involved are able to cope with family stress and go on to lead normal, productive lives.

Survey reports from young people themselves show that the majority are not depressed, alienated, or profoundly dissatisfied with their lives. Survey measures of young people's subjective well-being do not indicate that this situation has become notably worse (or better), at least not in the past ten years. In this section we review some of the evidence on these topics.

The Rise in Teen Suicide

The indicator of youthful emotional problems that has received the most public attention is the adolescent suicide rate, which has

Table 2.9 SUICIDE DEATHS AND DEATH RATES AMONG TEENAGERS

Age group	1960	1970	1975	1978	1980	1981	1982	1983	1984
					Number of deaths				
All teenagers									
Ages 12–14	n.a.	n.a.	n.a.	141	130	149	176	182	205
Ages 15–19	475	1,123	1,594	1,788	1,797	1,770	1,730	1,677	1,692
					Death rates[a]				
All teenagers									
Ages 12–14	n.a.	n.a.	n.a.	1.3	1.2	1.4	1.6	1.6	1.9
Ages 15–19	3.6	5.9	7.5	8.4	8.5	8.7	8.7	8.7	9.0
White males									
Ages 12–14	n.a.	n.a.	n.a.	1.8	2.1	2.1	2.7	2.5	3.0
Ages 15–19	5.9	9.4	12.9	14.3	15.0	14.9	15.5	15.1	15.8
White females									
Ages 12–14	n.a.	n.a.	n.a.	1.0	0.5	1.0	0.7	0.7	1.0
Ages 15–19	1.6	2.9	3.1	3.4	3.3	3.8	3.4	3.5	3.8
Black males									
Ages 12–14	n.a.	n.a.	n.a.	0.4	0.9	0.4	1.6	1.3	1.6
Ages 15–19	2.9	4.7	6.1	6.7	5.6	5.5	6.2	6.5	5.9
Black females									
Ages 12–14	n.a.	n.a.	n.a.	0.4	0.2	0.3	0.3	1.7	0.2
Ages 15–19	1.1	2.9	1.5	2.1	1.6	1.6	1.5	1.7	1.7

Source: National Center for Health Statistics, unpublished work tables prepared by the Mortality Statistics Branch, Division of Vital Statistics.
n.a. Not available.
a. Deaths per 100,000 persons in age group.

climbed dramatically in the past quarter-century. The suicide rate for teenagers ages 15 to 19 doubled between 1960 and 1975, going from 3.6 deaths to 7.5 deaths per year per 100,000 persons in that age range. It has risen by 20 percent since 1975, reaching a level of 9 deaths per 100,00 in 1984. The rate for younger adolescents (ages 12 to 14) is considerably lower, but it, too, has been climbing, going from 1.3 to 1.9 deaths per 100,000 between 1978 and 1984.[131]

Suicide rates have traditionally been highest among the elderly and lowest among adolescents and young adults. But although the rates for the elderly have declined somewhat, rates for adolescents and young adults have soared. Suicide has surpassed homicide to become the second leading cause of death (following accidents) among adolescents. Nearly 1,900 teenagers (ages 12 to 19) took their own lives in 1984.[132]

■ *GROUP DIFFERENCES*

For each instance in which a young person succeeds in killing him- or herself, there are many more attempts at suicide that do not succeed. Across all ages, it is estimated that there are 8 to 10 suicide attempts for every suicide completion. For teenagers and young adults, however, the ratio is more on the order of 25 to 50 suicide attempts for every suicide completion. Males who attempt suicide are more likely to use highly effective ways of killing themselves, such as guns, than are females. Females are likely to use less certain methods, such as wrist-slashing or drug overdoses. This is one reason why, even though suicide attempts are more common among females, the completed suicide rate is higher among males.[133]

Suicide is also more common among white teens than among black teens, the reverse of the situation with homicide. Thus, of the four sex–race subgroups, the highest rates of teen suicide by far are found among white males. The suicide rate in 1984 for white males ages 15 to 19 was nearly 16 per 100,000. Black males came next, with a 1984 suicide rate of about 6 per 100,000. They were followed by white females, with a rate of about 4 per 100,000, and black females, with a rate of less than 2 per 100,000.[134] Despite the sizable differences across subgroups, all groups except black females had a suicide rate in 1984 that was at least double the rate observed in 1960.

■ *REASONS FOR THE INCREASE*

The rise in youthful suicide has been attributed to a wide variety of causes, including "the increased availability of firearms, changing family patterns, the breakdown in traditionally stabilizing institutions, the dissolution of a sense of community, rapidly changing social mores that aggravate already turbulent adolescent development, and the intensive pressures of competing for limited educational and employment opportunities."[135] A weakening of religious prohibitions against taking one's own life, the increase in adolescent drug use, and coverage of teen suicide cases in the mass media are still other factors to which the epidemic of teen suicide has been linked.

Research has yet to sort out the individual significance and relative importance of these different influences. It has been found that family and cultural factors play a role in the genesis of suicidal behavior, but not in ways that are especially helpful in accounting for the secular trend. Suicide shows a tendency to "run" in families, perhaps as much for genetic as for environmental reasons. In addition, abusive families and families with persistently high levels of tension and disorganization seem to put their offspring at greater risk of self-destructive behavior. However, suicide does not seem particularly linked to divorce; about as many suicidal youngsters come from two-parent as from single-parent families. But rates of suicide do seem to be somewhat higher among young people who have lost both their parents through death or family breakdown.

■ *STRENGTHS AND WEAKNESSES OF SUICIDE AS AN INDICATOR*

The suicide rate has several advantages as an indicator of malaise in young people. It is an easily understandable and relatively objective measure (although determining whether or not a person intended to take his or her own life sometimes involves a considerable element of subjective judgment). Data on the incidence of suicide in the past and in various geographical areas are readily available. Moreover, teenage suicide is a public health problem and cause for community concern in its own right.

But using the suicide rate as an indicator of emotional well-being also has drawbacks, because it involves extrapolating from the extreme behavior of a small number of individuals to the alienation or unhappiness of large segments of the population. Such extrapolation may not be warranted. Substantial variations can occur in the suicide rate because of changes in the availability of different means of self-destruction (for example, guns or potentially lethal drugs). Inasmuch as the number of suicide attempts far exceeds the number of completed suicides, changes in the suicide death rate could take place without any change, or even an opposite change, in the rate of attempted suicide. The latter rate, which would probably be a better measure of the prevalence of severe emotional distress, is much less well documented. Finally, differences in suicide rates across population groups are not necessarily parallel to group differences in other measure of emotional well-being. In personal interview surveys, for example, high levels of depression are found among young black women, but as we have seen, this group has a comparatively low rate of suicide.[136]

Considerations such as these make it advisable to examine trends in measures of youthful emotional problems other than the teen suicide rate. There are several other indicators for which comparative national data are available from the 1960s. Although these measures have their limitations as well, they help to provide a fuller picture of how the emotional well-being of U.S. children has changed over time. One such indicator is a measure of the frequency with which U.S. parents have obtained professional help for psychological problems in their adolescent children.

Young People's Use of Mental Health Services

■ *MORE TEENS ARE SEEING PSYCHIATRISTS*

Survey data on young people's use of mental health services show that the frequency with which young people are taken to see psychiatrists or psychologists for emotional, mental, or behavioral problems has significantly increased since the 1960s. Between the late 1960s and 1981, the proportion of adolescents ages 12 to 16 who had received psychological help within the previous 12 months nearly doubled, going from 2 percent to almost 4 percent. The proportion of teens who had ever received help increased by 44 percent over the same period, going from just over 6 percent to nearly 9 percent of all teenagers (table 2.10). The increases were significant and roughly parallel for male and female adolescents. In both earlier and later surveys, males were about one-and-a-half times as likely as females to have received counseling or therapy within the previous year.

When the change over time in the receipt of psychological help by adolescents was analyzed according to the marital situations of the families in which the teenagers lived, the increase was found to have occurred primarily in families with a history of marital disruption. Teens from intact two-parent families showed essentially no change in their use of psychological help. Nearly 6 percent of adolescents from intact families received psychological help in the late 1960s, and 5 percent received such help in 1981.

By contrast, among teens from mother-only families, the proportion of adolescents ever receiving counseling went from about 9 percent in the late 1960s to almost 15 percent in 1981. Among teens from mother–stepfather families, the proportion receiving help went from 7 percent to more than 14 percent. Adolescents from father-only and father–stepmother families showed similar increases over time. Of course, there were also more teenagers living in single-parent or stepfamilies in the later survey. Because of this and because of the relationship between type of family and receipt of psychological

Table 2.10 PERCENTAGE OF ADOLESCENTS WHO HAVE RECEIVED PSYCHOLOGICAL HELP (percentage)

Type of family and when, if ever, adolescent received psychological help	1966–70	1981	Percentage change
All adolescents, ages 12–17			
Ever received psychological help	6.1	8.8	+44
Within last year	2.0	3.8	+90
More than a year ago	4.1	5.0	
Never received psychological help	93.9	91.2	
	100.0	100.0	
Adolescents in mother-father families			
Ever received psychological help	5.7	5.0	−12
Within last year	1.7	1.9	+12
More than a year ago	4.0	3.1	
Never received psychological help	94.3	95.0	
	100.0	100.0	
Adolescents in mother-only families			
Ever received psychological help	9.1	14.6	+60
Within last year	3.7	6.9	+86
More than a year ago	5.4	7.7	
Never received psychological help	90.9	85.4	
	100.0	100.0	
Adolescents in mother-stepfather families			
Ever received psychological help	7.1	14.3	+101
Within last year	2.3	5.7	+148
More than a year ago	4.8	8.6	
Never received psychological help	92.9	85.7	
	100.0	100.0	

Source: Analysis by Child Trends, Inc., of public use data from the Child Health Supplement to the 1981 National Health Interview Survey and Cycle III of the Health Examination Survey, 1966–70. Data collected by the National Center for Health Statistics, Divisions of Health Interview Statistics and Health Examination Statistics.

help, the majority of young people receiving help in 1981 came from disrupted or reconstituted families.

■ *IS IT GREATER NEED OR GREATER AVAILABILITY?*

These comparisons are based on parent responses to similar questions in two national surveys conducted by the National Center for Health

Statistics. Because the figures are based on parent reports, they are subject to error stemming from forgetfulness, reluctance to report psychiatric care, or even lack of understanding of what a psychiatrist or psychologist is. Nevertheless, the increase in psychological help appears to be genuine, and not merely the result of some methodological artifact. Indeed, it seems probable that the increase in lifetime utilization of psychological care is understated because parents may have forgotten care episodes that took place several years prior to the survey.

A more difficult question is whether the trend to more frequent use of psychologists and psychiatrists means that the need for psychological services has grown or, rather, that such services have become easier to obtain and more acceptable to use by families with teenagers than they were in the past. There is evidence to indicate that both processes have played a role in the increase.

■ *INCREASED CHILDHOOD STRESS*

Among the data that lend credence to the notion that the need for psychological help among the young has increased are survey reports from parents that show an increase in the proportion of children who have experienced seriously disturbing events in childhood. The 1976 National Survey of Children included a question to parents of children between the ages of 7 and 11 that had previously been asked in a survey conducted by the National Center for Health Statistics in 1963–65. The question was, "Has anything ever happened to seriously upset or disturb your child?" The proportion responding affirmatively rose from 27 percent in the earlier survey to 37 percent in the later one. The kinds of events that were most frequently cited in the 1976 survey as causes of childhood upset were instances of marital discord and family disruption.[137]

■ *REPORTS FROM TEACHERS*

Survey reports from teachers and annual counts by state educational agencies of the number of students receiving special educational resources also point to a growing need for psychological help among the nation's young people. The proportion of adolescent students who were described by their teachers as needing help for chronic emotional problems doubled between the Health Examination Survey of 1966 to 1970 and the 1981 National Survey of Children, from 1.3 percent to 2.7 percent.

The number of students who actually receive special educational assistance because of chronic emotional problems is only about one-half to one-third of the number that teachers identify as needing such assistance. But lately the number receiving help also has been expanding. As a fraction of total public school enrollment, the number of students receiving assistance for chronic emotional problems grew from 6.4 per 1,000 in 1976–77 to 9.2 per 1,000 in 1983–84, a 44 percent increase.[138]

■ *CHANGES IN THE AVAILABILITY AND ACCEPTABILITY OF PSYCHOLOGICAL HELP*

Although the need for help seems to have become more widespread, there is also ample reason to believe that psychological services have become more readily available and their use more acceptable to parents over the past quarter-century. The number of clinical psychologists and psychiatrists in the United States grew substantially over the period in question. These professionals could also be found in areas outside the major urban centers. Psychological services for children were more likely to be covered by private health insurance or Medicaid. In addition, psychological assessment and counseling services became more accessible through the public schools because of federal laws mandating the provision of such services for handicapped children.

In addition to these developments, public awareness of matters psychological has increased. Talk shows and soap operas on television, advice columns in newspapers, articles in popular magazines, movies, novels, and self-help books have all helped to spread information (and misinformation) about child development issues and family problems, including those of children experiencing their parents' divorce. As a result, parents probably are more sensitive to childhood disturbances and are more open to dealing with family problems that were formerly kept private.

Despite these changes, there is still some stigma attached to the notion that a child might need psychological help. Most families still have a bias against taking a child to see a psychologist or psychiatrist unless the child exhibits fairly serious and persistent behavior problems at home, or professional help is recommended by teachers or juvenile authorities. Thus, in the absence of better measures, it seems reasonable to use the receipt of psychological help as an indicator of a behavioral problem. Of course, whenever possible, it is preferable to have independent measures of emotional and behavior problems in addition to measures of service utilization.

Unfortunately, no time-series data from the 1960s on youthful behavior problems are available.

In summary, the use of psychological services by young people seems to have increased both because the number of persons needing help has increased and because helping services are more accessible and acceptable to families with children.

Self-Reports of Happiness and Life Satisfaction

As we have seen, there is evidence that the number of young people with severe emotional problems has grown over the past three decades. The evidence also indicates, however, that most young people are able to cope successfully with family stress and other pressures of modern childhood and adolescence. Surveys in which young people are asked to report their feelings about various aspects of their lives find that the majority are not angry, alienated, or depressed. On the contrary, most seem reasonably happy and satisfied with how their lives are going.

■ *MOST ARE "PRETTY HAPPY"*

In each year since 1976, for example, as part of the Monitoring the Future project, a national sample of high school seniors has been asked this question: "Taking all things together, how would you say things are these days—would you say you're very happy, pretty happy, or not too happy these days?" In 1986, 18 percent of the seniors surveyed described themselves as "very happy"; 69 percent as "pretty happy"; and 13 percent as "not too happy." In other words, more than 85 percent said they were at least "pretty happy." By way of comparison, when the same question was put to national samples of U.S. adults (age 18 and older), a typical response distribution has been 34 percent, "very happy"; 53 percent, "pretty happy"; and 13 percent, "not too happy." Although a larger fraction of adults describe themselves as "very happy," the same relatively small proportion of adults and high school students choose the most negative category, "not too happy," to characterize the current state of their lives.[139]

There is significant variation in self-reported happiness across different groups of high school seniors. Black students, for example, have been only about half as likely as white students to rate themselves as "very happy" and twice as likely as the whites to describe themselves as "not too happy." Nonetheless, 80 percent of black students in 1986 classified themselves as at least "pretty happy."[140]

■ *LITTLE CHANGE IN THE PAST TEN YEARS*

The fact that adolescent students tend to be somewhat less happy than older persons who have left school and moved into adult occupational and social roles is not a recent development. Nor has there been much change over the past 10 high school classes in students' responses to the happiness question. The response distribution in 1976—19 percent, "very happy"; 68 percent, "pretty happy"; and 13 percent, "not too happy"—was practically identical to the one found a decade later in 1986. Answers to other questions put to the high school seniors concerning their feelings and sense of life satisfaction have shown similar stability over successive classes. When asked to rate their overall life satisfaction on a 7-point scale, for example, almost two-thirds of both the class of 1976 and the class of 1986 selected one of the three positive rating categories.[141]

A sizable minority of high school seniors, about 37 percent, have described themselves as feeling lonely a lot of the time, but this proportion also has not changed since 1977, when the question was first asked.[142] There has been some negative movement in the distribution of responses to a question about trust in people. This item, which has been used as an indicator of alienation, asks whether, in general, most people can be trusted or "you can't be too careful in dealing with people." Between 1976 and 1986, the proportion of high school seniors choosing the response "most people can be trusted" fell from 32 percent to 25 percent, while the proportion choosing "you can't be too careful" rose from 38 percent to 47 percent. (The remainder of the students could not or would not decide between the alternatives presented.)[143]

Although this trend appears to indicate growing alienation among young people, other, related items in the high school surveys have not shown the same degree of negative movement. The change in this particular item may simply reflect young people's response to recent admonitions to be cautious of others in connection with public health and safety campaigns on missing children, sexual abuse, and AIDS. The predominant impression one receives from examining trends in the subjective well-being items in the annual high school surveys is that things have not changed much in the past 10 years, despite the continuing changes in marital disruption, maternal employment, and other aspects of young people's family environments.

■ SATISFACTION WITH FAMILY LIFE

The largely positive picture that is obtained from the annual surveys of high school seniors is reinforced by the results of other recent surveys of young people, such as the National Survey of Children, the General Mills American Family Reports, and the American Chicle Youth Poll. These surveys were based on households rather than schools, covered a broader range of ages than the surveys of high school seniors, and included young people who may have dropped out of school before their senior year. Despite differences in samples and methods, these youth surveys also find the majority of American young people to be fairly happy and pleased with most aspects of their lives.

Some negative feelings, such as fear of crime, fear of parental arguments, and anxieties about schoolwork, are extremely common, especially among preadolescent children. But few children seem paralyzed by fear or overwhelmed by sadness or anger. Indeed, a striking finding of the youth surveys, in light of the continuing turbulence in American family life, is the positive feelings that most young people express about their families. For example, three-quarters of the 11 to 16 year olds interviewed in the National Survey of Children said they were "very satisfied" with their families. Children whose parents have divorced or remarried are somewhat less likely to be positive about family matters than children in intact families. Thus, 64 percent of teens in mother–stepfather families, as opposed to 82 percent of those in mother–father families, were "very satisfied" with their families. But, as this result illustrates, even in disrupted families, the majority have good things to say about their family relations.[144]

SUMMARY OF TRENDS IN YOUNG PEOPLE'S WELL-BEING

In this section we summarize the trends in children's well-being that have occurred since 1960. First, in the area of childhood poverty and economic well-being, the situation improved during the 1960s, stagnated or gradually deteriorated during the 1970s, markedly deteriorated and then partially recovered in the 1980s. Although the average value of cash benefits available from state welfare programs for indigent families with dependent children has declined, the economic security of families with children has been bolstered by the introduction during the late 1960s and 1970s of noncash benefit programs, such as food stamps, subsidized housing, and Medicaid. Despite cuts, these programs continue to provide benefits to substantial numbers of families with children. Thus, children as a group are now better off economically than they were at the beginning of the 1960s, although they have gained less ground than some other groups in the society.

In the area of *physical health*, the situation improved during the 1960s, 1970s, and 1980s, although on some indicators the rate of improvement has declined in recent years. Nevertheless, the physical health of U.S. children is clearly better today than it was in 1960.

In the area of *academic achievement*, two divergent trends are evident. As far as *high achievement* is concerned, the situation deteriorated in the late 1960s and early 1970s, then leveled off or slightly improved in the late 1970s and 1980s. The achievement of today's best students appears to be significantly lower than that of the best students of the early 1960s. In contrast, the *achievement of students from minority and lower class family backgrounds* improved during the 1960s and 1970s, and apparently further improved during the 1980s, although at a slower pace. The achievement levels of today's minority and lower-class nonminority students are better than those of comparable groups in the early 1960s, but they remain well below those of middle-class nonminority students.

The past three decades have seen profound changes in young people's *social behavior and social attitudes*. Many forms of *youthful misconduct*, including violence, theft, drug use, and early sexual activity, became much more prevalent during the late 1960s and early 1970s, then leveled off or diminished somewhat during the late 1970s and early 1980s. Although deviant behaviors have not continued to increase, most forms of misconduct remain more common in the 1980s than they were in the early 1960s.

Changes in the *fertility-related behavior and attitudes* of young Americans include trends toward postponement of first marriage and first childbearing, increases in the use of contraceptive devices and abortion to prevent or terminate pregnancy, a weakening of the link between pregnancy and marriage, and a decrease in the number of children young women eventually wish to have. Young people's *sex role attitudes* have also shifted toward greater endorsement of equal opportunity for both sexes and greater acceptance of maternal employment outside the home.

Despite these changes, there is little indication that young people are turning away from family life per se. Indeed, several different surveys of young people's *goals and values* have shown that substantial majorities of high school and college students of both sexes consider it very important in their own lives that they find the right person to marry, rear children, and have a happy family life. Surveys of high school seniors and college freshmen have found evidence that the students of the 1980s are more concerned with material success than were the students of the 1960s, and less interested in goals such as helping the unfortunate or developing a meaningful philosophy of life. However, the surveys also show that a majority of today's students endorse humanitarian values and think that American society is too materialistic.

Two behavioral indicators of the *emotional well-being and life satisfaction* of children and adolescents suggest that young people are less well off now than in the past. One is the teenage suicide rate, which more than doubled between 1960 and the mid-1980s. The other is a measure of the frequency with which adolescents receive psychological help for emotional, mental, or behavioral problems, which nearly doubled between the late 1960s and the early 1980s. However, both the suicide rate and the psychological help measure are problematic as indicators of the well-being of the general youth population. In contrast to the negative picture provided by these indicators, national survey data show that the majority of today's young Americans are not anxious, depressed, alienated, or profoundly dissatisfied with their lives. Although high school students are somewhat less likely than their elders to describe themselves as "very happy," most young people appear to be reasonably content with their families, their schools, their communities, and their lives in general.

FAMILY POLICY AND CHILDREN'S WELL-BEING

The Fit between the Trends and the Theories about the Family

■ *THE FACTS DON'T FIT*

How well do the trends in young people's well-being and behavior just summarized accord with popular ideas about the effects of family changes on children and youth? And what are the implications of the trends for policies aimed at strengthening families and improving the lot of children? As mentioned at the beginning of this chapter, many people in the United States believe that the institution of the family is falling apart; the condition of children is deteriorating; and changes in the family, especially increases in divorce, single parenthood, and maternal employment, are the principal causes of the ills of children. But all three of these assumptions are challenged by the trend data reviewed in this chapter.

What the trend data seem to show instead is that the family is changing, not disintegrating; trends in children's well-being have been mixed, with deterioration in some areas but stability and even improvement in others; and the links between family trends and trends in children's well-being are weaker than commonly supposed. For example, as the proportions of children affected by divorce, out-of-wedlock child rearing, and maternal employment have increased over the past three decades, the physical health of U.S. children has improved, not deteriorated. So has the academic achievement of black youth, many of whom have grown up in single-parent families or families with mothers who worked full-time outside the home, or both.

To be sure, there have been negative trends in high-level academic achievement; in youthful crime, drug use, and sexual behavior; and in indicators of young people's emotional well-being. But even in these areas, the sequence of events suggests that other forces were at work, not a causal mechanism based on "family disintegration." If there were a strong causal link between, say, divorce rates and juvenile crime rates, one would expect some temporal lag between the rise in divorce and the rise in juvenile crime. If a divorce occurs when the child is three or four years old, as it often does, it would take at least 10 to 15 years before the child was old enough to appear in juvenile crime statistics. Yet the increase in teen crime during the late 1960s and early 1970s coincided with, rather than followed, the surge in the number of divorces.

The leveling off of the negative behavioral indicators that took place in the late 1970s and 1980s would certainly not have been predicted by "family disintegration" hypotheses. If anything, these hypotheses would call for further escalation of negative teen behavior during the 1980s, with leveling off not expected until the 1990s, if then. (The arguments against a simple, family-based explanation of the increase in youthful behavior and achievement problems are developed at greater length in chapter 3.)

■ REASONS FOR THE LACK OF FIT

There are a number of reasons why the trend picture has not conformed to popular expectations. First, commonly held views about the family and how it works to influence children have proven to be erroneous or overly simple. Second, children themselves have turned out to be more adaptable and resilient than they are often credited with being. Thus, although the net effects on children of increased divorce and out-of-wedlock child rearing have probably been negative, the effects have been considerably less than the devastating impact that was anticipated. As far as increased maternal employment is concerned, it may have contributed to rising rates of family disruption, but thus far it has been found to have little, if any, direct detrimental effect on children's well-being.

In addition, it has become increasingly clear that young people's development is influenced by forces other than the treatment and tutelage they receive at home. The other forces include the school, peer culture, mass media, and general social climate. Recent social changes have generally worked to decrease the influence of the family on children, and to increase the influence of these other forces.

Finally, in focusing on the negative (or supposedly negative) changes that were occurring in American families, commentators have either overlooked or underestimated a number of positive developments that have taken place in our society. Yet some of these developments seem to have had more of an effect on children's well-being than has the movement away from traditional family patterns. Among the positive developments are changes that have affected families, such as the trends toward higher levels of parent education, later marriages, smaller family size, more equality between the sexes, more democratic patterns of family interaction, increased openness about family problems, and greater willingness to do something about these problems. Other trends that have had beneficial effects on indicators of young people's well-being are the reduction in the size of the youth population since the mid-1970s and the improvement in the economic picture since the early 1980s.

■ THE ROLE OF GOVERNMENT PROGRAMS

Government social programs also have helped to ameliorate the situation of children and counteract the effects of family turbulence.

Although it is fashionable to think that welfare programs have contributed to the weakening of the family and that the antipoverty programs of the 1960s and 1970s were failures, we have seen that significant progress has been made since 1960 in improving child health, minority educational achievement, and the economic situation of families with children. Antidiscrimination laws, equal opportunity programs, government-sponsored biomedical research, immunization drives, health and safety regulations, Medicaid, food stamps and child nutrition programs, compensatory education, and other federal and state programs have played a role in these advances.

Equality among ethnic groups has not been achieved, to be sure. The efficacy of some of the aforementioned programs has yet to be demonstrated by evaluation research. Moreover, it is certainly possible to argue that government social programs have had at least some counterproductive effects. But there can be little doubt that, taken together, these programs have made a positive difference in the lives of children, especially poor and minority children.

Helping Children At Risk

Nonetheless, the family remains the central institution in children's lives and a significant minority of today's children are being reared in less than optimal family environments. As we have seen, parental conflict and family disruption are major sources of stress for many children and cause long-term developmental difficulties in some. In addition, growing numbers of children are being born and reared outside marriage. These children are more likely than other children to have to contend with financial hardship, and some have the additional burdens of parental ignorance and immaturity, lack of intellectual stimulation, poor supervision, and lax or erratic discipline. The prospects of children who must grow up in multiple-risk families, be they single-parent or two-parent families, are considerably worse than those of children who grow up in more favorable family environments.

■ *GOING BEYOND SURVIVAL NEEDS*

Policies aimed at reducing the negative financial and emotional consequences of family disruption for children certainly seem warranted, as do attempts to alleviate the plight of children in multiple-risk families. However, the trends reviewed in this chapter suggest that it is necessary for public policy on children at risk to go beyond current preoccupations, which are mainly with family economic resources and children's physical health and basic academic achievement. Policymakers must wrestle with the thornier issues of how children are being reared in their families; what effects family turmoil and undesirable child-rearing practices are having on young people's social behavior and emotional well-being; and what, if anything, public policy can do to improve or compensate for negative socialization patterns.

■ *HELPING CHILDREN NOW AND IN THE FUTURE*

Child welfare policies should aim not only to help the children who are in high-risk situations at present, but also to ensure that fewer children will be in such a situation in the future. Unfortunately, these two goals can be contradictory, because the provision of resources to families at risk may encourage the formation of more such families in the future. Even taking the widely supported step of making sure that absent parents meet their child support obligations could have the unintended effects of increasing the number of family breakups or prolonging or intensifying conflict between parents.

The challenge to policymakers is twofold: to find ways to help children at risk without producing incentives for undesirable behavior on the part of parents or potential parents, and to discourage the formation of high-risk families without trampling on reproductive rights or hurting the children who have already been born into such families. These are not easy tasks, but neither is the situation hopeless. The trend toward later and, hence, more stable marriages augurs somewhat more favorable family environments for children in the near future. So does the increase in the use of family planning techniques by women of all social classes and ethnic groups, including low-income, minority women who have had one or two babies as teenagers or young adults. Although examples of welfare mothers who continue to have babies may still be found, this stereotypical figure has become much less common.

Balancing Work and Family

What are the implications of trend data on children's lives for policy issues concerning parental employment and child care? Both the trend data and the results of family research studies suggest that it is time to move the policy debate beyond the question of whether mothers should or should not work outside the home to questions like these: What is the optimal balance between work and family responsibilities? How can public policies help more families to achieve such an optimal balance? There are, to be sure, still some people who would like to turn back the clock and return women to full-time motherhood and homemaking, but the trends in women's labor force behavior and in youthful attitudes toward maternal employment strongly indicate that this is not going to happen.

Powerful economic and ideological factors make it likely that levels of women's labor force participation will increase, not decrease, in the future. These factors include the increases in women's wage rates, the entrance of women into a broader range of occupations, the growth of those sectors of the economy where women are already heavily employed, the need for dual incomes to meet inflated living costs, and the feminist drive to increase the independence of women and expand their educational and career opportunities. There is now widespread public acceptance of maternal employment when children are of school age. There is still considerable opposition to the notion of employment for mothers of infants or preschoolers, but, as we have seen, this opposition has been steadily eroding among high school students over the past 11 years. Similar shifts in attitude have been occurring among adults. And the actual growth in rates of employment among mothers of very young children over the past decade has been nothing short of phenomenal.

Unlike the situation with divorce and single parenthood, there is little in the research literature to indicate direct negative effects of maternal employment on children. Moreover, data from time-use surveys and observational studies show that most working mothers go out of their way to spend time with their children and fulfill parental responsibilities, even if it means sacrifice of the mother's sleep, personal care, and leisure time. Yet preconceived notions about children and families make it difficult for some to accept these research findings. It is not unusual to hear pronouncements about the detrimental effects of maternal employment that are at best unfounded and at worst downright insulting to employed women.

Of course, when maternal employment is said not to be harmful to children, the proviso is that adequate child care is available at an affordable price. Proponents of subsidized child care claim that many families experience difficulties in finding suitable care for their children, turnover in child care arrangements is high, and the demand for good-quality care at a reasonable price far exceeds the supply. Others dispute these claims, arguing that market forces are sufficient to provide the needed workers and facilities. It seems likely, though, that pressure will mount for government action—

federal or state or both—aimed at increasing the supply, subsidizing the cost, and ensuring the quality of child care. However, some of the government actions that have been proposed, specifically those involving the imposition of training and licensing requirements on child care workers, could have the ironic effect of decreasing rather than increasing the supply of day care.

Adamant opposition to maternal employment and policies aimed at making day care more readily available seems unreasonable (as well as politically unwise), given the trends just described. It seems perfectly reasonable, however, for people who wish to preserve the family's traditional role in child rearing to seek policies that try to ensure that working parents can and do remain closely involved in the care and upbringing of their children, and that institutions that provide day care and early childhood education respect parental preferences and values. These goals might be furthered by expanding opportunities for mothers and fathers to work part-time while their children are young without hurting the parents' chances for career advancement or fringe benefits; limiting the total hours per week that children could be left in subsidized care; requiring that parents assist at group care facilities periodically; insisting that businesses give fathers as well as mothers time off to attend to parental responsibilities, such as taking the child to the doctor or meeting with the child's teacher; and requiring child care providers to ascertain and, to the extent feasible, support the values that parents are trying to inculcate in their children.

As the number of children being reared in two-career families increases and more families make use of group care facilities, it becomes more desirable for families and child care institutions to cooperate closely. Yet the experience of the public schools has been that, as school systems have grown larger and more bureaucratic, they have developed their own agendas and become less responsive to parental goals and preferences. This is one reason why parents turn to private schools. It would be unfortunate, but hardly surprising, if government involvement in substitute child care were to hasten the bureaucratization of that enterprise. Child care policymakers should seek ways to preserve the flexibility and responsiveness of child care organizations while upgrading the quality of care. The goals should be to expand, not contract, the range of care options available to parents.

Flexibility and diversity are also desirable in policies that affect parental employment patterns and job benefits. Generally speaking, the younger the child, the greater the need for care. But child development research indicates that children have a greater need for the special attention that parents provide when they are one to three years old than when they are infants. The need for special attention also varies with the child and as the child encounters health problems or passes through periods of developmental difficulty. Thus, rather than establishing certain patterns of work and leave as norms for all parents, employment and benefit policies should aim at making a variety of work schedules possible for parents.

Despite the growth of maternal employment in the United States, most children have mothers who do not work full-time, full-year. Some of these women would work full-time if they could arrange it, but many find it preferable to limit the time they devote to the labor market in order to spend more time with their children. And although full-time homemakers have become less common, they have certainly not disappeared. We appear to be moving into an era, however, where many more mothers will work full-time, year-round from the time their children are born right through adolescence. We hope that, in this new era, part-time employment and full-time homemaking will remain economically and socially viable options for women with children—and, indeed, become viable options for men with children.

As we move into the new period, we should continue to monitor the development and well-being of children in order to detect possible untoward effects of more intensive parental employment. Obviously, current conclusions about the benign effects on children of both parents being employed are based on research done when part-time or part-year work was the predominant pattern for mothers. Recently, there has been a highly publicized dispute among child psychologists about whether extended infant day care has negative effects on children's social development. Although this particular debate appears to have been blown out of proportion by the news media, the public attention reflects the real concern that many working parents have about their children. Monitoring children's well-being would also help in the evaluation of public policies regarding child care, parental leave, and the like.

The research on which this chapter was based was supported by Grant Number SES-8501616 from the National Science Foundation (NSF) and by supplementary funds and programming assistance from the Office of the Assistant Secretary for Planning and Evaluation of the U.S. Department of Health and Human Services (DHHS/ASPE). The opinions expressed herein are those of the authors and do not necessarily reflect the positions of these federal agencies. We gratefully acknowledge the intellectual guidance and moral support provided by our program officers, Murray Aborn of NSF and William R. Prosser of DHHS/ASPE. In preparing the chapter, the authors drew heavily on data and trend assessments contained in a statistical report titled: U.S. Children And Their Families: Current Conditions and Recent Trends, prepared by Child Trends, Inc., for the Select Committee on Children, Youth and Families of the U.S. House of Representatives. We thank Representative George Miller, chairman of the Select Committee, and Ann Rosewater, staff director, for the use of these materials. We are deeply indebted to our colleagues at Child Trends, Kristin A. Moore, James L. Peterson, Christine Winquist Nord, and Nancy O. Snyder, who participated in the preparation of the select committee report and provided additional assistance to us while this chapter was being prepared. Any errors of fact or interpretation that are present are the responsibility of the authors.

Notes

1. Samuel H. Preston, "Children and the Elderly: Divergent Paths for America's Dependents," *Demography* 21, no. 4 (1984): 435–57.

2. Marian Wright Edelman, *Families in Peril: An Agenda for Social Change* (Cambridge Mass.: Harvard University Press, 1987).

3. Gary L. Bauer. *The Family: Preserving America's Future*, Report of the Working Group on the Family (Washington, D.C.: U.S. Department of Education, Office of the Under Secretary, November 1986).

4. Barbara Vobejda, "Education Leaders Warn of Crisis for U.S. Youth," *Washington Post*, June 2, 1987, p. A-16; Congressional Research Service, *Changes in the Rate of Child Poverty: Possible Implications for Chapter 1, Education Consolidation and Improvement Act* (Washington, D.C., 1986); George S. Masnick, "The Nation's Children: A Demographic Profile," prepared for a conference on Children in a Changing Health Care System, sponsored by the Division of Health Policy Research and Education, John F. Kennedy School of Government, Harvard University, November 20–21, 1986; Daniel Patrick Moynihan. *Family and the Nation: The Godkin Lectures at Harvard University* (New York: Harcourt, Brace, Jovanovich, 1986); Congressional Budget Office, *Reducing Poverty Among Children* (Washington, D.C., 1985); and J. Merrow, "In Defense of the Young," *re:act* (Action for Children's Television News Magazine), 11, nos. 3 and 4 (1982): 6–7.

5. Albert D. Biderman, "Social Indicators and Goals," in Raymond A. Bauer, ed., *Social Indicators* (Cambridge Mass.: MIT Press, 1966), pp.122–25; and Richard A. Easterlin, *Birth and Fortune: The Impact of Numbers on Personal Welfare* (New York: Basic Books, 1980).

6. U.S. Bureau of the Census, "Household and Family Characteristics," *Current Population Reports*, various issues.

7. Data Resources, Inc., unpublished tables using annual data from the Current Population Survey, prepared for the Assistant Secretary for Planning and Evaluation, U.S. Department of Health and Human Services.

8. U.S. Bureau of the Census, "Population Profile of the United States: 1984–85," *Current Population Reports*, Series P-23, no. 150, Washington, D.C., April 1987.

9. National Center for Health Statistics, "Advance Report of Final Mortality Statistics, 1985," *Monthly Vital Statistics Report* 36, no. 4 (1987); and U.S. Bureau of the

Census, "Fertility of American Women: June 1985," *Current Population Reports*, Series P-20, no. 406, Washington, D.C., June 1986.

10. National Center for Health Statistics, "Advance Report of Final Mortality Statistics, 1985," *Monthly Vital Statistics Report* 36, no. 5 (1987).

11. U.S. Bureau of the Census, "Projections of the Population of the United States: 1983 to 2080," *Current Population Reports*, Series P-25, no. 952, (Washington, D.C., May 1984).

12. U.S. Bureau of the Census, "Marital Status and Living Arrangements," *Current Population Reports*, Series P-20, annual issues, table 9; and unpublished data from the Current Population Survey, U.S. Bureau of the Census.

13. U.S. Bureau of the Census, "Marital Status and Living Arrangements: March 1985," *Current Population Reports*, Series P-20, no. 410, Washington, D.C., November 1986.

14. William H. Frey, "Mover Destination Selectivity and the Changing Suburbanization of Metropolitan Whites and Blacks," *Demography* 22, no. 2 (1985): 223–43; Larry H. Long and Daphne Spain, "Racial Succession in Individual Housing Units," *Current Population Reports*, Series P-23, no. 71, Washington, D.C., 1978; Larry H. Long and Paul C. Glick, "Family Patterns in Suburban Areas: Recent Trends," in Barry Schwartz, ed., *The Changing Face of the Suburbs* (Chicago: University of Chicago Press, 1976), pp.39–67; and Reynolds Farley, "The Changing Distribution of Negroes within Metropolitan Areas: The Emergence of Black Suburbs," *American Journal of Sociology* 75 (January 1970): 512–29.

15. William Julius Wilson, *The Truly Disadvantaged: The Inner City, the Underclass, and Public Policy* (Chicago: University of Chicago Press, 1987).

16. Margot Hornblower, "South Bronx, 10 Years After Fame," *Washington Post* (August 25, 1987): A-1 and A-8.

17. Masnick, "The Nation's Children."

18. Nicholas Zill, "Behavior, Achievement, and Health Problems Among Children in Stepfamilies: Findings from a National Survey of Child Health," in E. Mavis Hetherington and J. Arasteh, eds., *The Impact of Divorce, Single Parenting, and Step-Parenting on Children* (in press).

19. Sandra L. Hofferth, "Updating Children's Life Course," *Journal of Marriage and the Family* 47, no. 1 (1985): 93–115; Larry Bumpass, "Children and Marital Disruption: A Replication and an Update," *Demography* 21, no. 1 (1984): 71–82; and Frank F. Furstenberg, Jr., Christine W. Nord, James L. Peterson, and Nicholas Zill, "The Life Course of Children of Divorce: Marital Disruption and Parental Contact," *American Sociological Review* 48, no. 2 (1983): 656–68.

20. National Center for Health Statistics, "Advance Report of Final Divorce Statistics, 1984," *Monthly Vital Statistics* Report 35, no. 6 (1986).

21. U.S. Bureau of the Census, "Marital Status and Living Arrangements: March 1986," *Current Population Reports*, Series P-20, no. 418, Washington, D.C., December 1987.

22. Kristin A. Moore, *Children of Teen Parents: Heterogeneity of Outcomes* (Washington, D.C.: Child Trends, Inc., 1986); and Nicholas Zill, *American Children: Happy, Healthy, and Insecure* (forthcoming).

23. Zill, "Behavior, Achievement, and Health Problems among Children in Stepfamilies."

24. Ibid.

25. Furstenberg, Nord, Peterson, and Zill, "The Life Course of Children of Divorce."

26. Ibid.

27. Nicholas Zill, "Child Custody, Child Support and Parental Visitation in a National Sample of Children," research summary prepared for the Women's Legal Defense Fund, Wingspread Conference on Child Custody and the Legal System (March 1984); and Frank F. Furstenberg, Jr., and Christine W. Nord, "Parenting Apart: Patterns of Childrearing After Marital Disruption," *Journal of Marriage and the Family* 47, no. 4 (1985): 893–904.

28. Eleanor Maccoby, Charlene Depner, and Robert H. Mnookin, "Co-Parenting After Divorce: Communication, Cooperation and Conflict," draft paper for the Stanford Child Custody Study, August 1987; and Robert H. Mnookin and Kimberly K. Powlishta, "The Interests of Children in Divorce: What Custodial Arrangements Are Parents Negotiating?" presented to the University of Wisconsin Conference on Child Advocacy (September 1987).

29. Michael Rutter, *Maternal Deprivation Reassessed* (New York: Penguin, 1972).

30. U.S. Bureau of the Census, unpublished data from the 1986 Current Population Survey; and U.S. Bureau of the Census, *Census of Population: 1960*, Subject Reports, Final Report, "Persons by Family Characteristics," PC(2)-4B, Washington, D.C., table 1.

31. Voluntary Cooperative Information Systems (VCIS), American Public Welfare Association (APWA), Washington, D.C., unpublished data.

32. U.S. Social Security Administration, unpublished data.

33. VCIS and APWA, unpublished data.

34. U.S. Bureau of Labor Statistics, "Half of Mothers with Children Under 3 Now in Labor Force," *News*, August 20, 1986; idem, "Labor Force Activity of Mothers of Young Children Continues at Record Pace," *News*, September 19, 1985; and unpublished data from the Bureau of Labor Statistics.

35. Howard Hayghe, "Rise in Mothers' Labor Force Activity Includes Those with Infants," *Monthly Labor Review* 109, no. 2 (1986): 43–45; and unpublished data from the U.S. Bureau of Labor Statistics.

36. Ibid.

37. U.S. Department of Education, Center for Education Statistics, *The Condition of Education, 1985 Edition* (Washington, D.C., 1986), table 1.3.

38. U.S. Bureau of the Census, "Child Care Arrangements of Working Mothers: June 1982," *Current Population Reports*, Series P-23, no. 129 (Washington, D.C.: U.S. Government Printing Office, November 1983).

39. U.S. Bureau of the Census, "Household and Family Characteristics," *Current Population Reports*, various issues; and unpublished data from the Current Population Survey, Bureau of the Census.

40. U.S. Bureau of the Census, "Marital Status and Living Arrangements: March 1985," *Current Population Reports*, Series P-20, no. 410 (Washington, D.C.: U.S. Government Printing Office, November 1986); idem, "Social and Economic Characteristics of Students," *Current Population Reports*, Series P-20, no. 360 (Washington, D.C., April 1981); and idem, "School Enrollment: October 1970," *Current Population Reports*, Series P-20, no. 222 (Washington, D.C., June 1971).

41. Ibid.

42. Congressional Budget Office, "Trends in Family Income: 1970–1986," Washington, D.C., 1988; U.S. Bureau of the Census, "Money Income of Households, Families, and Persons in the United States," *Current Population Reports*, various issues; and unpublished data from the U.S. Bureau of the Census.

43. U.S. Bureau of the Census, "Characteristics of American Children and Youth: 1980," *Current Population Reports*, Series P-23, no. 114, Washington, D.C., January 1982; and unpublished data from the U.S. Bureau of the Census.

44. U.S. Bureau of the Census, "Money Income and Poverty Status of Families and Persons in the United States: 1986," *Current Population Reports*, Series P-60, no. 157, Washington, D.C., 1987.

45. Sheldon Danziger and Peter Gottschalk, *How Have Families with Children Been Faring?* Discussion Paper no. 801-86 (Madison, Wis.: Institute for Research on Poverty, University of Wisconsin—Madison, January 1986); and idem, "The Poverty of Losing Ground," *Challenge* 28, no. 2 (1985): 32–38.

46. U.S. Bureau of the Census, *Statistical Abstract of the United States*, various issues; and unpublished data from the Office of Family Assistance, Department of Health and Human Services.

47. U.S. Bureau of the Census, "Money Income and Poverty Status of Families and Persons in the United States: 1986."

48. Social Security Administration, Office of Research and Statistics, *Aid to Families with Dependent Children: 1979 Recipient Characteristics Study, Part I, Demographic and Program Characteristics* (Washington, D.C.: U.S. Department of Health and Human Services, 1982); U.S. National Center for Social Statistics, *Findings of the 1969 AFDC Study, Part I, Demographic and Program Statistics* (Washington, D.C.: National Center for Social Statistics, 1970); U.S. Bureau of the Census, *Statistical Abstract of the United States, 1985* Washington, D.C., December 1984; Department of Health and Human Services, *AFDC Quality Control Survey* (Washington, D.C.: Department of Health and Human Services, 1983); and unpublished data from the Office of Family Assistance, Department of Health and Human Services.

49. U.S. Bureau of the Census, "Receipt of Selected Noncash Benefits: 1985," *Current Population Reports*, Series P-60, no. 155, Washington, D.C., 1987.

50. Analysis by Child Trends, Inc., of public use data from the March 1985 Current Population Survey, U.S. Bureau of the Census, in Select Committee on Children, Youth, and Families, U.S. House of Representatives, *U.S. Children and Their Families: Current Conditions and Recent Trends, 1987* (Washington, D.C.: U.S. Government Printing Office, March 1987).

51. U.S. Bureau of the Census, "Characteristics of Households and Persons Receiving Selected Noncash Benefits," *Current Population Reports*, Series P-60, various issues, 1979–85.

52. Analysis by Child Trends, Inc., of public use data from the March 1985 Current Population Survey.

53. U.S. Bureau of the Census, "Child Support and Alimony: 1985 (Advance Data from March–April 1986 Current Population Surveys)," *Current Population Reports*, Series P-23, no. 152, Washington, D.C., 1987.

54. Department of Health and Human Services, "Child Support Payments Increase," *Youth Policy* 9, no. 9 (September 1987), 38.

55. U.S. Bureau of the Census, "Child Support and Alimony: 1985."

56. Ibid.

57. National Center for Health Statistics, *Health: United States, 1985* and *Health: United States*, annual issues (Hyattsville, Md.: U.S. Public Health Service); U.S. Bureau of the Census, *Statistical Abstract of the United States, 1982–83;* and Centers for Disease Control, *United States Immunization Survey*, annual data.

58. U.S. Department of Health and Human Services, Public Health Service, Centers

for Disease Control, Division of Immunization, unpublished data from annual School Enterer Assessment.

59. Population Reference Bureau, Inc., *1988 World Population Data Sheet* (Washington, D.C.: Population Reference Bureau, Inc., 1988).

60. Ibid.

61. Population Reference Bureau, Inc., unpublished data, 1986.

62. Institute of Medicine, *Preventing Low Birthweight* (Washington, D.C.: National Academy Press, 1985).

63. National Center for Health Statistics, "Advance Report of Final Natality Statistics, 1984," *Monthly Vital Statistics Report* 35, no. 4 (1986); and National Center for Health Statistics, *Health, United States, 1982,* and "Advance Report of Final Natality Statistics," *Monthly Vital Statistics Report,* annual issues.

64. National Center for Health Statistics, "Current Estimates from the National Health Interview Survey: United States," *Vital and Health Statistics,* Series 10, nos. 150, 154, 156, and 160 (1982–1985 issues).

65. National Center for Health Statistics, "Current Estimates from the National Health Interview Survey, United States, 1985," *Vital and Health Statistics,* Series 10, no. 160; idem, "Dental Visits—Volume and Interval Since Last Visit: United States, 1978 and 1979," *Vital and Health Statistics,* Series 10, no. 138; and unpublished data from the Health Interview Survey Statistics Branch, National Center for Health Statistics.

66. Ibid.

67. Analysis by Child Trends, Inc., of public use data from the March 1985 Current Population Survey.

68. Bernard Guyer and Susan S. Gallagher, "An Approach to the Epidemiology of Childhood Injuries," *Pediatric Clinics of North America* 32, no. 1 (February 1985): 5–15.

69. National Center for Health Statistics, unpublished work tables prepared by the Mortality Statistics Branch, Division of Vital Statistics.

70. Guyer and Gallagher, "An Approach to the Epidemiology of Childhood Injuries"; Susan P. Baker, Brian O'Neill, and Ronald S. Karpf, *The Injury Fact Book* (Lexington, Mass.: D.C. Heath, 1984); Ross Roundtable on Critical Approaches to Common Pediatric Problems, *Preventing Childhood Injuries: Report on the Twelfth Ross Roundtable on Critical Approaches to Common Pediatric Problems,* in collaboration with the Ambulatory Pediatric Association, Abraham B. Bergman, ed. (Columbus, Oh.: Ross Laboratories, 1982); Alan K. Done, "Aspirin Overdosage: Incidence, Diagnosis and Management," *Pediatrics* 62, no. 5 (November 1978): 890–897; and National Safety Council, *Accident Facts* (Chicago: National Safety Council, 1977–1984 editions).

71. National Center for Health Statistics, unpublished work tables prepared by the Mortality Statistics Branch, Division of Vital Statistics.

72. National Academy of Sciences, Committee for the Study of the Benefits and Costs of the 55 mph National Maximum Speed Limit, "55: A Decade of Experience," *Transportation Research Board Special Report,* no. 204 (Washington, D.C.: National Academy Press, 1984); Elizabeth McLoughlin, Mary Marchone, Pearl German, and Susan P. Baker, "Smoke Detector Legislation: Its Effect on Owner Occupied Homes," *American Journal of Public Health* 75, no. 8 (1985): 858–862; and National Safety Council, *Accident Facts.*

73. "Unintentional Ingestions of Prescription Drugs in Children Under Five Years

Old," *Morbidity and Mortality Weekly Reports* 36, no. 9 (March 13, 1987): 124–32; and Consumer Products Safety Commission, unpublished data, 1986.

74. U.S. Department of Justice, Bureau of Justice Statistics, "International Crime Rates," *Statistical Bulletin,* May 9, 1988.

75. National Center for Health Statistics, unpublished work tables prepared by the Mortality Statistics Branch, Division of Vital Statistics.

76. Ibid.

77. American Association for Protecting Children, Inc., *Highlights of Official Child Neglect and Abuse Reporting, 1984* (Denver, Colo.: American Humane Association, 1986); and Select Committee on Children, Youth, and Families, *Abused Children in America: Victims of Official Neglect* (Washington, D.C., 1987).

78. Philip J. Cook and John H. Laub, "Trends in Child Abuse and Juvenile Delinquency," unpublished manuscript, May 1985; and National Center for Health Statistics, unpublished data.

79. Robert Haggerty, Klaus Roghmann, and I. Barry Pless, *Child Health and the Community* (New York: John Wiley and Sons, 1975).

80. Paul W. Newacheck, Peter P. Budetti, and Neal Halfon, "Trends in Activity-Limiting Chronic Conditions among Children," *American Journal of Public Health* 76, no.2 (February 1986): 178–84; and National Center for Health Statistics, "Current Estimates from the National Health Interview Survey: United States," *Vital and Health Statistics,* Series 10, annual issues.

81. Nicholas Zill, "How Is the Number of Children with Severe Handicaps Likely to Change Over Time?" Testimony prepared for the Subcommittee on Select Education of the Committee on Education and Labor, U.S. House of Representatives, June 25, 1985; and U.S. Department of Education, *Eighth Annual Report to the Congress on the Implementation of the Education of the Handicapped Act* (Washington, D.C., 1986).

82. Ibid.

83. U.S. Bureau of the Census, "School Enrollment—Social and Economic Characteristics of Students: October 1983," *Current Population Reports,* Series P-20, no. 413, Washington, D.C., March 1987; and unpublished 1987 data from the Current Population Survey.

84. Ibid. The Current Population Survey dropout rate is estimated by dividing the number of dropouts (the number of persons ages 14 to 24 who reported that they had completed 9, 10, or 11 years of school, had been enrolled in October of the previous year, but were not currently enrolled) by the total number of persons assumed to have been enrolled the year before in grades 10, 11, and 12. The denominator is estimated as all current enrollees in grades 11 and 12, plus all high school graduates and all estimated dropouts in the previous year.

85. National Center for Education Statistics, U.S. Department of Education, *High School and Beyond: A National Longitudinal Study for the 1980's, Two Years in High School: The Status of 1980 Sophomores in 1982,* table 1, and *Two Years After High School: A Capsule Description of 1980 Seniors,* table 3 (Washington, D.C., 1984).

86. Congressional Budget Office, *Educational Achievement: Explanations and Implications of Recent Trends* (Washington, D.C.: Congressional Budget Office, 1987); Gilbert R. Austin and Herbert Garber, eds., *The Rise and Fall of National Test Scores* (New York: Academic Press, 1982); National Assessment of Educational Progress, *Technical Report, Change in Student Performance by Achievement Class and Modal Grade: A Different Look at Assessment Data in Reading, Science and Mathematics,*

No. SY-RSM-21 (Denver, Colo.: Education Commission of the States, December 1982); Advisory Panel on the Scholastic Aptitude Test Score Decline, *On Further Examination* (New York: College Entrance Examination Board, 1977); and Leo A. Munday, *Declining Admissions Test Scores* (Iowa City: American College Testing Program, 1976).

87. Congressional Budget Office, *Educational Achievement: Explanations and Implications of Recent Trends* (Washington, D.C.: Congressional Budget Office, 1987); and Albert E. Beaton, Thomas L. Hilton, and William B. Schrader, *Changes in the Verbal Abilities of High School Seniors, College Entrants, and SAT Candidates between 1960 and 1972* (New York: College Entrance Examination Board, 1977).

88. Leonard Ramist and Solomon Arbeiter, *Profiles, College-Bound Seniors, 1985* (New York: College Entrance Examination Board, 1986); College Entrance Examination Board, *Profiles, College-Bound Seniors*, annual issues; and *New York Times*, Letters to the Editor, April 25, 1981.

89. National Assessment of Educational Progress, *The Reading Report Card, Progress Toward Excellence in Our Schools: Trends in Reading Over Four National Assessments, 1971–1984*, Report no. 15-R-01 (Princeton, N.J.: Educational Testing Service, 1985); idem, *Three National Assessments of Reading: Changes in Performance, 1970–80*, Report No. 11-R-01 (Denver, Colo.: Education Commission of the States, April 1981); and idem, *Changes in Mathematical Achievement, 1973–78* (Denver, Colo.: Education Commission of the States, 1979).

90. National Assessment of Educational Progress, *The Third National Mathematics Achievement, Trends and Issues*, Report no. 13-MA-01 (Denver, Colo.: Education Commission of the States, April 1983); and idem, *Changes in Mathematical Achievement, 1973–78*.

91. National Assessment of Educational Progress, *Three National Assessments of Reading: Changes in Performance, 1970–80*.

92. Arthur N. Applebee, Judith A. Langer, and Ina V.S. Mullis, *The Writing Report Card: Writing Achievement in American Schools* (Princeton, N.J.: Educational Testing Service, 1986); National Assessment of Educational Progress, *Three National Assessments of Reading: Changes in Performance, 1970–80;* and idem, *Writing Achievement, 1969–79* (Princeton, N.J.: Educational Testing Service, 1980).

93. Appleby, Langer, and Mullis, *The Writing Report Card;* Gene I. Maeroff, "Students' Knowledge of Arts Found to Decline," *New York Times*, December 30, 1981; National Assessment of Educational Progress, *Music 1971–79: Results From the Second National Music Assessment*, Report no. 10-MU-01 (Denver, Colo.: Education Commission of the States, November 1981); idem, *Citizenship/Social Studies Technical Summary, 1969–76* (Denver, Colo.: Education Commission of the States, 1979); idem, *Three Assessments of Science, 1969–77: Technical Summary* (Denver, Colo.: Education Commission of the States, 1978); and idem, *Changes in Political Knowledge and Attitudes, 1969–76* (Denver, Colo.: Education Commission of the States, 1978).

94. Allan Bloom, *The Closing of the American Mind* (New York: Simon and Schuster, 1987); and Eric D. Hirsch, Jr. *Cultural Literacy: What Every American Needs to Know* (Boston: Houghton Mifflin, 1987).

95. National Assessment of Educational Progress, *Three National Assessments of Reading;* idem, *Writing Achievement, 1969–79;* and idem, *Changes in Mathematical Achievement, 1973–78*.

96. National Assessment of Educational Progress, *The Reading Report Card*.

97. Appleby, Langer, and Mullis, *The Writing Report Card;* National Assessment of Educational Progress, *The Reading Report Card;* and idem, *The Third National Mathematics Achievement*.

98. Edward B. Fiske, "Steady Gains Achieved by Blacks on College Admission Test Scores," *New York Times* (September 23, 1987), A-1 and D-30; and Ramist and Arbeiter, *Profiles, College-Bound Seniors, 1985.*

99. Philip J. Cook and John H. Laub, "The (Surprising) Stability of Youth Crime Rates," *Journal of Quantitative Criminology* 2, no. 3 (1986): 265–77; Michael J. Hindelang and M. Joan McDermott, *Juvenile Criminal Behavior: An Analysis of Rates and Victim Characteristics* (Albany, N.Y.: Criminal Justice Research Center, 1981); and Franklin E. Zimring, "American Youth Violence: Issues and Trends," in N. Morris and M. Tonry, eds., *Criminal Justice: An Annual Review of Research* 1 (Chicago and London: University of Chicago Press, 1979): 67–107.

100. U.S. Department of Justice, Bureau of Justice Statistics, *Teenage Victims: A National Crime Survey Report* (Rockville, Md.: Justice Statistics Clearinghouse); and John H. Laub, *Trends in Juvenile Criminal Behavior in the United States: 1973–1981* (Albany, N.Y.: Criminal Justice Research Center, SUNY, 1983).

101. National Center for Health Statistics, *Health, United States, 1982,* table 21, and *Health, United States: 1985*, table 24; and unpublished data provided by the Statistical Resources Branch, National Center for Health Statistics.

102. U.S. Department of Justice, Bureau of Justice Statistics, *Children in Custody* (Rockville, Md.: Justice Statistics Clearinghouse, October 1986).

103. Ibid.; and Katherine M. Jamieson and Timothy J. Flanagan, eds., *Sourcebook of Criminal Justice Statistics—1986* (Washington, D.C.: U.S. Department of Justice, Bureau of Justice Statistics, 1987).

104. U.S. Department of Justice, *Teenage Victims: A National Crime Survey Report,* tables 3 and 13.

105. Ibid., tables 3 and 14.

106. Cook and Laub, "The (Surprising) Stability of Youth Crime Rates"; and U.S. Department of Justice, Bureau of Justice Statistics, *Children in Custody.*

107. U.S. Bureau of the Census, *Statistical Abstract of the United States: 1987,* Washington, D.C., 1986, table 171; *National Institute on Drug Abuse, National Household Survey on Drug Abuse: 1985 Population Estimates* (Rockville, Md.: National Institute on Drug Abuse, 1987); National Center for Health Statistics. *Health: United States, 1985* (Hyattsville, Md.: U.S. Public Health Service, 1985); Lloyd D. Johnston, Jerald G. Bachman, and Patrick M. O'Malley, "National Trends in Drug Use and Related Factors among American High School Students: 1975–1986," (Rockville, Md.: National Institute on Drug Abuse, 1987); and idem, *Monitoring the Future* (Ann Arbor, Mich.: Institute for Social Research, University of Michigan, annual volumes, 1975–1985).

108. National Institute on Drug Abuse. *National Household Survey on Drug Abuse: 1985 Population Estimates;* and Johnston, Bachman, and O'Malley, "National Trends in Drug Abuse and Related Factors among American High School Students: 1975–1986."

109. Ibid.

110. Ibid.

111. Melvin Zelnik and John F. Kantner, "Sexual Activity, Contraceptive Use and Pregnancy Among Metropolitan-Area Teenagers: 1971–1979," *Family Planning Perspectives* 12, no. 5 (September/October 1980): 230–37.

112. National Center for Health Statistics, unpublished tabulations from the 1982 National Survey of Family Growth, Cycle III, 1984.

113. Margaret E. Ensminger, "Adolescent Sexual Behavior as It Relates to Other

Transition Behaviors in Youth," in Sandra L. Hofferth and Cheryl D. Hayes, eds., *Risking The Future: Adolescent Sexuality, Pregnancy, and Childbearing* (Washington, D.C.: National Academy Press, 1987): 36–55; Sandra L. Hofferth, "Social and Economic Consequences of Teenage Childbearing," in Hofferth and Hayes, eds., *Risking The Future:* 123–44; and Kristin A. Moore and Martha Burt, *Private Crisis, Public Cost: Policy Perspectives on Teenage Childbearing* (Washington, D.C.: Urban Institute Press, 1982).

114. National Center for Health Statistics, unpublished tabulations from the 1982 National Survey of Family Growth, Cycle III.

115. Calculations by Jacqueline D. Forrest from vital statistics data from the National Center for Health Statistics, in Hofferth and Hayes, eds., *Risking The Future,* table 3.3.

116. Calculations by Sandra L. Hofferth, Center for Population Research, National Institute for Child Health and Human Development, National Institutes of Health, in Select Committee on Children, Youth, and Families, U.S. House of Representatives, *U.S. Children and Their Families: Current Conditions and Recent Trends, 1987* (Washington, D.C., March 1987), 75.

117. Kristin A. Moore. *Facts at a Glance* (Washington, D.C.: Child Trends, Inc., 1987).

118. Martin O'Connell and Carolyn C. Rogers, "Out-of-Wedlock Births, Premarital Pregnancies and Their Effect on Family Formation and Dissolution," *Family Planning Perspectives* 16, no. 4 (July/August 1984): 157–62.

119. Moore, *Facts at a Glance;* Wilbur Weder, U.S. Department of Health and Human Services, Family Support Administration, unpublished tabulations, September 1987; and Gina C. Adams, "The Dynamics of Welfare Recipiency Among Adolescent Mothers," Human Resources and Community Development Division, Congressional Budget Office, memorandum, March 17, 1987.

120. U.S. Bureau of the Census, "Household and Family Characteristics," *Current Population Reports,* Series P-20, annual issues; and Andrew J. Cherlin, *Marriage, Divorce, Remarriage* (Cambridge, Mass.: Harvard University Press, 1981).

121. National Center for Health Statistics, "Trends and Variations in Post Partum Sterilization in the United States, 1972 and 1980," *Monthly Vital Statistics Report* 36, no.7 (1987); and Christine A. Bachrach, "Contraceptive Practice among American Women, 1973–1982," *Family Planning Perspectives* 16, no. 6 (November/December 1984): 253–59.

122. U.S. Bureau of the Census, "Fertility of American Women: June 1985," *Current Population Reports,* Series P-20, no. 406, Washington, D.C., June 1986; Eugenia Eckard, "Wanted and Unwanted Births Reported by Mothers 15–44 Years of Age: United States, 1976," *Advance Data,* no. 56 (1980); and National Center for Health Statistics, unpublished data from the 1982 National Survey of Family Growth, Cycle III.

123. Lloyd D. Johnston, Jerald G. Bachman, and Patrick M. O'Malley, *Monitoring the Future: Questionnaire Responses from the Nation's High School Seniors* (Ann Arbor, Mich.: Survey Research Center, Institute for Social Research, University of Michigan, annual issues, 1975–85).

124. Ibid.

125. Ibid.; F. Thomas Juster and Frank P. Stafford, eds., *Time, Goods, and Well-Being* (Ann Arbor, Mich.: Survey Research Center, Institute for Social Research, University of Michigan, 1985); Nicholas Zill and James L. Peterson, "Learning to Do Things without Help," in Luis M. Laosa and Irving E. Sigel, eds., *Families As Learning*

Environments For Children (New York: Plenum Publishing Corporation, 1982); and John P. Robinson, *How Americans Use Time: A Social-Psychological Analysis of Everyday Behavior* (New York: Praeger, 1977).

126. U.S. Department of Education, National Center for Education Statistics, *High School and Beyond: A National Longitudinal Study for the 1980's, Two Years After High School: A Capsule Description of 1980 Seniors* (1984), and *A Capsule Description of High School Students* (Washington, D.C., 1981).

127. Alexander W. Astin, Kenneth C. Green, William S. Korn, and Marilyn Schalit, *The American Freshman—National Norms for Fall 1985* (Los Angeles: Higher Education Research Institute, Graduate School of Education, UCLA, December 1985 and annual volumes); and Johnston, Bachman, and O'Malley. *Monitoring the Future: Questionnaire Responses from the Nation's High School Seniors.*

128. Ibid.; and National Center for Education Statistics, *High School and Beyond: A National Longitudinal Study for the 1980's, A Capsule Description of High School Students.*

129. Johnston, Bachman, and O'Malley, *Monitoring the Future: Questionnaire Responses from the Nation's High School Seniors.*

130. Ibid.; and Astin, Green, Korn, and Schalit, *The American Freshman.*

131. National Institute of Mental Health, *Useful Information On . . . Suicide* (Washington, D.C.: U.S. Department of Health and Human Services, 1986); and unpublished work tables prepared by the Mortality Statistics Branch, Division of Vital Statistics, National Center for Health Statistics.

132. Ibid.

133. Ibid.

134. Ibid.

135. National Institute of Mental Health, *Useful Information On . . . Suicide*, p. 13.

136. Frank Godley and Ronald W. Wilson, "Health Status of Minority Groups," in U.S. Department of Health and Human Services, *Health: United States, 1979* (Hyattsville, Md.: U.S. Public Health Service, 1980): 3–36.

137. Zill and Peterson, "Learning to Do Things without Help".

138. Nicholas Zill, *The School-Age Handicapped, Contractor Report*, National Center for Education Statistics (Washington, D.C., 1985); and Lance Federer and Nicholas Zill, "Educating Handicapped Children," in Valena W. Plisko and Joyce D. Stern, eds., *The Condition of Education: 1985 Edition* (Washington, D.C., 1985): 177–200.

139. Johnston, Bachman, and O'Malley. *Monitoring the Future: Questionnaire Responses from the Nation's High School Seniors;* and James A. Davis, *General Social Surveys, 1972–1978: Cumulative Codebook* (Chicago: National Opinion Research Center, University of Chicago, 1978), 100.

140. Ibid.

141. Ibid.

142. Ibid.

143. Ibid.

144. Data tabulations from the 1981 National Survey of Children: Child and Parent Questionnaire Responses by Sex, Age, Ethnic Group, Parent Education, and Family Structure (Washington, D.C.: Child Trends, Inc., 1985); Roper Organization, Inc., *The American Chicle Youth Poll* (Morris Plains, N.J.: Warner-Lambert Company, 1987); and Yankelovich, Skelly, and White, *Raising Children in a Changing Society* (Minneapolis: General Mills, Inc., 1977).

Chapter Three

FAMILY CHANGE AND ADOLESCENT WELL-BEING: A REEXAMINATION OF U.S. TRENDS

Frank F. Furstenberg, Jr.
Gretchen A. Condran

Concerns about a decline in the authority of the family and the well-being of American youth are not new. Family historians document that in the seventeenth century, religious and community leaders worried about the "failures of the family to produce the right kind of habits and beliefs in its young" (Scott and Wishy 1982, p.137; see also Demos and Demos 1969). Joseph Kett, tracing the changing role of youth throughout American history, cautions against romanticizing the past by conjuring up "a kind of Golden Age in intergenerational relations" (Kett 1974, p.17). He argues that nineteenth century unrest among youth rivaled twentieth century manifestations (Kett 1977).

In the 1950s, now remembered as an era of domestic stability and tranquillity, both the popular and professional literature described the shrinking authority of parents and the precarious situation of youth. Sociologists worried that high delinquency and school drop-out rates reflected the alienation and isolation of the young. Edgar Friedenberg's *The Vanishing Adolescent* (1959) linked the troubles of youth to the loss of parental authority and elaborated an earlier thesis, presented by David Riesman and his colleagues in *The Lonely Crowd* (1953), that children, deprived of character-building chores, had lost meaning in their lives.

In comparison with the decades that followed, the 1950s seem like a benign time for young people, and, in retrospect, family life appears to have been relatively stable. Drawing a contrast to that period of domestic tranquillity, many authorities regard the problem behavior of recent teenagers as having reached unparalleled levels due in large measure to the disarray of the family (Bronfenbrenner 1986; Shorter 1975). A new set of writings on the family have set forth a gloomy portrayal of family life in the 1980s and an even gloomier prognosis for its future if present trends continue (Lasch 1977; Davis 1985).

The previous chapter mentioned Peter Uhlenberg and David Eggebeen's widely cited article (1986) which assembled data from a variety of demographic and social surveys to support their thesis that the circumstances of youth, specifically those of 16- and 17-year-olds, have steadily worsened in recent decades, and that the decline in the well-being of youth can be linked to the loss of parental controls associated with rising rates of divorce and maternal employment.

The importance of the Uhlenberg and Eggebeen article lies in its claim to provide the empirical data to support ideas that have been expressed by many others in both the popular and academic presses (Winn 1983). In this chapter we review their evidence on changing patterns of teenage behavior and the link between that behavior and rates of divorce and maternal employment. Using more extensive data than Uhlenberg and Eggebeen have used, we show that trends in various indicators of adolescent behavior are less uniform than they suggest and that the causal link to divorce and maternal employment is not supported by the evidence.

THE UHLENBERG–EGGEBEEN THESIS

Uhlenberg and Eggebeen offer three separate premises for which they present supporting empirical data from a variety of sources. First, they contend that several aspects of adolescents' social environment thought to be important for their well-being have been steadily improving since the 1960s. In particular, parental economic and educational status and family size have become more favorable. Moreover, expenditures for education and welfare programs targeted for youth increased during the past two decades. As they put it, "If the creation of programs to assist the young is a measure of public concern, then the last several decades demonstrate an unparalleled commitment." (p. 30)

Second, Uhlenberg and Eggebeen describe patterns of youth behavior from 1960 to 1980 as heading in the "wrong direction." Drawing statistics from a variety of secondary sources, they provide an overview of changes in educational and intellectual performance, moral character, and physical health. Using a wide range of indicators—Scholastic Aptitude Test (SAT) scores, rates of school dropout, delinquency, substance abuse, adolescent pregnancy and childbearing, and mortality—they point to "a uniform and serious decline in the well-being of adolescents between 1960 and 1980." They conclude, "There may be some good news somewhere, but we could not locate it in any of the available statistics." (p.34)

Third, Uhlenberg and Eggebeen provide an explanation for the decline in well-being of youth. Having ruled out changes in the economic circumstances of families or in the resources available to young people, and drawing on several public opinion surveys, they identify the waning commitment of individual parents to child rearing as the source of the decline in adolescent well-being. They conclude that the rising rates of maternal employment and marital instability represent "an erosion of the bond between parent and child—one characterized by parental commitment and willingness to sacrifice self-interest." That erosion is, in turn, a "significant cause of the declining well-being of adolescents after 1960." (p.38)

Uhlenberg and Eggebeen support their contention that the well-being of youth has declined by comparing a number of behaviors at three points in time: 1960, 1970, and 1980. We will focus on these same (or similar) behavioral trends but depart from Uhlenberg and Eggebeen in our interpretation and analysis of these trends. First and most important, we do not assume that all the behaviors examined are indicators of one dependent variable, adolescent well-being. Education, crime, mortality, and sexuality are disparate phenomena: they are certainly related, but do not necessarily have a common cause or one-dimensional explanation. In addition, these behaviors are not universally accepted indicators of well-being. The definition of well-being and an assessment of its decline necessarily involve value judgments. Most people would agree that rising suicide rates represent a decline in well-being; there might be less agreement that increasing abortion rates, and even less that increasing motor vehicle death rates, are appropriate indicators. However, for the task of assessing Uhlenberg and Eggebeen's causal model, we will not take issue either with their choice of indicators or with their premise that changes in these behaviors are tantamount to a decline in well-being.

Our data differ from Uhlenberg and Eggebeen's in a number of respects (see annex). First, we have constructed annual series rather than relying on data for only three dates. Second, our data cover a longer period of time than Uhlenberg and Eggebeen's; whenever possible, the time series has been extended both backward (to 1940 or 1950) and forward (through the early 1980s). Finally, data have been collected for a number of age groups and, whenever possible, for blacks and whites separately. How much we were able to extend the information on each variable depended on the availability of data. We have occasionally supplemented Uhlenberg and Eggebeen's measures with an alternative one because theirs could not be extended back in time or because an additional measure seemed more appropriate to tap a particular area of youth behavior. Of course, some of the data are not available before 1960 or, in the case of substance abuse and abortion, before the 1970s. For most indicators we can fill in the picture only as far as 1984 or 1985, but the recent figures are quite informative.

Uhlenberg and Eggebeen's comparison points, presumably selected to match the dates of the decennial censuses conducted during the period under review, indicate an almost uniform pattern of deterioration across time in all the behaviors that purport to measure well-being. However, a comparison of only three points in time simplifies what is, on closer inspection, a more complex pattern of change. Because Uhlenberg and Eggebeen limit their discussion to white youth, we begin our discussion with an examination of the trends for white youth using data that are separately available by race.

Trends in academic achievement are shown in figures 3.1 and 3.2, which contain SAT scores and the number of high school graduates related to the number of 18-year-olds, the two indicators used by Uhlenberg and Eggebeen. In figure 3.3 we have added another measure, the percentage of 18- to 24-year-olds who are high school graduates, a more appropriate measure of educational attainment than the one Uhlenberg and Eggebeen used, because not all adolescents graduate high school at 18 even when they remain at grade level.

The annual series of SAT scores shows a decline starting in 1963. According to the evaluation by the Educational Testing Service (ETS), the decline between 1963 and 1970 is largely compositional: that is, explained by the increase in the number of students taking the exam. After 1970, the decline shows up in every category of test taker. Only about a quarter of the change can be attributed to changes in the number and the composition of those taking the exam. ETS collected no data relevant to the independent variables that we will be examining later, namely, mother's labor force participation or marital stability, but in general ETS related the decline in SAT scores to changes in pedagogy and school requirements (College Entrance Examination Board 1977; also, Congressional Budget Office, 1987). The important point for our argument, however, is that SAT scores began to rise again after 1980.

The percentage of whites between the ages of 18 and 24 who are high school graduates declined slightly between 1976 and 1980 but has since returned to only 0.2 percent lower than its high point. Moreover, as shown in the previous chapter, scores from a reading test administered to a national sample of 7-, 13-, and 17-year-olds, a measure with less selection bias than SAT scores, did not decline at all during the period for which data are available. A recent analysis undertaken by the Congressional Budget Office (1987) reveals a general upward trend in test scores beginning in the mid-1970s. Finally, high school graduates as a percentage of 18-year-olds declined in the late 1970s, leveled off, and then rose again. (See also U.S. Bureau of the Census, *Current Population Reports*, Series P-20, no. 426, 1988.) The positive trend after 1980 is a prominent feature in figures 3.4 through 3.10, containing trends in a number of other teenage behaviors. Although data on drug and alcohol use (figures 3.4 and 3.5) are available only for fairly wide age groups and for limited years, a rise during the 1970s is clear; but so is the decline starting in 1979 and continuing through 1984, the last year for which we have data. The drop in marijuana use is especially evident. As seen in figure 3.5, cocaine use rose for some time but has remained fairly constant since 1979.

The rate of delinquency (figure 3.6) shows a similar trend. It began to rise among 10- to 17-year-olds between 1961 and 1962 and rose quite sharply until 1980 when it turned down.

The death rates for three causes among 15- to 19-year-olds also show a rise followed by a leveling off or decline in the most recent years. Homicide rates (figure 3.7) began to rise gradually in the early 1960s and at a faster rate during the late 1960s and early 1970s, before dropping off sharply. Motor vehicle death rates (figure 3.8) rose sharply in the early 1960s showed large fluctuations but no trend in the 1970s, and dropped off steeply after 1980. Suicide rates (figure 3.9) began to rise earlier (about 1955) than either motor vehicle or homicide death rates and have leveled off since 1980 but have declined less sharply than the youth mortality rates.

Abortion ratios (figure 3.10) are available only since 1972. They rose sharply until 1978, then rose more slowly, and leveled off after 1980. The final indicator, rates of birth to unmarried white women ages 15 to 19 (figure 3.11), is an exception to the pattern of reversing trends after 1980; it rose in the 1950s and even before, and rose more steeply until the last available date, 1983, with no sign of a downturn. These series suggest three main points:

□ First, annual figures show that the patterns of change over time are less uniform than is suggested by data for three points in time.

For example, the death rates among teenagers from motor vehicle accidents look quite different from other indicators, although they, too, peak in 1980 and decline thereafter.

□ For all indicators except out-of-wedlock birthrates and possibly suicide, deterioration in the condition of youth is followed by a rise in well-being as measured by these indicators in the late 1970s or early 1980s.

□ Although it is impossible to draw any definitive conclusion because of the limitations of the available data, some indicators evidently were changing adversely in the decades before the 1960s. Out-of-wedlock birthrates began their upward trend for white youths in the 1940s. Suicide, homicide, and motor vehicle death rates all showed some rise in the 1950s, while the other indicators for which we have data before 1960 generally show no decline in well-being until the 1960s or 1970s. The limited available data before 1960 again point to the fact that all indicators are not alike; and some of the behaviors started to change before the period of family change that, according to Uhlenberg and Eggebeen, caused the trends in teen behavior.

EVALUATING THE UHLENBERG–EGGEBEEN HYPOTHESIS

Uhlenberg and Eggebeen assert that parental commitment has been waning and that the strength of the parent–child bond has weakened over the past two decades. Erosion in the willingness of parents to sacrifice for their children is evident, they say, in rising levels of divorce and maternal employment since the mid-1960s. But Uhlenberg and Eggebeen do not specifically describe the link between family deterioration and problem behavior. Presumably, structural changes in the family—marital instability and two-earner families—are both causes and consequences of a lessened commitment to child-rearing responsibilities. Apparently, as the family in recent years has offered less protection and security, teenagers have become more vulnerable to problem behavior than those raised in an era of lower divorce and maternal employment—when parents had a greater commitment to their offspring.

If Uhlenberg and Eggebeen are right and the trends in youth behavior are caused by waning levels of parental commitment as measured by divorce rates and women's labor force participation, what empirical results would support their thesis?

Uhlenberg and Eggebeen deliberately confined their analysis to white youth. But a look at blacks should be revealing, for if their explanation is correct, we might expect that rates of problem behavior among black youths should have risen sharply between 1960 and 1985. Throughout this period, the rates of labor force participation have been much higher—and the rise, steeper—for black mothers with young children than for white mothers of young children. The reverse is true for mothers of older children; whites increased their labor force participation more than blacks. For both groups, however, the rates rose throughout the early 1980s (see figures 3.12 and 3.13). Rates of marital disruption and single-parenthood also have risen more sharply for blacks than whites.

Blacks and whites can be compared on five of the indicators that we have used, and the results are not uniform. Suicide, motor vehicle accident, and homicide death rates rose in the late 1960s for blacks as they did for whites but began to decline much earlier for blacks (figures 3.7, 3.8, and 3.9). Out-of-wedlock births among black teenagers began a steep rise in the 1940s, leveled off in the 1960s, rose again in the early 1970s and then declined from 1975 to 1983, while both divorce rates and mothers' labor force participation rates were rising. This pattern is quite different from the pattern for white teenagers of a slow steady rise early on and an acceleration in the 1970s (figure 3.11). The proportion of 18- to 24-year- olds who are high school graduates rose much more for blacks than for whites during the period when their family conditions were deteriorating (figure 3.3). Overall, even less correspondence exists between family change and the indicators of well-being for blacks than for whites.

Even more important than the differential by race, the Uhlenberg–Eggebeen hypothesis would lead us to expect the trends in the indicators for young people to be different from those for older people who presumably did not experience the weakening of parental involvement that caused the trends. Uhlenberg and Eggebeen singled out adolescents and presented evidence on the trends in their well-being, ignoring the behavior of older adults. This decision seems reasonable enough because youth are the subject of their analysis, but we asked whether the changes in these indicators were the same for people in other age groups as for youth. Data showing similar patterns of change for older age groups would cast some doubt on attributing the changes in indicators to a decline of parental commitment to young people.

Figures 3.14 through 3.20 contain the available data on the set of behaviors examined earlier, but this time for people 20 to 24, 25 to

29, and 35 to 39 as well as for 15- to 19-year-olds. For adults, as for teenagers, the 1960s and early 1970s represented a period of declining well-being as defined by these indicators. Indeed, the trends for adults and youth bear an uncanny resemblance. For all age groups, the rates for suicide and homicide, substance abuse, and abortion rose precipitously. For most behaviors except abortion, the rise for young people was usually steeper than for adults. Consistent with the pattern we detected among the teenage population, adult rates indicate an end to the decline or an improvement in well-being shortly before or just after 1980. The timing of this reversal is strikingly similar for all age groups under age 45, although the slope of the trends varies somewhat.

One indicator, birthrates to unmarried women (figure 3.20), is an exception to the general pattern of similarity between adult and teenage behavior. Until the mid-1960s the pattern of change in out-of-wedlock childbearing was similar for women of all ages, but from 1965 to 1980, the rate declined for older women and continued to rise for teens. After 1980, older women's nonmarital fertility reversed course again and showed the same upward trend as in the adolescent population.

Thus, neither the decline in well-being from 1960 to 1980 that Uhlenberg and Eggebeen reported nor the general improvement in well-being after 1980 that we observed was unique to youth. Whatever accounted for the trends in youth behavior affected adults as well, at least those adults not yet middle-aged. Because these adults grew up during the post-World-War II period of unusual family stability, their rising rates of problem behavior cannot be explained by changing family environments. If it is difficult to fit the facts to Uhlenberg and Eggebeen's thesis for youth, it is impossible to reconcile them with trends in the behavior of younger adults.

Furthermore, the patterns of change in the presumed causal variables—divorce rates and labor market participation of women—cast further doubt on Uhlenberg and Eggebeen's interpretation. If they are right, we ought to see a reversal in divorce rates and labor force participation preceding the improvements in well-being in the 1980s. The trends in divorce rates and women's labor force participation by family status are shown in figures 3.12 and 3.13. The labor force participation rates of married, spouse present, women with children have risen continuously since 1947 and were continuing to rise through the latest year for which data are available.

Divorce rates (figure 3.21), however, do decline slightly in the 1980s and therefore, at first glance, seem like a possible explanation for at least those indicators that show "improvement" after 1980: suicide, homicide, and motor vehicle death rates, abortion ratios, drug and alcohol use, and SAT scores. However, this line of reasoning is undercut by a closer examination of the data on divorce trends. First, although rates have leveled off or declined in recent years, this change has occurred too recently to affect teenagers who were growing up in an era when divorce rates reached peak levels. The cumulative risk of divorce has continued to rise for birth cohorts who reached their teens during the early 1980s. In other words, a 16-year-old in 1985 was significantly more likely to have experienced a divorce during childhood than a 16-year-old in 1980 or 1975. Even if divorce rates continue to decline, it will take another 10 years or so before the cumulative rate of divorce begins to drop off for the teenage population.

It might be argued that divorce during the teen years is the relevant predictor of problem behavior among adolescents. But, as we will discuss later, evidence generally suggests that the divorce of parents has stronger and more persistent negative effects on young children than on older children (Emery 1988).

In examining the effects of divorce on problem behavior, it makes sense to correlate behavior with a divorce rate lagged 10 years or so. Figure 3.22 contains the 10-year-lagged divorce rates, the labor force participation rates for women with children under age 6 and two indicators of well-being, annual rates of marijuana and alcohol use. Lagging the divorce rates puts their downturn far too late to explain the improvements in the drug-use variable. In fact, divorce rates have the same timing of change as the teen behaviors, suggesting that a common explanation of both may be appropriate.

In summary, when we extend the time frame and look at the data for older age groups and blacks, the evidence on the behavior of adolescents differs from the evidence presented by Uhlenberg and Eggebeen. The picture of change is not nearly so uniform, so continuous, or so confined to the period of family change as data for white teenagers at three points in time would imply. This more complex picture of change casts serious doubt on Uhlenberg and Eggebeen's explanation of the trends. The dependent variables selected as measures of the well-being of youth do not consistently vary when changes occur in the presumed explanations of the behavior—divorce and mothers' labor force participation. Uhlenberg and Eggebeen may still be correct that waning parental commitment is the underlying cause of the trends in the behavior of teenagers. Perhaps parental commitment is simply not well measured by divorce rates and women's labor force participation. Indeed, Uhlenberg and Eggebeen present evidence from two separate sources—a mid-1970s survey conducted by Yankelovich, Skelly, and White and opinion data for 1957 and 1976 from a study done by Veroff, Douvan, and Kulka (1981)—to show that parents are less willing to make sacrifices for their children today than previously.

According to Uhlenberg and Eggebeen, a majority of Americans agreed with the statement, "It is important for parents to lead their own lives even if it means spending less time with their children," an attitude measured in the Yankelovich survey. However, the majority supporting this statement was obtained by combining respondents who were reported in the original study as strongly agreeing and partially agreeing with the statement, and contrasting them with the residual category of those who disagreed. Of course, those who partially agree also partially disagree, and therefore it is equally correct to say that a majority disagreed with the statement. In fact, more respondents in the survey disagreed with the statement than agreed with it (32 percent vs. 22 percent), if the middle category of those with mixed feelings are excluded. More important, data from a single point in time do not provide evidence of a decline in the willingness of parents to sacrifice for their children.

The Veroff, Douvan, and Kulka study (1981) contains data on Americans' attitudes about parenthood from surveys taken in 1957 and 1976. Americans expressed more reservations and ambivalence about parenthood in 1976 than in 1957. The proportion of parents who report that they have at sometime felt inadequate as parents and who have experienced problems in relating to their children also increased slightly. Yet, these responses do not necessarily indicate that parents have devalued their role. Parents assigned a much higher importance to their family roles—marriage and parenthood—as sources of value fulfillment and social validity than to work or leisure-time activities in 1976. Unfortunately, trends in these attitudes cannot be traced because the question was new to the 1976 survey. Today's parents are probably more likely to view parenthood as voluntary, and therefore may be more cognizant of the trade-offs or personal costs in having a family. But there is no evidence from the survey data that parents today are less committed to rearing children once they have decided to have them than were parents in the past. According to Veroff et.al., parenthood may have become more demanding, especially for men, but any shifts in the recent past appear to be minor.

A final weakness in the Uhlenberg and Eggebeen argument is its failure to refer to the large literature linking family conditions—maternal employment and marital instability—and the well-being of children on an individual level. They maintain that the social scientific evidence on the links is unclear. In fact, the evidence on the consequences of maternal employment on children's well-being is about as consistent as any set of findings on child development. In general, children of employed mothers are no more likely to experience developmental difficulties or behavioral disorders than children whose mothers do not work (Bronfenbrenner and Crouter 1982). In 1983, a select panel of the National Academy of Sciences which reviewed the research on the consequences of maternal employment on children's well-being concluded, "There is no compelling evidence to suggest that mothers' or fathers' labor force participation has only good or only bad consequences for all children in all social, economic, and cultural circumstances." (Kamerman and Hayes 1982, pp. 311–12.)

Research on the consequences of marital disruption for children has produced more ambiguous results, partly because it is difficult to separate the effects of family instability from conditions surrounding marital dissolution—particularly parental conflict preceding separation and economic deprivation following divorce.

Clinical studies of children and theories of child development have suggested that the disruption of their parents' marriage should have severe negative consequences for the well-being of children. However, empirical research using large, nationally representative samples of children has failed to document persistent and pervasive differences. Separation and divorce have moderate negative effects on a number of aspects of children's behavior, such as performance in school or reports of problem behavior at home or at school, but the expected powerful relationship between marital disruption and problem behavior has not been found as yet (Furstenberg, Morgan and Allison 1987). In addition, a number of studies suggest that high-conflict but intact marriages produce the same negative effects on children as disruption (Emery 1988).

ALTERNATIVE EXPLANATIONS OF THE TRENDS IN YOUTH BEHAVIOR

If changes in the family as measured by divorce and mothers' labor force participation do not explain patterns of adolescent problem behavior from 1960 to 1985, what does? As we noted earlier, Uhlenberg and Eggebeen dismiss for lack of evidence several other possible explanations of the observed trends. They contend that the social environment of teenagers has been steadily improving since the 1960s. Family size and the number of siblings with whom teenagers have to compete has declined over time, although the decline has been less steady than Uhlenberg and Eggebeen imply (Blake 1981). In addition, parents' education has risen. But we agree with Uhlenberg and Eggebeen that trends in teen behavior cannot be explained by these kinds of population changes, which would generally have produced patterns quite different from those which we observed.

Uhlenberg and Eggebeen are also correct that the resources directed toward children have grown over the past two decades, although the United States has had relatively low public expenditures for youth compared with those of most West European countries (Kamerman and Kahn 1981). The lion's share of the increase in expenditures in the 1960s and early 1970s was channeled into education. The growth of educational expenditures may, however, have been inadequate to meet the demands made on the public school system when baby boom children reached school age (Coleman 1974). Preston (1984), among others, has argued that increases in expenditures went to maintaining aging buildings and paying higher administrative and energy costs rather than improving the quality of education, which probably deteriorated as the real income of teachers declined during this period. He claims that children have fared poorly in both relative and absolute terms, in the competition for resources with the elderly, and he contends that some adverse trends in youth behavior might be attributed to the quantity and quality of supportive services for youthful dependents. (See also, Bane and Ellwood 1983.)

Finally, Uhlenberg and Eggebeen's assertion that poverty has declined for 16- and 17-year-olds is true for the 1960s and early 1970s, although the proportion of teenagers living in poverty has increased since the late 1970s. Still, the economic status of youth does not seem to explain in any direct way, changes in teenage behavior.

We have no explanation for the trends in the behavior of youth. Rather, our empirical work suggests several important considerations in seeking explanations. A plausible account of the trends described in this chapter must apply not only to youth but to young adults as well. There are striking similarities in the trends in the behavior of young people and adults at least to age 35 or 40. Although many of the variables have similar trends, the patterns of change are not identical, suggesting that a one-dimensional explanation for the changes in all these behaviors may be inappropriate. For many of the behaviors, the explanation must fit with a reversal of trends after 1980.

These empirical facts suggest that specific historical conditions in the 1960s and the early 1970s that might have been powerful enough to produce sudden and fairly dramatic changes in a variety of behaviors. Without going into a detailed review of recent U.S. history, we can say that the Vietnam War precipitated a cultural crisis that sent shock waves through a number of institutions (Flacks 1971). Public opinion polls document a growing skepticism of authority and an increasing tolerance for so-called countercultural lifestyles (Yankelovich 1974). During these years public support for liberalizing prohibitions against drug use, certain sexual behaviors, and divorce. Youth were certainly in the forefront of many of these cultural changes, although young adults and even some people in their middle years also embraced the changes. To be sure, the family was affected by these trends, but so were schools, religious institutions, voluntary associations, and government. Thus, it is tempting to attribute at least some of the changes in behavior to a relaxation in social control during the historical period stretching from the Vietnam War through the Watergate scandal.

Even a cursory look at trends during the same period in Europe however, shows remarkably similar, if somewhat attenuated, changes in some of the behaviors catalogued by Uhlenberg and Eggebeen. Thus, although the period of the late 1960s and early 1970s was a turbulent time throughout much of Europe as well, explanations of the trends in the United States must also account for parallel changes throughout the West and therefore extend beyond specific cultural conditions in the United States.

One explanation put forth by demographers and sociologists is that sharp imbalances in the size of cohorts can create radical shifts in the availability of actual and perceived opportunities (c.f. Easterlin 1980; Ryder 1974). As the baby boom generation came of age in both the United States and Western Europe, there was considerable competition for scarce resources. In 1974, Ryder observed that the potential for generational conflict and youth alienation is exacerbated when large cohorts of youth must be absorbed into productive positions. If parents and teachers are, in effect, temporarily outnumbered by the huge size of the youthful cohort, "a disproportionate share in the process of socialization will be assumed by the contemporaries themselves" (Ryder 1974).

Easterlin (1978; 1980), drawing some of the same conclusions, contends that the restriction of objective opportunities caused by cohort crowding is further aggravated by the perception of young people that they are likely to be worse off than their parents were at a similar stage in life. In a recent analysis of economic trends in the period from 1950 to 1980, Levy (1987) argues that young adults did indeed lose out financially relative to their elders. This explanation, attributing changes in behavior to the entrance of large cohorts into the teenage years, would account for the similarity of changes in the United States and other Western nations that also faced less severe but still substantial demographic imbalances in the 1960s and 1970s. In addition, reversals in trends after the late 1970s can be explained by the cohort-crowding hypothesis.

Simultaneous trends in behavior among a large number of age groups and the lack of a clear cohort pattern of change are harder to explain. It is possible that the behavior of the baby boom cohorts influenced the behavior of other age groups by influencing norms more generally. Thus, a period change in behavior affecting a large number of age groups may have been triggered by the arrival at teenage of the baby boom cohorts.

An adequate test of this explanation for the changing trends in problem behavior is beyond the scope of this paper and requires much more empirical work. For example, it would be useful to compare trends in the behavior of teenagers and young adults among countries with varying baby boom experiences. A more refined analysis of the differing trends in behavior across age groups also would be instructive. A direct examination of normative changes by age and their relationship to trends in behavior would help establish whether there is any evidence for the diffusion of normative change across age groups or even across national boundaries.

A final comment can be made on Uhlenberg and Eggebeen's thesis which this chapter has questioned. While we take issue with their depiction and interpretation of trends in adolescent problem behavior, we do not necessarily disagree with their contention that the situation of youth today is far from ideal. Even if indicators of adolescent well-being continue to improve somewhat in the next decade, as we suspect that they might, rates of problem behavior are likely to remain high. Moreover, the proportion of children living below or near the poverty line is a distressing symptom of our country's questionable commitment to the well-being of the next generation.

However, a call for greater sacrifice on the part of individual parents, while rhetorically appealing in a politically conservative era, appears to us to offer little promise for improving the situation of youth. In the unlikely event that parents heeded this appeal and restored the "traditional family," we seriously doubt that levels of drug use, alcohol consumption, or crime would return to the levels of the 1950s. The circumstances facing youth today are quite different from a generation ago, and it is difficult for us to imagine a return to the status quo ante.

References

Bane, Mary Jo, and David T. Ellwood. 1983. "The Dynamics of Dependence: The Routes to Self-Sufficiency." Report prepared for Assistant Secretary for Planning and Evaluation, Department of Health and Human Services. Cambridge, Mass.: Harvard University Press.

Blake, Judith. 1981. "Family Size and the Quality of Children." *Demography* 18: 421-42.

Bronfenbrenner, Urie, and Ann C. Crouter. 1982. "Work and Family Through Time and Space." In *Families That Work: Children in a Changing World*, Sheila B. Kamerman and Cheryl D. Hayes, eds. Washington, D.C.: National Academy Press: 39-83.

Bronfenbrenner, Urie. 1986. "Alienation and the Four Worlds of Childhood." *Phi Delta Kappan* 67, no. 6:430-36.

Coleman, James S. 1974. *Youth: Transition to Adulthood*. Report of the Panel on Youth of the President's Science Advisory Committee. Chicago: University of Chicago Press.

College Entrance Examination Board. 1977. *On Further Examination: Report of the Advisory Panel on the Scholastic Aptitude Test Score Decline*. New York: College Entrance Examination Board.

Congressional Budget Office. 1986. *Trends in Educational Achievement*. Washington, D.C.

Davis, Kingsley, ed. 1985. *Contemporary Marriage*. New York: Russell Sage Foundation.

Demos, John, and Virginia Demos. 1969. "Adolescence in Historical Perspective." *Journal of Marriage and the Family* 31:632-38.

Easterlin, Richard A. 1978. "What Will 1984 Be Like? Socioeconomic Implications of Recent Twists in Age Structure." *Demography* 15, no. 4:397-432.

———.1980. *Birth and Fortune: The Impact of Numbers on Personal Welfare*. New York: Basic Books.

Emery, Robert E. 1988. *Marriage, Divorce, and Children's Adjustment*. Beverly Hills: Sage Publications.

Flacks, Richard. 1971. *Youth and Social Change*. Chicago: Markham Publishing Company.

Friedenberg, Edgar Z. 1959. *The Vanishing Adolescent*. New York: Dell.

Furstenberg, Frank F., Jr., S. Philip Morgan, and Paul Allison. 1987. "Paternal Participation and Children's Well-being After Marital Dissolution." *American Sociological Review* 52:695-701.

Henshaw, Stanley. 1986. "Trends in Abortion, 1982-1984." *Family Planning Perspectives* 18, no. 1, 34.

Kamerman, Sheila B., and Cheryl D. Hayes, eds. 1982. *Families That Work: Children in a Changing World*. Washington, D.C.: National Academy Press.

Kamerman, Sheila B., and A.J. Kahn. 1981. *Child Care, Family Benefits, and Working Parents*. New York: Columbia University Press.

Kett, Joseph F. 1974. *Youth: Transition to Adulthood*. Report of the Panel on Youth of the President's Science Advisory Committee. Chicago: University of Chicago Press.

———. 1977. *Rites of Passage: Adolescence in America 1970 to the Present*. New York: Basic Books.

Lasch, Christopher. 1977. *Haven in a Heartless World: The Family Besieged*. New York: Basic Books.

Levy, Frank. 1987. *Dollars and Dreams: The Changing American Income Distribution*. New York: Russell Sage Foundation.

National Center for Health Statistics. 1985(a). "Advance Report of Final Natality Statistics: 1983." *Monthly Vital Statistics Report* 34, no. 6, 20 September. DHHS Publication no. (PHS) 85-1120. Washington. D.C.

———.1985(b). Vital Statistics of the United States: 1981. Vol. III, *Marriage and Divorce*. DHHS Publication no. (PHS) 85-1121. Washington, D.C.

———.1986(a). "Advance Report of Final Divorce Statistics, 1984." *Monthly Vital Statistics Report* 35, no. 6, 25 September. DHHS Publication no. (PHS) 86-1120. Washington, D.C.

———.1986(b). Unpublished Statistics.

——— .Various years. Vital Statistics of the United States. Vol. I, Natality. Vol. II, Mortality. Washington, D.C.

National Institute of Drug Abuse. 1985. *Use of Illicit Drugs by American High School Students, 1975-1984*. DHHS Publication no. (ADM) 85-1394. Washington, D.C.

Nimick, Ellen H., Howard N. Snyder, Dennis P. Sullivan, and Nancy J. Tierney. 1985. *Juvenile Court Statistics: 1982*. U.S. Department of Justice. Washington, D.C.

Preston, Samuel. 1984. "Children and the Elderly: Divergent Paths for America's Dependents." *Demography* 21, no. 4:435-57.

Riesman, David, Nathan Glazer, and Reuel Denney. 1953. *The Lonely Crowd: A Study of the Changing American Character*. New York: Doubleday.

Ryder, Norman B. 1974. *Youth: Transition to Adulthood*. Report of the Panel on Youth of the President's Science Advisory Committee. Chicago: University of Chicago Press.

Scott, Donald M., and Bernard Wishy, eds. 1982. *America's Families: A Documentary History*. New York: Harper and Row.

Shorter, Edward. 1975. *The Making of the Modern Family*. New York: Basic Books.

Snyder, Howard. 1986. Personal Communication.

Uhlenberg, Peter, and David Eggebeen. 1986. "The Declining Well-being of American Adolescents." *The Public Interest* 82:25-38.

U.S. Bureau of the Census. 1974(a). "Characteristics of the Low-Income Population: 1973." *Current Population Reports*, Series P-60, no. 94. Washington, D.C.

———.1974(b). "Supplementary Report on the Low-Income Population: 1966 to 1972." *Current Population Reports*, Series P-60, no. 95. Washington, D.C.

———.1985. "School Enrollment–Social and Economic Characteristics of Students: October 1984 (Advance Report). *Current Population Reports*, Series P-20, no. 404. Washington, D.C.

———.1988. "School Enrollment-Social and Economic Characteristics of Students: October 1985 and 1984." *Current Population Reports*, Series P-20, no. 426. Washington, D.C.

———.Various years(a). "Characteristics of the Population Below the Poverty Level." *Current Population Reports*, Series P-60, nos. 102 (1974), 106 (1975), 115 (1976), 119 (1977), 124 (1978).

———.Various years(b). "Marital and Family Status of Workers." *Current Population Reports*, Series P-50, nos. 11 (1948), 22 (1949), 29 (1950), 44 (1952), 62 (1954-55), 73 (1956). Washington: D.C.

———.Various years(c). "Estimates of the Population of the United States by Age, Color, and Sex." *Current Population Reports*, Series P-25, nos. 146 (1950-56), 212 (1957-59). Washington, D.C.

———.Various years(d). "Household and Family Characteristics." *Current Population Reports*, Series P-20, nos. 381 (1982), 388 (1983), 398 (1984), 411 (1985). Washington, D.C.

———.Various years(e). "Money Income and Poverty Status of Families and Persons in the United States." *Current Population Reports*, Series P-60: nos. 127 (1980), 134 (1981), 140 (1982), 145 (1983), 149 (1984). Washington, D.C.

———.Various years(f). *Statistical Abstract of the United States: 1979, 1980, 1982-83, 1984, 1985, 1986, 1987*. Washington, D.C.

U.S. Department of Labor. 1985. "Family Characteristics of Workers." *Special Labor Force Reports*, no. 7. Washington, D.C.

———.1983. "Marital and Family Patterns of Workers: An Update." *Bulletin* 2163. Washington, D.C.

———.1985. Handbook of Labor Statistics. *Bulletin* 2217. Washington, D.C.

———. Various years. "Marital and Family Characteristics of Workers." *Special Labor Force Reports*, nos. 13 (1960), 20 (1961), 26 (1962), 40 (1963), 50 (1964), 64 (1965), 80 (1966), 94 (1967), 130 (1970), 144 (1971), 153 (1972), 164 (1973), 173 (1974), 183 (1975), 206 (1976), 216 (1977), 219 (1978), 237 (1979). Washington, D.C.

Veroff, Joseph, Elizabeth Douvan, and Richard A. Kulka. 1981. *The Inner American: A Self-Portrait from 1957 to 1976*. New York: Basic Books.

Winn, Marie. 1983. *Children Without Childhood: Growing Up Too Fast in the World of Sex and Drugs*. New York: Penguin Books.

Yankelovich, Daniel. 1974. *The New Morality: A Profile of American Youth in the 70's*. New York: McGraw-Hill Book Company.

Yankelovich, Skelly, and White, Inc. 1977. *Raising Children in a Changing Society*. The General Mills American Family Report, 1976-1977. Minneapolis: General Mills, Inc.

Annex: Chapter Figures

Figure 3.1 SCHOLASTIC APTITUDE TEST SCORES

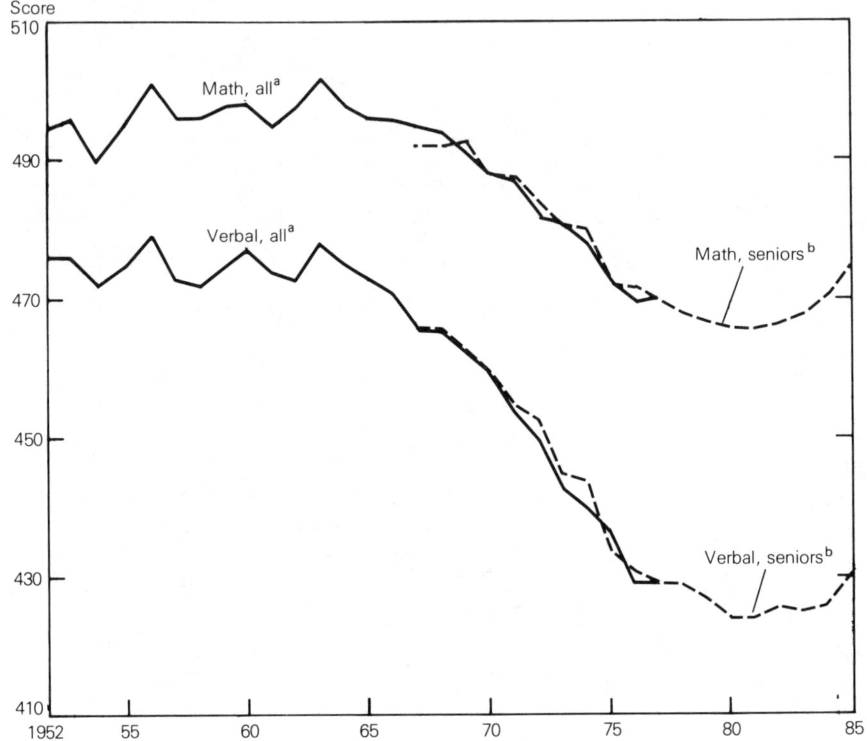

Source: 1951–76: College Entrance Examination Board (1977), p. 6. 1977–84: U.S. Bureau of the Census (various years [f]); *Statistical Abstract: 1986*, p. 147.

Figure 3.2 HIGH SCHOOL GRADUATES AMONG 18-YEAR-OLDS

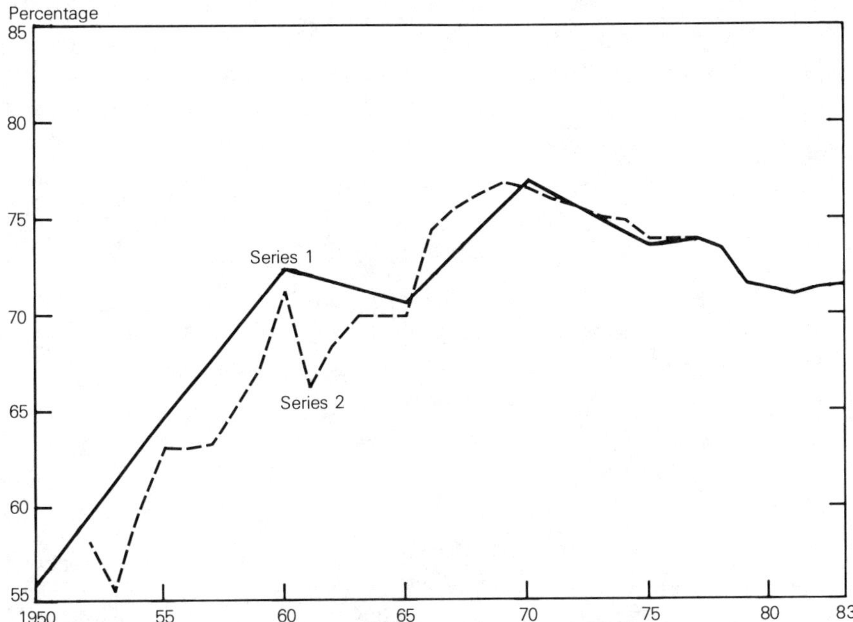

Source: 1952–77 (Series 1): College Entrance Examination Board (1977), p. 4. 1953–83 (Series 2): U.S. Bureau of the Census (various years [f]); *Statistical Abstract: 1986*, p. 149.

Note: The two lines represent different sources that varied in their estimated number of 18-year-olds.

Figure 3.3 COMPLETERS OF 12 YEARS OF SCHOOLING, AGES 18 TO 24

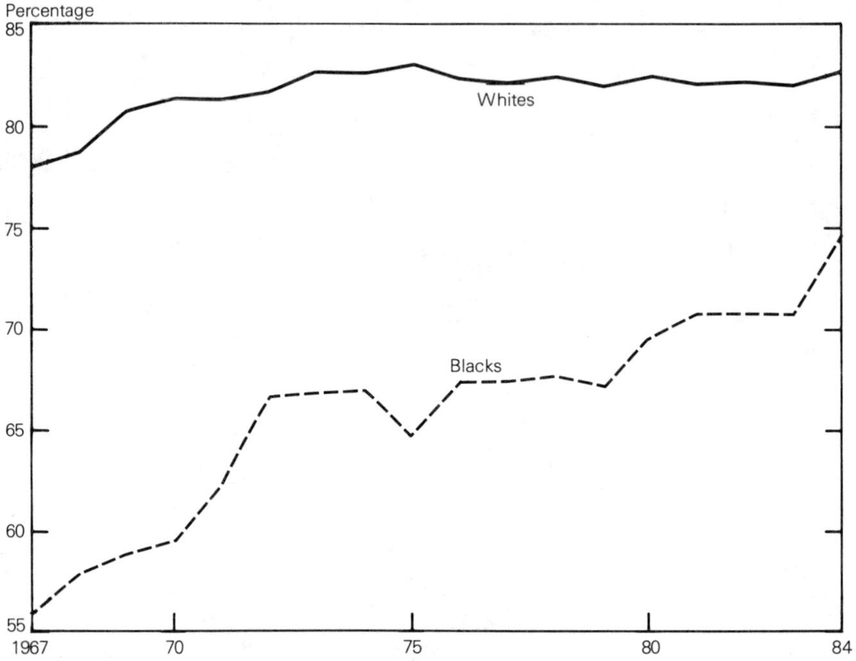

Source: 1967–84, U.S. Bureau of the Census (1985).

Figure 3.4 MARIJUANA AND ALCOHOL USE[a] AMONG 12- TO 17-YEAR-OLDS

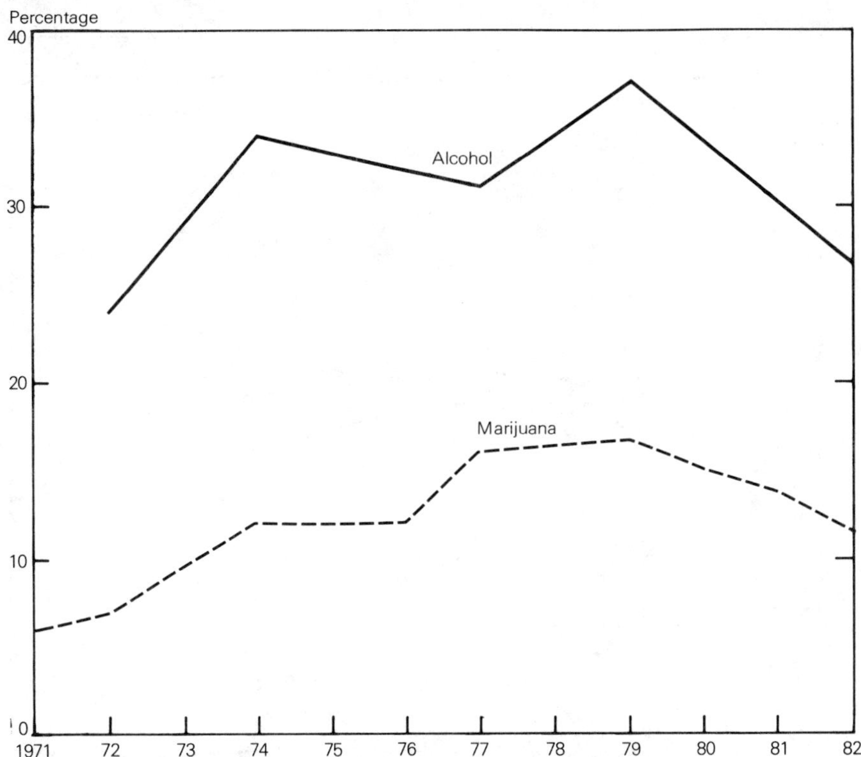

Source: 1972–74: 1976, 1979, 1982, U.S. Bureau of the Census (various years [f]); *Statistical Abstract: 1986*, p. 118. 1971, 1977: U.S. Bureau of the Census (varous years [f]) and *Statistical Abstract: 1980*, p. 129.

a. In month prior to the study.

Figure 3.5 HIGH SCHOOL STUDENTS USING ILLICIT DRUGS AND ALCOHOL

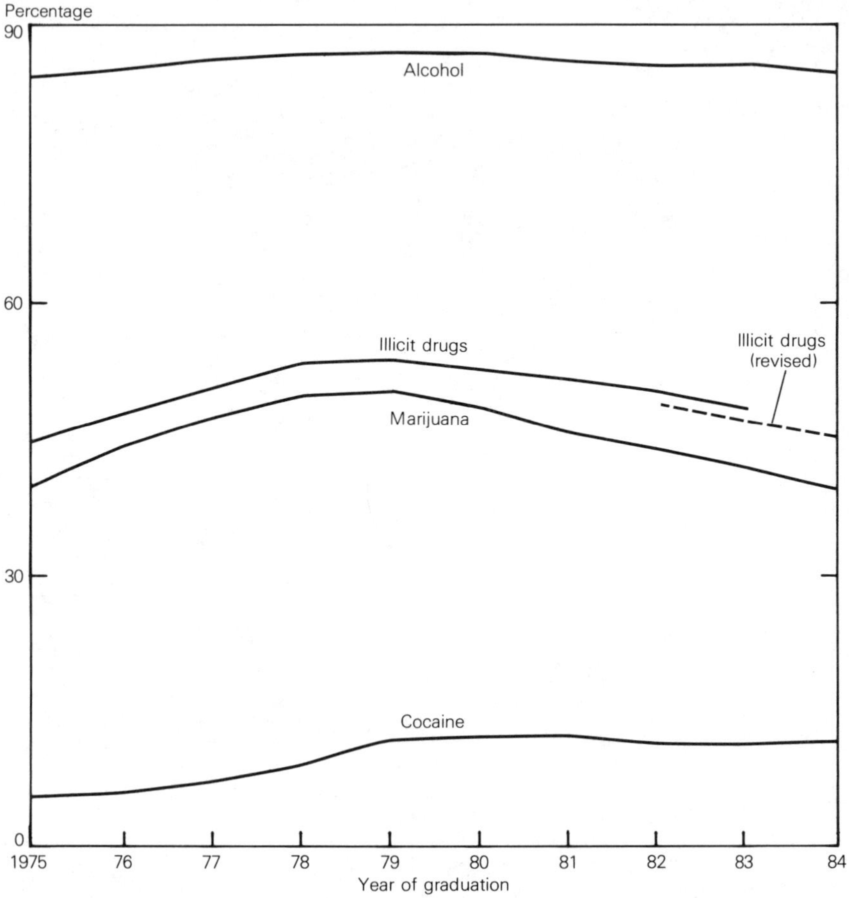

Source: National Institute of Drug Abuse (1985).

Figure 3.6 DELINQUENCY CASE DISPOSITIONS, 10- TO 17-YEAR-OLDS

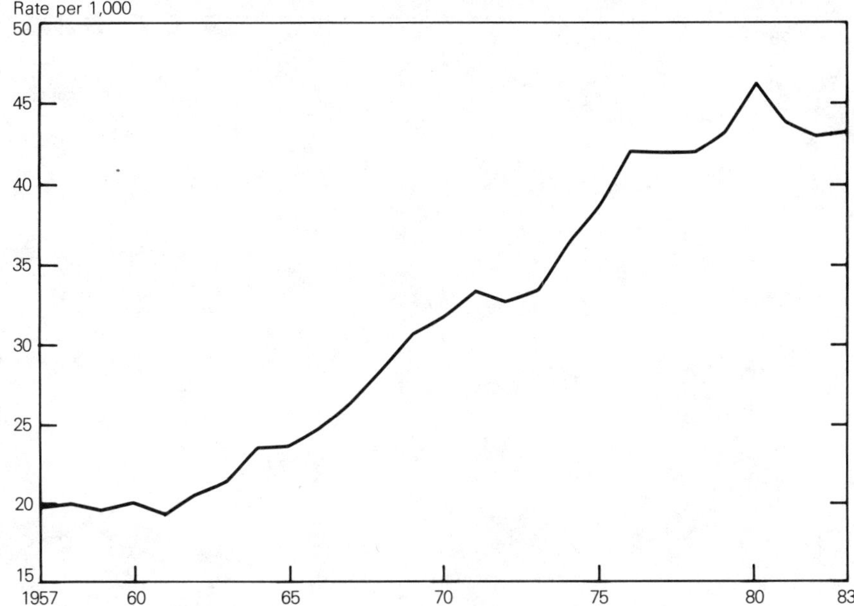

Source: 1957–82, Nimick et al. (1985); 1983, Snyder (1986).

Figure 3.7 HOMICIDE DEATH RATES, AGES 15 TO 19

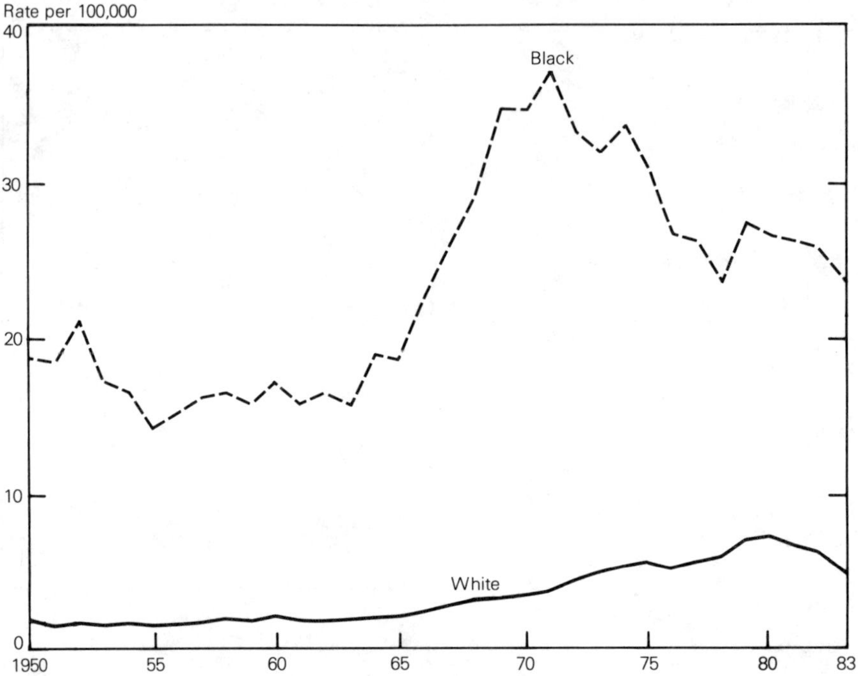

Rate per 100,000

40
30
20
10
0

Black

White

1950 55 60 65 70 75 80 83

Source: 1950–59: National Center for Health Statistics (various years); U.S. Bureau of the Census (various years [b] and [c]).

1960–80: National Center for Health Statistics (various years).

1981–82: National Center for Health Statistics (1986b).

Figure 3.8 MOTOR VEHICLE DEATH RATES, AGES 15 TO 19

Rate per 100,000

60 50 40 30 20 10

White

Black

1950 55 60 65 70 75 80 83

Source: See figure 3.7.

Figure 3.9 SUICIDE DEATH RATES, AGES 15 TO 19

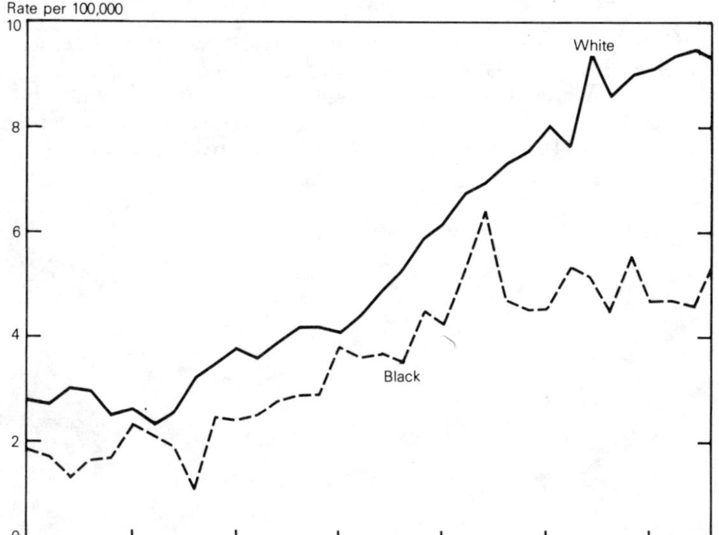

Source: See figure 3.7.

Figure 3.10 ABORTION RATES,[a] AGES 15 TO 19

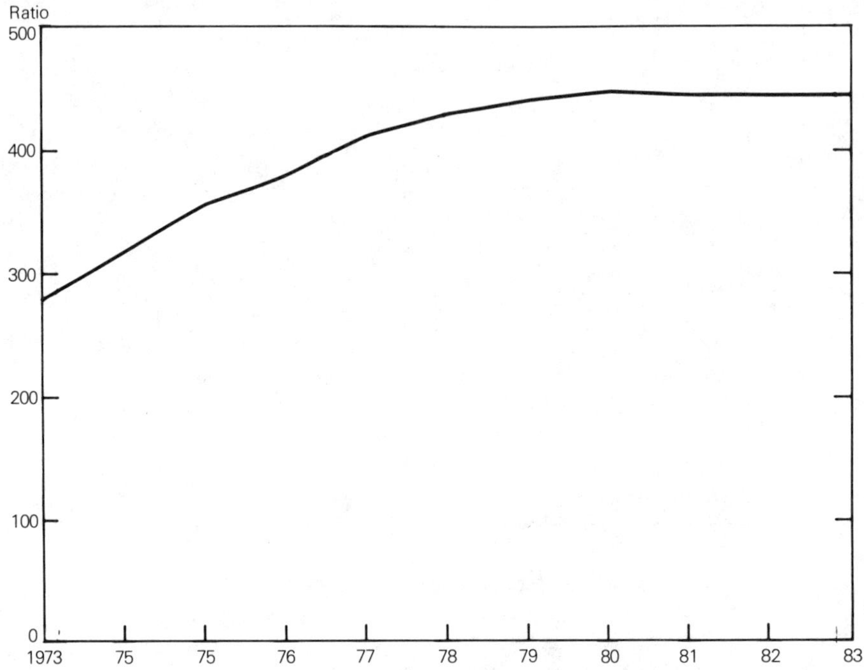

Source: 1973, 1980, 1981: U.S. Bureau of the Census (various years [f]); *Statistical Abstract: 1985.*

1974–77: U.S. Bureau of the Census (various years [f]); *Statistical Abstract: 1984;* National Center for Health Statistics (various years).

1978: U.S. Bureau of the Census (various years [f]); *Statistical Abstract: 1980.*

1979: U.S. Bureau of the Census (various years [f]); *Statistical Abstract 1982–83.*

1982–84: Henshaw (1986); U.S. Bureau of the Census (various years [f]); *Statistical Abstract: 1987.*

Figure 3.11 UNMARRIED BIRTH RATES, WOMEN, AGES 15 TO 19

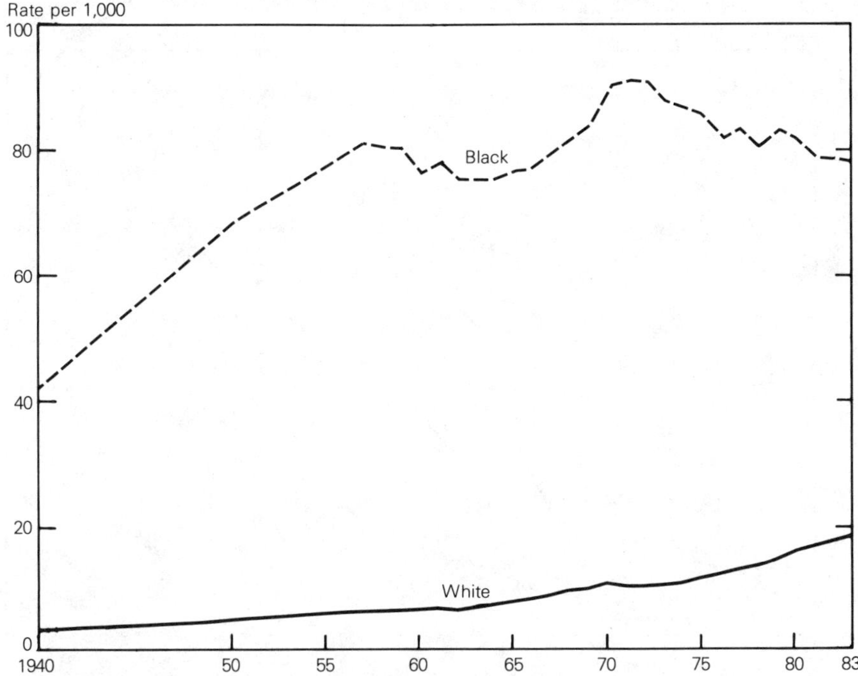

Source: 1940, 1950, 1960–80: National Center for Health Statistics (various years); 1981–83: National Center for Health Statistics (1985a).

Note: Two points in 1980 based on different definitions; after 1980 the new definition is used.

Figure 3.12 LABOR FORCE PARTICIPATION RATES, MARRIED, SPOUSE PRESENT, MOTHERS WITH CHILDREN UNDER AGE 6

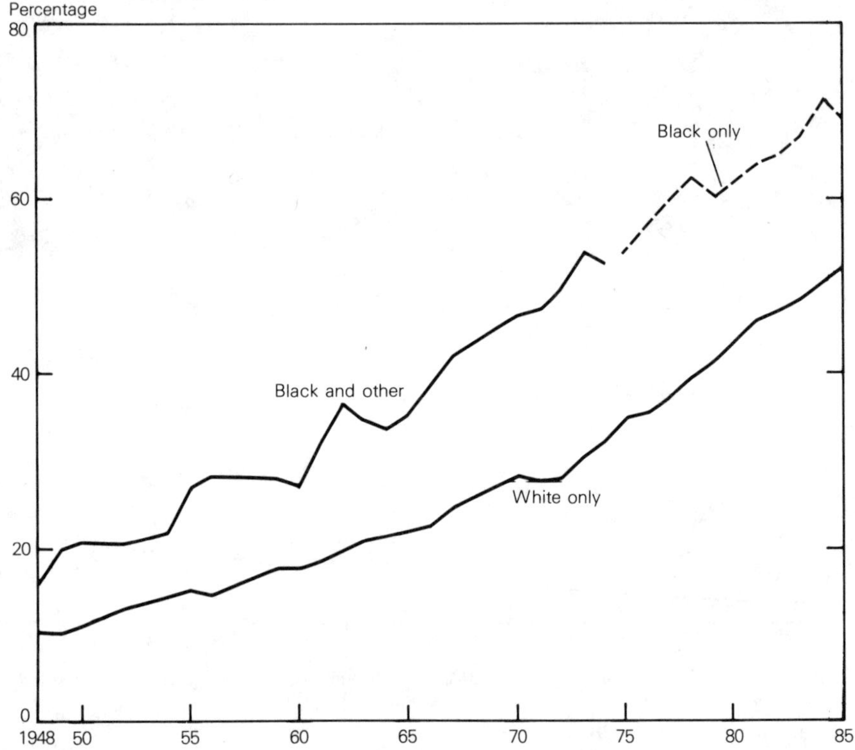

Source: All races, 1948–84: U.S. Department of Labor (1985).

Whites, blacks, and other races, 1948–56: U.S. Bureau of the Census (various years [b]); 1959, U.S. Department of Labor (1960); 1960–79, U.S. Department of Labor (various years); 1981, U.S. Department of Labor (1983); 1982/85, U.S. Bureau of the Census (various years [d]); 1986, U.S. Bureau of the Census (various years [f]) and *Statistical Abstract:1987*.

Figure 3.13 LABOR FORCE PARTICIPATION RATES, MARRIED, SPOUSE PRESENT, MOTHERS WITH CHILDREN AGES 6 TO 17

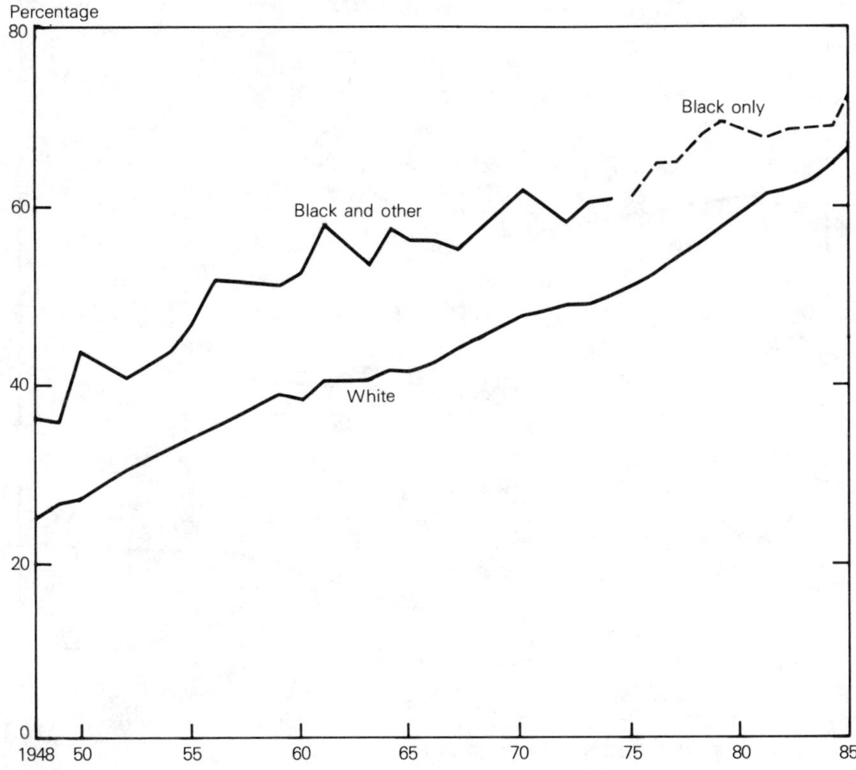

Source: See figure 3.12.

Figure 3.14 USE[a] OF MARIJUANA, BY AGE

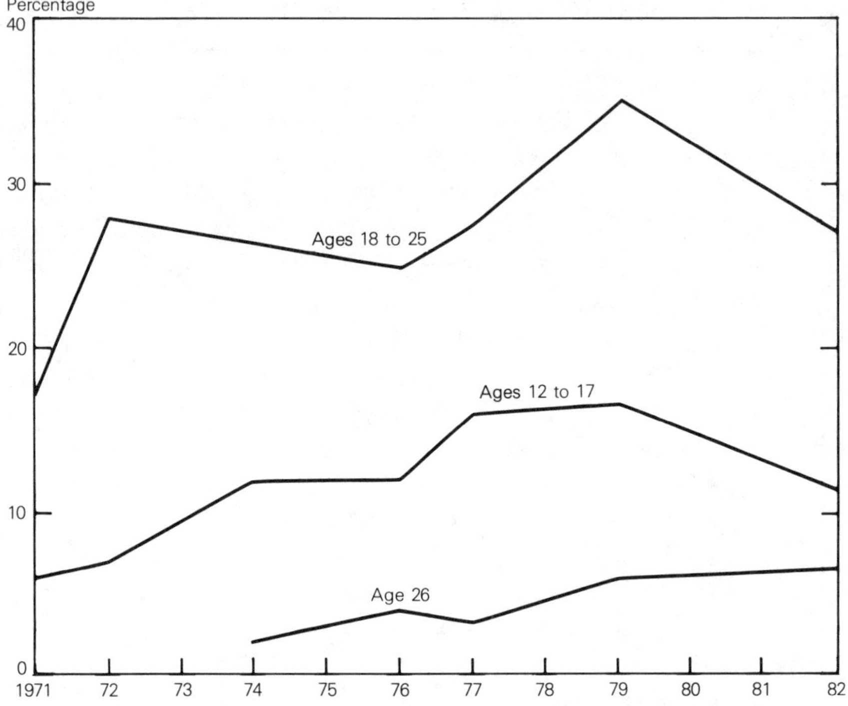

Source: 12 to 17 age group, 1972–74, 1976, 1979, 1982; 18 to 25 age group, 1974, 1976, 1979, 1982; 26 age group, 1974, 1976, 1979, 1982: U.S. Bureau of the Census (various years [f]); *Statistical Abstract: 1986,* p. 118.

12 to 17 age group, 1971, 1977; 18 to 25 age group, 1977; 26+ age group, 1977: U.S. Bureau of the Census (various years [f] and *Statistical Abstract: 1980,* p. 129.

18 to 25 age group, 1971: U.S. Bureau of the Census (various years [f]) and *Statistical Abstract: 1979,* p. 125.

a. In the month prior to the study.

Figure 3.15 ALCOHOL USE,[a] BY AGE

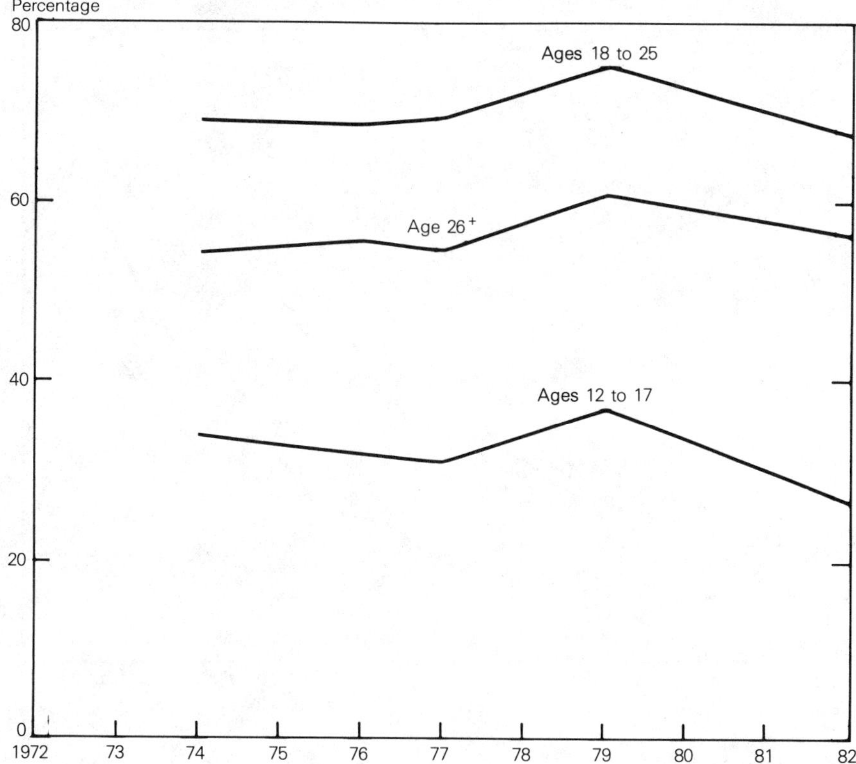

Source: See figure 3.14.
a. In the month prior to the study.

Figure 3.16 HOMICIDE DEATH RATES, WHITES

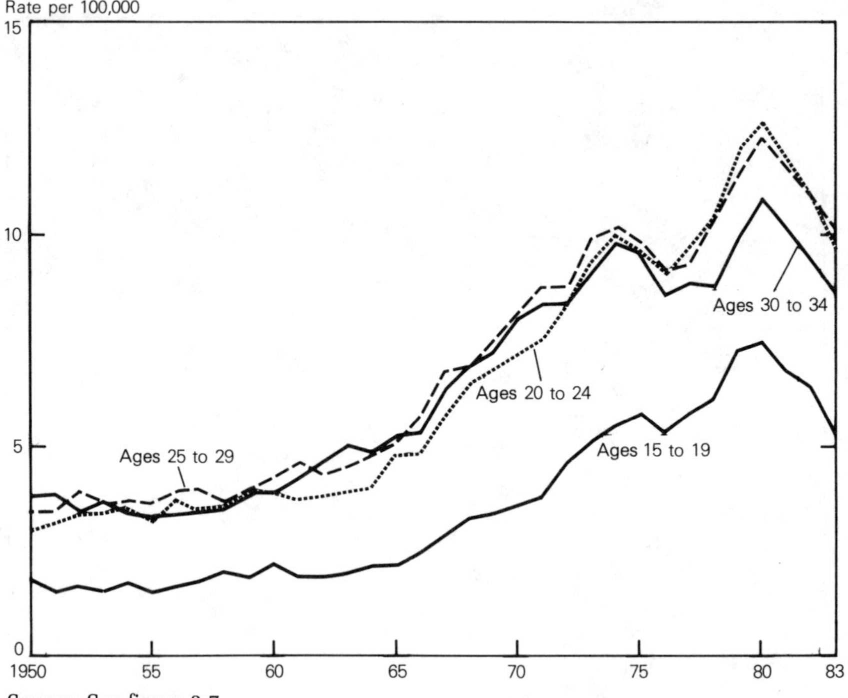

Source: See figure 3.7.

Figure 3.17 MOTOR VEHICLE DEATH RATES, WHITES

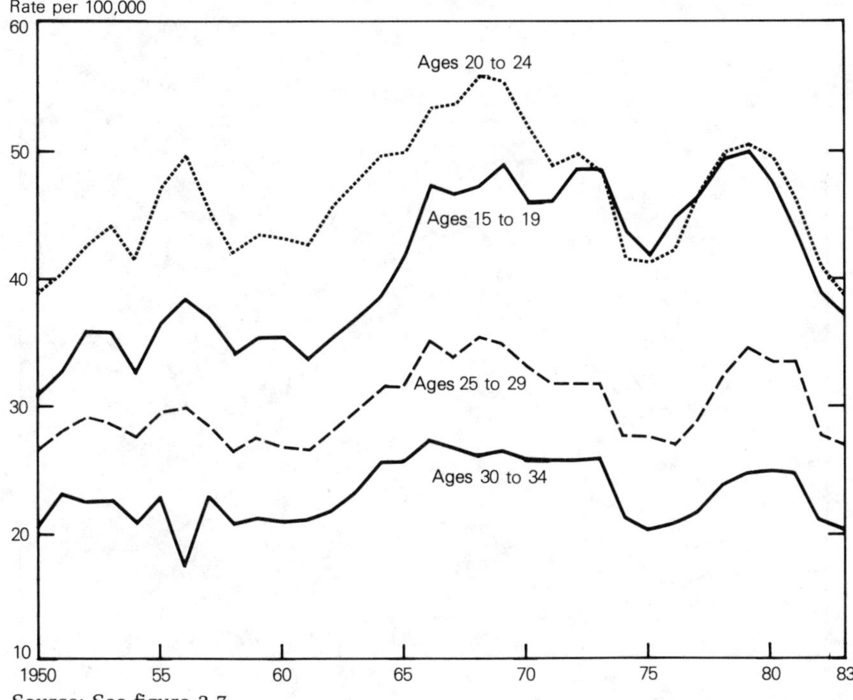

Source: See figure 3.7.

Figure 3.18 SUICIDE DEATH RATES, WHITES

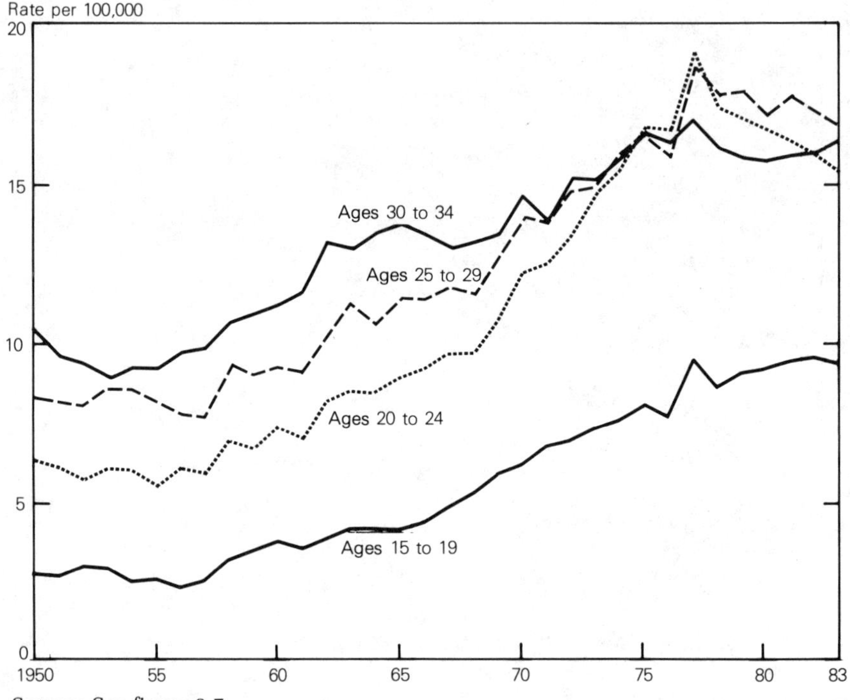

Source: See figure 3.7.

Figure 3.19 ABORTION RATIOS[a]

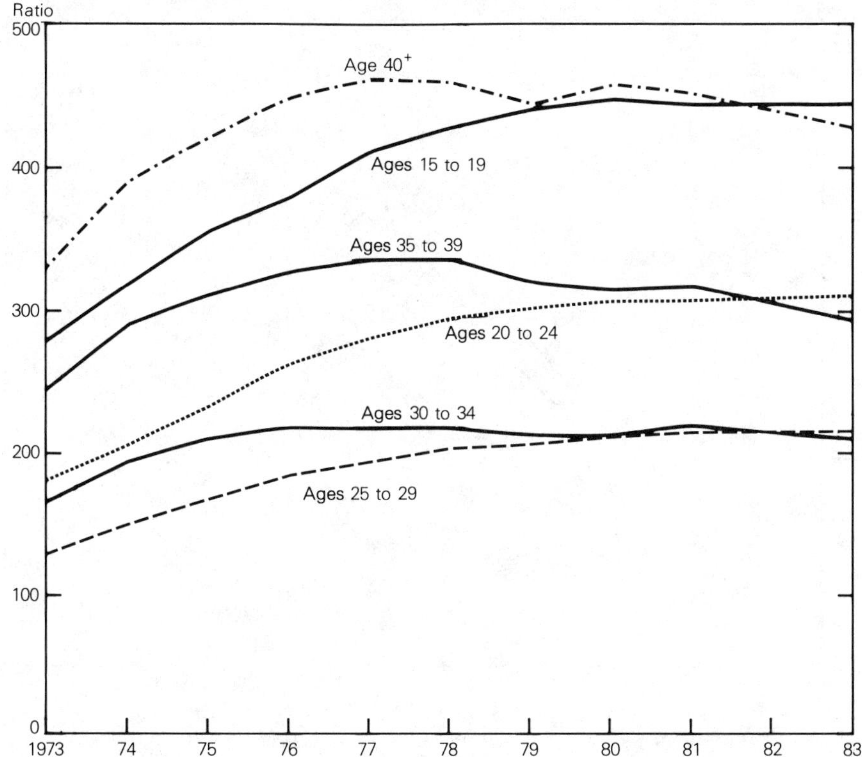

Source: See figure 3.10.

a. Abortions divided by live births plus abortions.

Figure 3.20 UNMARRIED BIRTH RATES, WHITES

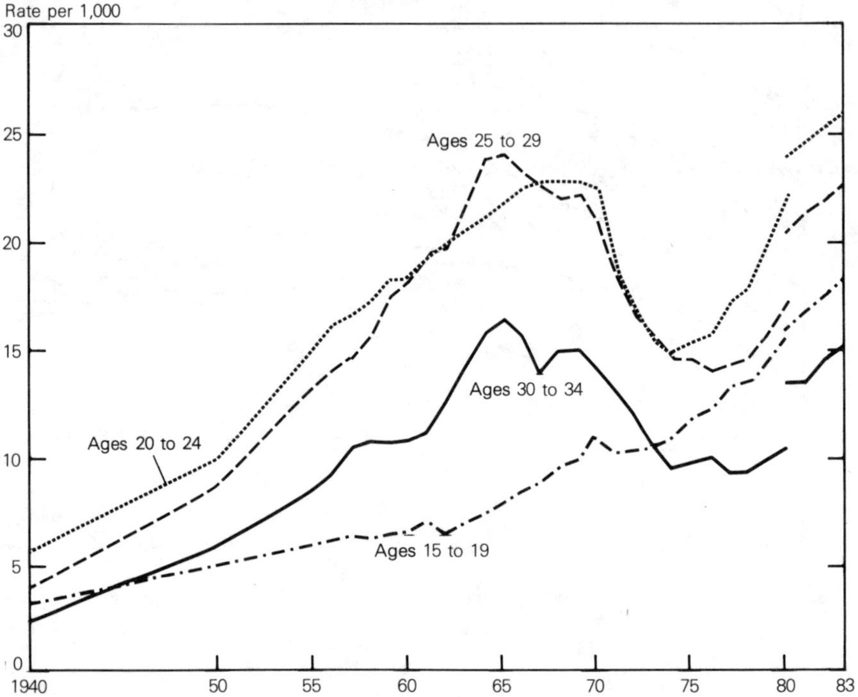

Source: See figure 3.11

Note: Two points for 1980 are based on different definitions; after 1980 the new definition is used.

Figure 3.21 DIVORCE AND CHILDREN

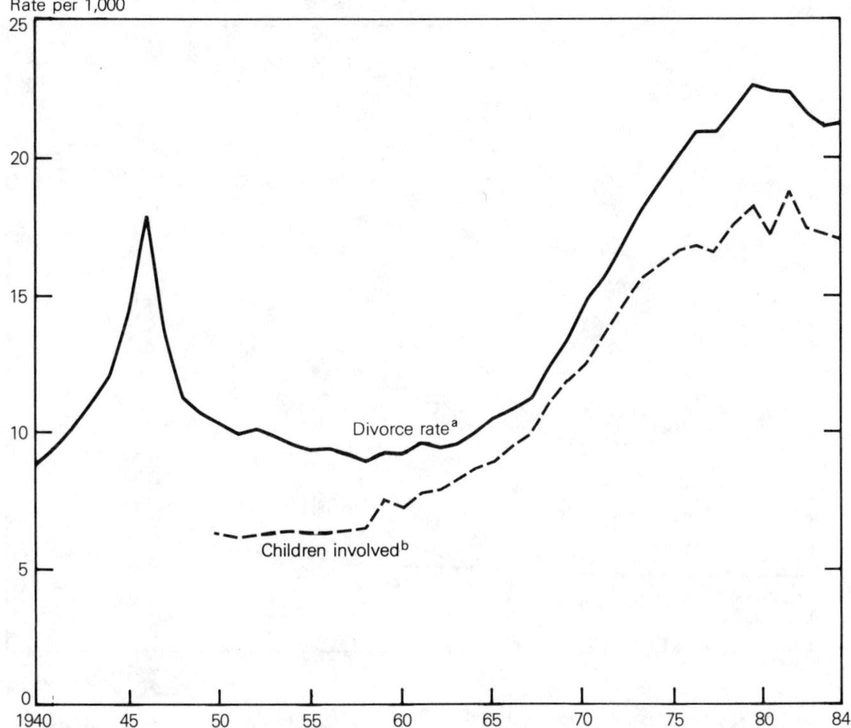

Source: Divorce rate, 1930–81, National Center for Health Statistics (1985b); 1982–84, National Center for Health Statistics (1986a).

Children under age 18 involved in divorce, 1950–84, National Center for Health Statistics (1986a).

Figure 3.22 WORKING MOTHERS, ADOLESCENT DRUG USE, AND DIVORCE

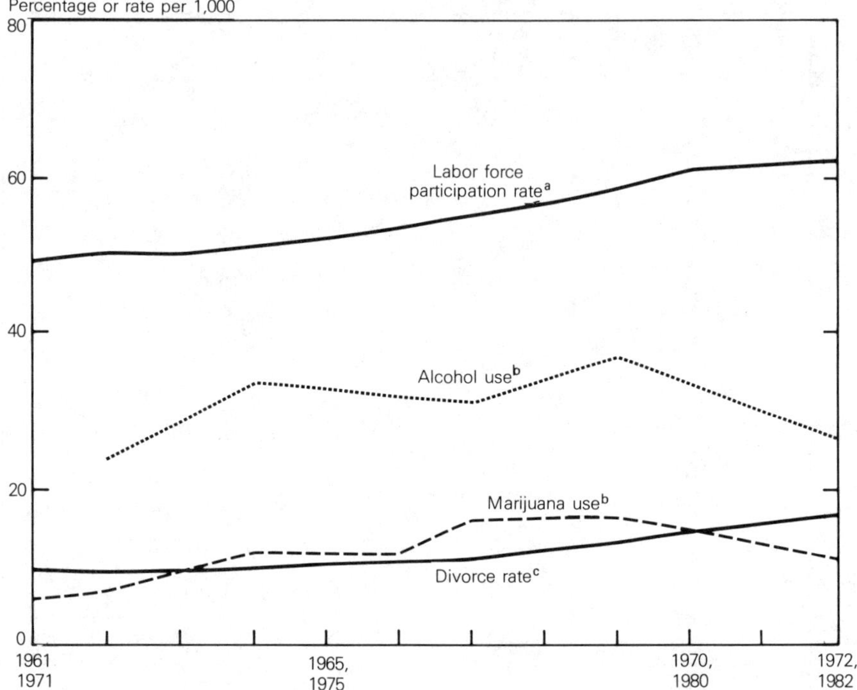

Source: See figures 3.4, 3.12, and 3.21.
Note: Percentage of 12- to 17-year-olds reporting marijuana and alcohol use, labor force participation rate per 1,000 mothers of children ages 6 to 17, and lagged divorce rates per 1,000 married women.

Figure 3.23 WHITE AND BLACK 16- TO 17-YEAR-OLDS LIVING BELOW THE POVERTY LEVEL

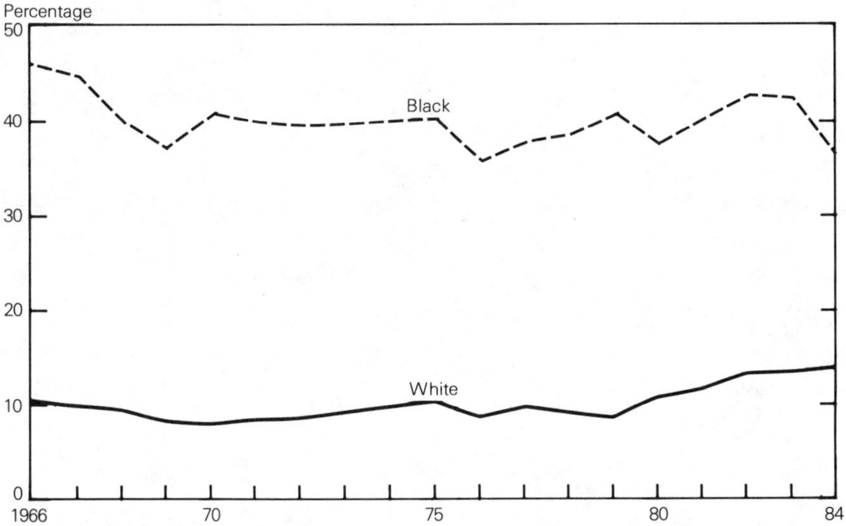

Percentage
50
40
30
20
10
0
Black
White
1966 70 75 80 84

Source: 1966–72, U.S. Bureau of the Census (1974b); 1973, U.S. Bureau of the Census (1974a); 1974–78, U.S. Bureau of the Census (various years [a]; 1979–84, U.S. Bureau of the Census (1980 and various years [e]).

Chapter Four

TOWARD A FAMILY POLICY: CHANGES IN MOTHERS' LIVES

Cynthia Fuchs Epstein

Apart from such women as the Old Testament prophet Deborah, Catherine the Great, Hypat a, Susan B. Anthony, and a few others, women in history have been noted for their association with men as mothers and wives. Family roles have defined women and have also constituted the focus of social science research about them. Only recently have women been able to assume other roles—occupational and political—that are as important in the definition of who they are. However, regarding women as wives and mothers continues to be a cultural theme with prescriptions to accompany it, and there has been a slight shift of focus recently toward motherhood in particular. This is so for two reasons. First, the demands of motherhood conflict more seriously with occupational and political roles than the demands of being a wife. Second, political leaders are concerned that women should continue to perform motherhood functions for the sake of reproducing the society, their social class, and the labor force.

One can speculate whether the status of wife or of mother has traditionally come first in the ranking of women's status sets, for marital status has certainly defined women's position both legally and in the social hierarchy. Of course, in most societies and throughout most of history, marriage has been associated with motherhood. Most women married and most women had children. This is still true today of course, but the new options for women have produced a major change in motherhood, not only because the norms have changed but also because women no longer suffer the consequences of uncontrolled fertility. Patterns of fertility have been altered by knowledge and technology, by cultural views, and by norms regarding family size.

In addition, fertility has been altered by the intervention of the state, whose interest in reproduction has always been pertinent to women's position in society. The state has also been responsible for alterations in the social ranking of women by offering or limiting their economic and political rights and opportunities. This chapter, like the others in this volume, is concerned with social policy as determined by the state, in negotiation with interest groups and the social mass that becomes activated from time to time. When considering policy one ought to be aware of the intentions and policies of powerful actors and institutions in determining the situation of men, women, children, and the family.

As a result of the emphasis on women's family roles, scholars have neglected the study of men as decisionmakers in the family, of their behavior as husbands and fathers, and of the consequences of their involvement or disengagement from family life. Influenced by values that affirm what some people regard as the "traditional" division of labor, family studies have overemphasized men's roles as breadwinners outside the home and women's as homemakers within it, inadequately considering men's behavior in the family and women's roles as economic providers. Thus, the division of roles in the family and the study of it conform to the dichotomous categories that characterize men and women in the rest of social life. But these "traditional" models of the family increasingly have been subjected to critical evaluation, partly on the basis of new scholarship in the burgeoning field of social history and partly by recent scholarship in sociology and anthropology. "We now possess more accurate information about the family than Marx, Durkheim, or Weber ever knew—we also know more than did the family scholars of the 1950's and 1960's," observed William Goode in his most recent book on the family.[1] Furthermore, a reordering of family patterns over the past decade[2] has resulted in a reanalysis of the frameworks that guide research.

In this chapter we consider some visions of the family with particular reference to women's roles within it and their relationship to men's roles. We analyze models of the "normal" family and perspectives on motherhood and on the division of labor in the household. These topics, although not comprehensive, highlight some of the issues that have surfaced recently because of social concerns about women's rights, the care of children, and social obligations. These hotly debated concerns about women's roles reflect conflicts in the values and institutions in our society that have torn scholarly and feminist circles apart.

MYTH AND REALITY IN THE FAMILY

Idealized families and idealized relationships within families, including myths of the good and bad woman, the good and the bad mother, have formed the basis of models followed by novelists, theologians, of lawmakers, national propagandists, and social service practitioners. Social scientists also have been responsible for selective visions of families and their members, with consequences for the behavior and attitudes of the very individuals they have studied. For many people, an orderly family with a clear division of labor, authority, and even emotions—between husband and wife and between parents and children—has been the ideal.

In his overview of research on families throughout the world more than two decades ago, Goode cautioned scholars against using stereotypical views of the family as a basis for assessing change.[3] In the United States, for example, he suggested there was a nostalgic vision of the extended family living in one large, rambling house,[4] providing warmth, comfort, security, and discipline for its members administered by a strong father and a nurturant mother. Such families were "havens in a heartless world" in the words of Christopher Lasch, who sees in the idealization a model that makes deviations aberrant.[5] Those who believe their mandate is to remedy social change have attempted to restore the "impaired" contemporary family to the ideal form. For example, the political scientist Jean Bethke Elshtain has taken a traditional "profamily" stance that affirms gender differentiation and celebrates qualities, such as mothering, that are seen as distinctive to women.[6] And making traditional marriage "work" has been a core concern among many family sociologists.

Comparative studies of the family by sociologists and psychologists have documented variations in family forms throughout the world for some time. But not all social scientists apply to their own research the lessons offered by comparative analysis. Unfortunately, those who devote their efforts to the search for "universal" family patterns have paid insufficient attention to variations in the experiences of members of different kinds of family groups. Too often, stability and order have been stressed to the exclusion of other virtues: members of stable families are assumed to be happy, and unhappiness is assumed to be the outcome of the lower number of stable marriages today. These assumptions have been made without recognizing the emotional and sometimes physical costs to women when order is derived from patriarchal authority. "Order may be based on tyranny," wrote Mirra Komarovsky in 1953. "We shall probably never know, though some writers presume to tell us, just how happy our grandmothers were. There were no Kinseys to record their sexual frustrations, no psychiatrists to unravel their neuroses, no novelists to indict them for monism."[7]

There has been, rather, the characterization of a harmonious nuclear family in which members play complementary roles. This form, with its sharp division of labor between husband and wife, became most associated with Talcott Parsons, who focused on the sexual and socialization functions of the family. He believed that the nuclear family with a breadwinner father and a homemaker mother provided an optimal structure for the care of children and anchoring of the "secure" adult.[8] Key aspects of Parsons' work were criticized after they appeared.[9] Parsons, replying to his critics, claimed that the statistical portrait of American family life did document a "normal American family."[10]

Betty Friedan's[11] critique of Parsons' work in her 1963 book, *The Feminine Mystique*, touched off a spirited discussion of the negative consequences to women of their restriction to the roles of homemaker and mother (as they suffered from "the problem that has no name"). It was particularly influential among the feminist activists organizing in groups ranging from the National Organization for Women (founded by Friedan), which sought an equal partnership with men in the family and society, to radical separatist groups such as the Red Stockings and New York Radical Women. NOW, the mainstream organization, saw itself as the women's counterpart to the black civil rights movement. Radical groups, inspired by theorists in their ranks, called for destruction of the traditional family in order to restructure society and abolish gender roles.[12]

But feminists of all political persuasions subscribed to a core of feminist ideology. The writings of the 1960s and 1970s focused on sexual politics, which aimed at transforming gender and sexuality both in the public sphere and in the home. Like the activities of the first women's movement in the 1900s, the battle over the family and women's roles in it was fought largely through books, journal articles, position papers, philosophical tracts, and sociological explorations. The discussions began to affect cultural visions at the same time that structural changes were occurring. In the social sciences, particularly in sociology, scholars began examining women's real roles in the family and the consequences of the power structure for women. More recently, research attention has been directed to power relationships within the family, to women's labor within the home, and to motherhood. Each of these topics is explored in more detail later in this chapter.

Of course, the demographic portrait today is very different from the one on which Parsons based his analysis of the "normal American family." By 1977, only 16 percent of families in the United States fit the model described by Parsons in 1960,[13] that is, father as sole wage earner, a full-time homemaker mother, and at least one child living at home. As the "traditional family" was eclipsed, social scientists were provoked into considering a new reality, one reflecting the increase in women's labor force participation, dual-earner families, and female-headed households; delay in the age of marriage; an increase in divorce and separation; and the aging of the society. There was more research attention to alternative arrangements of family life, including single-parent families, households without children, and homosexual and lesbian couples with or without children. Further "rethinking" offered in a collection of studies edited by Thorne and Yalom[14] denied that the organization of the family is biologically determined in any direct or immutable way. Writing in that volume, anthropologists Collier, Rosaldo, and Yanagisako asserted:

> The Family (thought to be universal by most social scientists today) is a moral and ideological unit that appears, not universally, but in particular social orders. The Family as we know it is not a "natural" group created by the claims of "blood" but a sphere of human relationships shaped by a state that recognized families as units that hold property, provide care and welfare, and attend particularly to the young—a sphere conceptualized as a realm of love and intimacy in opposition to the more "impersonal" norms that dominate modern economies and politics.[15]

This feminist perspective contributed to the rowing body of analysis that led the anthropologist Rayna Rapp to write: "One of the more valuable achievements of feminist theory has been its effort 'to deconstruct the family as a natural unit, and to reconstruct it as a social unit'—as ideology, as an institutional nexus of social relationships and cultural meanings."[16] For example, the bias toward the breadwinner–homemaker nuclear family supported a cultural belief that women quite naturally perform the mothering role competently, with ease, and with great emotional satisfaction. This view has since been challenged in feminist writings that have questioned the "motherhood cult."[17] Although admittedly it is difficult to do "objective" research on women's views of mothering because they are so entangled with normative prescriptions, people have attempted to try it. However, many social scientists, like lay people, make assumptions that correspond with normative views. For example, Sylvia Hewlett, in decrying a "lesser life" for mothers who work outside the home, presupposes that a better life exists for women who do not work outside the home, a notion posed without supporting evidence.[18] In fact, there is evidence to the contrary. Women's current economic opportunities can lead to greater satisfactions even as women also play roles as wives and mothers,[19] as we shall see later.

THE ISSUE OF ROLE STRAIN

There are good reasons to question the common assertion that mothers who work outside the home suffer inordinately from the "strain" of multiple roles. To be sure, there are disharmonies between the demands of the work world and those of the family, each with its set of institutions that are "greedy" of the time and emotional commitment of its members.[20] The assumption has been, of course, that it is women who suffer the most strain from these disharmonies, because it is their responsibility to run the home and be primary caretakers for the children.

Probably at no time in history have women had the opportunity to take on so many demanding and disparate roles—to try their hand at what some people define as "having it all." (Tradition and law have limited the number and variety of roles women could take on, although the amount of work women have been required to perform roles has often been unlimited.) The notion of "having it all" refers to women's assumption of roles outside the home in addition to traditionally ascribed roles—engaging in economically productive activity as well as being wives and having a family. This is the big issue of the 1980s, just as the big question of the 1970s was whether women could break down the barriers to the good jobs in society and have real careers.

But this issue is certainly not new. Through the ages women have had to perform a balancing act, handling their roles as wives and mothers and doing the multitude of chores historians remind us were typical of the premechanized household.[21] In the past, women raise chickens as well as children. Women might also work in the fields at harvest, make soap, preserve food, and cook for farmhands. Yet all these tasks were considered to be part of one status—housewife. Thus women worked at many jobs, and worked very hard ("woman's work is never done"). Today, as many of the traditional tasks of the housewife are now done outside the home, women are also moving away from the home to perform them, and in so doing are adding to their roles. Women are still housewives, but they are also workers in the formal economy, which society treats as a separate and distinct domain.

From the beginning of industrialization, some women have had to negotiate the demands of multiple roles: caring for aging parents and siblings and doing housework, while also working in the mills and offices of a growing society. Although few mothers of small children worked outside the home, many engaged in he economically productive labor force by taking in boarders[22] or working in family businesses, although their work there often went undocumented. We do not have much data on what women who were previously homemakers did in later periods. Poor women worked outside the home or inside the home taking in laundry and engaging in other activities that brought in some money. Middle-class women contributed their labor in the voluntary sector in schools and hospitals and engaged in charitable work that went largely unacknowledged as well as uncompensated.

What is new is that most women now work away from the home as well as in the home, and, as we have learned, the fastest-growing sector of the labor force is composed of married women with children under the age of six.[23] Furthermore, a good proportion of these women are assigning high priority to their work, ambitiously looking to excel and reap the rewards expected by men who do such work. The fact of women's lives today, as in the past, however, does not match the cultural image and certainly not the cultural ideal. It is considered objectionable, unhealthy, or immoral for women to assume unusual combinations of multiple statuses and roles, and they are subtly implored by national leaders and the media to reduce their number and rearrange their priorities in favor of "traditional" modes. These messages are extensions of ideological perspectives advocated by social philosophers and theologians who have long rationalized and justified women's primary attachment to family.[24] Such ideology has legitimated policies that have limited women's chances to become independent or to establish statuses that are not contingent on fathers' and husbands' statuses. Legal restrictions on women's rights to independent status in England and the United

States have been enunciated in the work of Albie Sachs and Joan Hoff-Wilson.[25]

The focus today in American popular culture on role strain may be seen as a form of resistance to women's assumption of unusual "status sets"[26] that offer the possibility of such independence. The focus on role strain and its accompanying stress may also result from the fact that many people feel threatened by the vitality and productivity of the people who accomplish the demands of multiple roles. In a society in which until very recently, people believed that the typical American woman was incapable of balancing a checkbook or driving a van, women's new competence as bank officers and truck drivers may encounter resistance.[27]

Social mechanisms that perpetuate limitations on women's freedom to assume multiple roles and statuses that deviate from traditional norms continue to reinforce women's low rank in society and their exclusion from male-dominated occupations. My study of women lawyers from the mid-1960s to the early 1980s provide illustrations of these phenomena.[28]

In modern society, the number of roles a person assumes is likely to be high. Meeting all the obligations attached to these roles may call for more time and energy than most people have. Juggling obligations can result in the state called role strain. Whether a person feels stressed or happily busy depends on the combination of roles the person has and whether society makes it easy or hard for the person to fulfill the expectations attached to them all. Role strain can rest not only from having a large number of roles to play, but also from holding a combination of statuses with which most people are unfamiliar or of which they do not approve. Robert K. Merton and Everett Hughes have pointed out that acquisition of some roles (attached to statuses) makes acquisition of others easy or difficult.[29]

Certain statuses combine more often than others, often resulting in normative expectations that they are the "right" or normal combination.[30] Hughes, in a classic paper titled the "Dilemmas and Contradiction of Status,"[31] analyzed how black doctors and women engineers were made to feel awkward by "role partners" who responded to their "inappropriate" status (as when patients responded to a woman doctor's female status rather than her professional one).

Robert K. Merton[32] and William J. Goode[33] have analyzed the techniques available to people for reducing role strain stemming from the assumption of multiple roles. My work on women professionals considered how women with deviant status sets managed to articulate their role sets.[34] My analysis[35] suggested (1) that society helps certain groups of people more than others in articulating role demands, depending on their rank and power, and (2) that because women had fewer resources on which to draw, they were more apt to suffer from role strain.

It is clear to me that gatekeepers (the people who control the entry to high level careers, and "society" made the cost of women's choosing a career rather than a job high before the 1970s. My research on lawyers showed that women who entered careers in a male-dominated profession in the 1960s and before had to face disapproval for aiming higher than it was believed they should or for getting "out of line." If the sum total of role demands created overload they could not expect sympathy. In fact, people were often appalled that women took on these "inappropriate" statuses, especially when they acquired the notice and money attached to them. Such choices, especially by mothers, were regarded as selfish; as a result, women felt guilty and this guilt remains.

The physical and time pressure overload of working and maintaining private lives are the same for women no matter what kind of work they do. Through much of history there has been little concern for the long hours women work in the household and in the laborious employment they have had as factory and clerical workers. Few people have thought it important to put limits on women's working hard at those tasks defined as "woman's work," circumscribed within a limited number of roles, but not on the *amount* of work encompassed by those roles.

Contemporary concern has been directed primarily to women who are competing for the good jobs society has to offer; suddenly, warnings are voiced about the mental health of the women doing the work that leads to power, authority, and money. Yet medical research has now established that the people who are most at risk to hypertension and its associated heart disease are those who work at jobs in which they are constrained from making decisions and which they face high demands—for example, white-collar jobs in which employees are ordered about.[36] Women clerical workers with nonsupportive bosses are found to be at high risk of coronary heart disease.[37] Similarly, unemployed men suffer from increased risk of heart attack, ulcers, hypertension, arthritis, diabetes, and elevations of serum cholesterol, as well as feelings of self-blame, hopelessness, depression, irritability, and malaise.[38] Some studies show that compared with housewives, employed married women report fewer psychiatric symptoms. Some studies show that compared with housewives, employed married women report fewer psychiatric symptoms. Other studies that compare the related mental health of women working for different kinds of employers, however, show no difference.[39] Social scientists today are finding that women gain a sense of well-being by accomplishing the tasks of many roles well[40] if they are roles of choice. This is the case for many women lawyers today.[41]

In the past, women who chose careers probably did have a certain amount of role strain to contend with, because the general view was that women's place ought to be primarily in the home. Thus women could not, and did not, expect much help from society in sorting out and coping with their role demands. They did not know how to delegate their duties, and family members usually refused to cut back on demands despite observing how busy women were. When there was conflict between work and family roles, women have been encouraged to use the ultimate mechanism—cutting off one of the roles causing the conflict. For women, it is usually their occupational role, and many women regard this as an option today, but more a theoretical option than a pragmatic one.

When I first did research on the obstacles women faced in becoming professionals two decades ago,[42] it seemed clear that women who left a profession or occupation at any level, from training to practice, did so with society's full approval. We are finding a visible but unknown percentage of middle-class women doing so today, a phenomenon widely reported in the media.

But my research and that of others studying "career women"[43] indicate an interesting paradox. The most successful women also have the most to do; they tend to be married and have children. Despite the absence of child care programs or flexible work schedules, many report that they feel effective and do not regard themselves as having serious problems. With money and resources at their disposal, they are gifted in handling multiple roles. Of course, above-average incomes allow the purchase of support services, and high-ranking jobs permit a certain amount of scheduling flexibility.

They also benefit from a changing culture. The women's movement had a lot to do with the fact that many women feel it is legitimate to work hard at a career. And society's awareness is growing that it is becoming normal for women, even those with families, to work for pay rather than only in the household, and to work at jobs with opportunity for growth.

Some people are defeated by the obligations of multiple roles and some are not. The differences lie in the situations in which women find themselves. Women who feel stress usually are confronted by role partners who act on two assumptions: first, that multiple roles for women—mixing work and home—will create strain; second, that this strain will cause women to do poorly in their family roles, their occupational roles, or both. When women believe this, too, they reduce their aspirations in the occupational sphere.

When people accept a zero-sum model, that time is limited and people can do only a limited number of tasks, these assumptions usually develop as a self-fulfilling prophecy. Strains may be created by the anticipation of having them. Strains may also be socially induced by a culture that is still suspicious of and hostile to women's acquisition of important and prestigious roles and by their independence, and by powerful people who see their interest as maximized by undermining the competition of women. The actual pressures of high-demand jobs, and the demands incurred when women must balance them with the obligations of family life, may be less of a problem than the symbolic impact of certain kinds of demands or the reactions of people to them.

High-level jobs are important routes to self-esteem, report Grace Baruch, Rosalind Barnett and Caryl Rivers studying women between the ages of 35 and 55.[44] Their findings dovetail with a study of stress and psychiatric disorder by the psychiatrist Frederic W. Ilfeld, Jr., who found that women exhibit twice as many stress symptoms as men, unless the men are poor, black, widowed, or single.[45] The only group of women who have as few problems as white, middle-class men are employed women whose occupational status is very high. This does not mean that these women are under less stress, just that stress does not overwhelm them.

Women at other occupational levels also benefit from performing multiple roles. Brigid O'Farrell and Sharon Harlan found that women doing nontraditional craft and technical work have a high degree of satisfaction.[46] Barnett and Baruch found the employed mothers of preschool-age children who are in a variety of occupations and are committed to their work rank high in well-being and satisfaction and that work contributes to a sense of mastery.[47] Melvin Kohn and his associates have discovered that women as well as men who work at jobs that encourage self-direction gain an increased ability to be flexible and intellectually adept.[48]

Acquiring multiple roles may even free a person from particular role obligations attached to some statuses. Adding the status of divorcee, for example, may free a woman from some obligations of motherhood. Judith Thomas shows how both ex-spouses in joint custody situations perform parental roles, but, by sharing these roles with ex-spouses, have more time ("time off" from parenting) to spend on work and other activities.[49] The notion that more roles create stress is clearly incorrect in this situation. Multiple roles can and do create pressure and permission to compartmentalize (one of the mechanisms Goode offered in his analysis of reduction of role strain). Otherwise, women often are prey to limitless expectations from the "greedy institution" of the family,[50] in which their role obligations follow a kind of Parkinson's Law that activities expand to fill the time available.[51]

These findings contrast strongly with the "stress" model common in our culture, which focuses only on the stress that can incapacitate. A new model offered by Stephen R. Marks[52] builds on Selye's observation that stress can also exhilarate. Marks proposes viewing human energy as renewable and able to be stimulated, not as a reservoir that can leak out or drain away altogether. He points out that many people with multiple roles tend to run out of time and energy, yet he finds it intriguing that a minority apparently do not fall victim to "strain" or "overload."

Marks identified the conditions under which people are energized or enervated. Most people seem to have time and energy to do things to which they are highly committed. Although commitment may be rooted in personal idiosyncrasy, Marks points out, the culture may encourage certain kinds of commitment. Society rewards success in these activities with wealth, power, and prestige, creating high-energy states in those who perform them. Many men have found that high-demand work in the professional and business community results in such high-energy states.

Now women are achieving the same kind of energy because they are in the same kind of stimulating jobs. The strengths provided by reward and recognition enable these women to juggle the roles in their lives. In the process, they may achieve personality enrichment and acquire greater personal capacity to cope well. The sociologist Sam Sieber has shown that role diversification may be essential to mental health, enhancing one's self-conception.[53] And Rose Laub Coser also has pointed out that expanding one's roles results in greater freedom and autonomy and rather than crushing a person with an overload of role demands, provides new options and a new breadth of vision.[54] Work by Peggy Thoits also shows that multiple identities contribute to people's well-being.[55]

Role strain is induced by ambivalence and stress. Women have taken on multiple roles for millennia. They are used to working hard and to doing many things at the same time. This era is no exception, and today's women probably include no more superwomen than the pioneers who preceded them.

CHANGING FAMILY DYNAMICS

Nevertheless, the increased occupational role of women has altered the dynamics of family life. The implications of this change for people's behavior and beliefs inside and outside the home are discussed in the remainder of this chapter. The increase in the number of mothers with preschool- or school-age children who work outside the home has affected the sharing of power in the home, the division of labor in the home, and the image and politics of motherhood.

Power in the Home

Studies of marital power[56] suggest that women's labor force participation and the economic resources that go with it increase their power in the home. In general, then, as large numbers of women move into the formal economic sector and it becomes less sex-segregated, the balance of power between the sexes in modern societies may shift. The value of women's contributions may be reassessed and the grounds for attaining power altered, affecting the standing of women in family life. For example, Rose Laub Coser has suggested that for the modern American family, more and more women enter the paid labor market in order to satisfy the family's desire for more material goods or increased educational opportunities for children. When this happens, Coser maintains, men lose power as women gain a measure of financial independence. She points out that because men improve their social standing when the family attains a middle-class standard as a result of the wife's earnings, there can be a trade-off between the husband's loss of power within the home and his gain in the community as family prestige improves.[57]

In the past, the movement of production to the factory and office building made it possible for women to increase their de facto power, according to Coser. In families in which the men worked away from home and women remained within it, the wives could make most of the decisions concerning the household. The wives were economically dependent on their husbands, but because the husbands were not at home during the day, the wives were free from the husbands' supervision. To be sure, both men and older women controlled wives' activities in traditional extended families, but in the relatively isolated suburban nuclear family, women could exercise a certain amount of autonomy in the home.

Of course, single women who now head their own households may have greater autonomy, but for most it is at the cost of economic well-being. Poverty is concentrated in single-parent families headed by women; almost one-half (44.3 percent) of all such families were poor in 1981, and the proportion who were poor rose with the number of children.[58] Similar conclusions emerge when either black or white families are considered, but black families suffer more and there has been an increase in their number (from 834,000 in 1970 to 1.4 million in 1981).[59] Two-thirds of all female-headed households rent their housing compared with one-fourth of all families. This is a problem because there is a growing trend toward excluding children from new housing. A 1980 study conducted by the Department of Housing and Urban Development (HUD) found that "no children" policies caused families to search longer for their housing and pay higher costs for lower quality. The HUD survey revealed that 22.5 percent of all rental units studied were closed entirely to children, and another 50 percent imposed restrictions limiting the age and number of children who could be admitted. Several studies have concluded that "no children" exclusionary practices actually may be used as a smokescreen for race or sex discrimination.[60]

Another factor to be considered in evaluating women's relative power is the age at which they have children. As age at marriage has increased, the average age at the birth of a first child has gone up. Thus, women are becoming mothers late than before, and they are bearing fewer children than before. This later start gives women the opportunity to obtain occupational training and job experience. Women could not invest this heavily in "human capital" when they had children early. Now the increase in human capital may also increase their power in the family. Their age and experience as workers can give them more self-assurance and greater resources to express their preferences. The wives' demonstrated ability to provide income and to improve the family's economic well-being can also increase husbands' interest and investment in their spouses' labor force activity. And in the case of wives who have excellent career possibilities, husbands may also have to strike a better bargain with wives by agreeing to increase their participation in child care or to procure paid helpers. The husband in couples may also be a source of political support for child care legislation.

The Division of Labor in the Home

Most husbands of wives who work outside the home still do only a modest amount more of child care and housework than do husbands of wives who are not in the labor force. The division of labor in the home became a feminist concern in the 1970s, particularly for those scholars and activists who emphasized that the unpaid tasks women performed in the home constituted "work." Ann Oakley's book on the sociology of housework examined the contemporary Western experience,[61] and it led to other studies on women's work outside the formal workplace and the industrialized world.[62]

The division of "emotional labor" in the family also became a concern for scholars who questioned the notion that the family was a haven for its members. They concluded that when men work outside the home, they can retreat to the family and enjoy some leisure there; for women, in contrast, the home may be a constant sphere of hard work, and only a relatively small percentage of privileged women enjoy leisure there. These scholars point out that although the home may provide emotional succor for many, it also generates tension and conflict; some flee it, some tolerate it, and others endure it.

In many parts of the world, anthropologists have observed men sitting in coffee houses or their equivalent while the women wash clothes and clean house, prepare meals, and care for children. In the United States, too, many men enjoy time spent in "hanging around."[63] Women's leisure activities tend to be less public and therefore more difficult to assess. Middle-class and working-class women who are full-time homemakers probably have time to socialize with other women when their children are in school. Increasingly, though, mothers are spending school day hours at work. It is important to remember that even women with full-time employment put in an additional 20 to 30 hours a week of work in the home.

In all countries wives' employment has been found to have only a modest effect on the household division of labor.[64] Wives usually retain responsibility for the daily organization of the household, for household work, and for the actual physical chores, including laundry, cleaning, and meals. However, wives who work outside the home receive somewhat more help from husbands than do wives who are not employed outside the home. This is particularly true for child care,[65] which tends to be shared more than routine housekeeping tasks.[66] Child care by the father also is related to the age and sex of the child and the number of hours a wife works. It is also contingent on whether the wife holds traditional sex-role attitudes, the extent to which she plays a gatekeeper role, and the husband's dissatisfaction with his own childhood experience.[67] On average, the husbands of employed wives do only slightly more housework (between 10 and 14 hours a week) than men whose wives are full-time homemakers.[68] Some social scientists cite these figures when arguing that there is a politics of housework:[69] that is, the sexual division of labor as more women enter the labor force is distorted by male privilege and places an unfair burden on women.[70]

There may be problems in acquiring accurate data about the division of labor in the home. Because jobs in the home, as in the labor market, are so stereotypically conceived, both the researchers and those who are the subjects of research report only the gender appropriate tasks that are done. I suspect that men often fail to report that they do traditionally "female" tasks such as washing dishes or making beds if they feel these would be regarded as unmanly. Furthermore, there are perceptual discrepancies.[71] Studies have shown that husbands and wives in the United States give different reports about what the other does.[72]

These discrepancies may be due to genuine unfamiliarity with how much work is done and who actually does it. Some of it is due, no doubt, to stereotypical views of who does what or ought to do what. Perception is also colored by how much prestige is attached to particular types of work and whether women and men feel proud or ashamed of what they do. It is not only a matter of altering the picture they give to others; they may also truly believe what they report.

Methodological considerations aside, it is no surprise that household tasks are sex-typed and that women do most of the housework.[73] Large-scale generalizations, however, tend to obscure class and regional differences in household work. Factors such as education, income, and employment are important in altering job segregation within the home, but there is disagreement about the impact of education and income on the extent to which the household work is allocated democratically. Young (under 35 years of age), well-educated couples seem to share household responsibilities more than older and less educated ones.[74] Husbands with high income are less likely to share in the housework. None of these studies reports on the use of paid household help. In my studies of high-income, highly educated women lawyers, few depended on assistance from husbands; almost all relied on paid housekeepers and child caretakers.[75]

Equity of resources between the couple is a basis for sharing house old tasks. Nowhere is this seen more clearly than among black couples, who tend to have less discrepancy in income. Farkas and Ericksen and colleagues find that black husbands do more housework than do white husbands.[76] In the Hispanic community, however, traditional views regarding the division of labor are more strongly held and relatively more so among women than men.[77]

Even when women do not actually perform household work themselves, they still have responsibility for it. We can speculate that this is because society requires it and maintains sanctions against women if they do not take on this responsibility, and because the reward structure of society is such that women also prefer it this way. The household has been women's only base of prestige and power until recent times, and women seem to retain a tenacious hold on the domain.

New research has also addressed the dynamic in the family with regard to child care and housework. A study by Baruch and Barnett,[78] for example, points out that high paternal involvement in child care is unlikely to occur unless there is support and approval for this behavior from significant others. Thus mothers' sex-role attitudes play a crucial "gatekeeping" role, either fostering or hindering fathers' participation in family work. This supports the view of the sociologist Sarah Festermaker Berk, who has conceptualized the family as a "gender factory" producing not only goods but also gender. In a study of the division of household work she finds that wives expect, and are expected to assume a vastly greater share of household tasks than other household members, and that wives and husbands are basically satisfied with the division of labor. Her analysis indicates that through housework, husbands and wives affirm their categorical status as male and female.[79]

Studies show that women receive more prestige in their roles as housewives than they do in their roles as workers, largely because the kinds of jobs they tend to have are poorly rewarded both absolutely and relative to the rewards men enjoy.[80] For example, despite women's attachment to the workplace and the growing proportion who work, women's earnings consistently lag behind men's earnings. Regardless of whether annual earnings, weekly earnings, or annual income is the base, women, on average, make

70 percent of what men make when both are working full-time. For reasons such as this, women often retreat to the home rather than face defeat in the workplace. It would be preposterous to suppose that women who are housewives hold high prestige. But they may receive recognition for being good homemakers and enjoy vicarious honor through marriage to a man who holds a respected occupational position. Today, as in the past, leaving work to care for children is an acceptable and often preferred option for the working woman, especially if her career is dead-ended or fails to meet her expectations. However, there are no indications, either honorific or monetary, that society regards housework as an enviable task.

People first learn about gender distinctions in the family, and all families, no matter what their form, specify roles for their members according to gender (as well as age). Families are, of course, influenced by the larger culture and by the political system that proposes and enforces various kinds of gender roles. Families also are affected by sentiments, those that occur through the normal affections and passions people have and those that are stimulated by norms informing which inform people about the "right" feeling to have. But, we have seen how wide the variation can be and to what extent the variation depends on views held by groups and subgroups. Typically, greater freedom in the political system and health in the economic system create a climate for greater freedom in the selection and performance of family roles.

The Image and Politics of Motherhood

The greater economic resources of mothers in the labor force, coupled with the availability of effective contraceptives and abortion, have given women more control over childbearing and child rearing. The decision about whether to have any children has become voluntary, perhaps for the first time in history. Yet there remains a strong emphasis on motherhood as a major social role for women.

Much of this emphasis has taken the form of an idealized vision of motherhood. The idealized mother—and her counterpart, the neglecting and erring mother—has been at the center of much public and social science attention. The roots of this concept in the United States date to the turn of the century, when mothers were viewed as technical experts whose marketable product was a well-adjusted and achieving child, according to Ehrenreich and English.[81] The studies that began in the 1940s and continued into the 1970s and beyond were of the social problem approach focused on improper mothering. They included accounts of the overprotective mother, who kept the child in a state of arrested development,[82] and of the schizophrenic mother, whose contradictory behaviors resulted in the mental illness of the child.[83] "Mother blaming" for the mental ills expressed by children appeared in major clinical journals during this period, according to a study by Caplan and Hall-McCorquodale covering the years 1970, 1976, and 1982.[84]

Some feminist writers shared these cause-and-effect assumptions, focusing attention almost exclusively on the mother as the agent responsible for the mental health and development of the child. Writers such as Dinnerstein and Flax[85] created a theme that Chodorow and Contratto[86] called the "fantasy of the perfect mother." They suggested that idealization and blame of the mother are two sides of the same belief in the all-powerful mother. They proposed that the focus on the mother as principally responsible for the psychological, emotional, and relational state of the child often led to a psychological determinism and reductionism, in which the mother–infant relationship was said to be at the root of the whole of history, society, and culture. They further noted that the perfect mother was not perceived as a person with other tasks, emotions, needs, or history, but was seen only as a mother:

> This creates the quality of rage we find in the "blame the mother" literature and the unrealistic expectation that perfection would result if only a mother would devote her life completely to her child and all impediments to doing so were removed. Psyche and culture merge here and reflexively create one another.[87]

Research and paradigms thus were oriented toward the presumed necessity for women to assume traditional sex roles lest "failure in mothering do something devastating to children."[88] But, as noted earlier, "over-mothering" or "momism"[89] brought its own dangers.

Subsequent studies have acknowledged many other factors that may contribute to or independently cause mental illness, homosexuality, or problems in children's adjustment. Some scholars have also noted the therapeutic effects of mothers' working outside the home, such as children's sense of independence and good school performance, effects that vary directly with mothers' feelings about their jobs.[90] Except for the research by these social scientists, most studies that attributed ill-effects to mothers' behavior did not clearly differentiate among the kinds of jobs mothers had, their education, their economic level, and their work experience. Here, as in countless other studies, insufficient disaggregation color the researchers' results.

The biological fact that women give birth, and for most of history have had to nurse children in their first year, has set the framework for judging women's roles primarily in terms of their reproductive function. Many scholars and lay people have considered the mothering role, to be an inevitable determinant of female personality.

Conceptions of the centrality of the mothering role for women, also have been derived from psychoanalytic writings (Parsons, for one, was influenced by Freud). Many psychoanalysts, particularly classical Freudians, claimed that women were best defined by their mothering role and that a retreat from this role made women neurotic.[91]

Alice Rossi's biosocial perspective claims that a special bond exists between mothers and infants because of women's physiological responses and their experiences in menstruation and childbirth.[92] Nancy Chodorow, a leading advocate for the idea that women's earliest relationships with their own mothers cause them to "reproduce mothering," asserts further that women, in contrast with men, develop distinct personalities featuring connectedness, a lack of separation or differentiation, and a lack of orientation toward "body-ego boundaries."[93] Chodorow acknowledges that the division of labor in society, women's inequality in terms of independence and income, and other social structural factors are important in determining and enforcing women's assumption of the mothering role. Still, Chodorow maintains that women have a need for an intensive "interpersonal, diffuse, affective relationship" with a child. More recently, Sylvia Ann Hewlett, an economist, has argued that "modern women—no matter how ambitious—yearn to have children."[94]

But Lorber, and others have argued that such a perspective is culture and time bound; its evidence is usually based on clinical case histories and on personal reflections of the social scientists speculating about motherhood.[95] Certainly, most people, men and women, are reared to want children, and therefore most married people do. But it is difficult to separate the "yearning" that is a direct product of social pressure and that which comes from a personal desire to rear children. For most people, motherhood and fatherhood are abstract concepts until they actually procreate. Many then find child rearing stressful (though they may be pleased to have a child). Jessie Bernard has noted that studies in the mental health field find that married women whose sole identity is as a wife and mother have higher rates of mental illness than do working women, single or married.[96] Theories ascribing a universal experience to women are more likely to be grounded in ideology or culture than in systematic observation.

We know that women's experiences in other cultures vary widely. Ethnographic evidence indicates that mothers are not the exclusive caretakers of children after infancy in many of the world's societies. Older children or grandparents are frequently assigned the responsibility;[97] of course, most caretakers are female.

Do all women want to be mothers? In the United States as well as elsewhere, there is no evidence to indicate consistent socialization patterns and consistent orientation toward motherhood for all women. In a recent study of middle-class and working-class women, *Hard Choices,* Kathleen Gerson shows that women's life decisions, including the decision to become mothers, are shaped and influenced by adult experiences rather than by childhood conditioning or predispositions. She challenges the view that all women share one "feminine personality" that compels them to prefer a domestic lifestyle and to rear children. Gerson believes that life circumstances, including a husband's interest in having children, influence women's decisions to become mothers, decisions sometimes incurring ambivalence and distress.[98] Elizabeth Badinger believes that childhood socialization has not produced a universal "mothering need," that not all women wish to mother, that many women are indifferent to children, and that some even abuse them.[99]

Certainly in other societies, women and men have been denied adult recognition until they had children. Sanctions are strong if they are unable to have them. Even in the United States, women who choose not to have children are the victims of disapproval and concern; clearly, motherhood is bolstered by many social controls that stigmatize women who do not have children and reward them with social approval for becoming mothers.

In every society, as Goode points out, there have been "various points at which custom or rationality put some brake upon fertility."[100] Notions of what constitutes the ideal family size also changes. Where contraception and other forms of fertility control are available, women seem to take advantage of them. Joan Huber and Glenna Spitze regard the dependable curtailment of fertility as the major turning point in the movement toward equality.[101] They suggest that the perceived inevitability of motherhood through history tethered women to the home, making them unable to engage in the kinds of activities that resulted in a wider distribution of wealth, or to enter and gain power in the political sphere.

Today, Americans are keenly aware of the debates in the society about women's rights to fertility control and restrictions on their rights. As Kristen Luker puts it, the family is contested terrain.[102]

The abortion issue, for example, is only the latest in a long history of debates over women's power to control their fertility, that is, to select the circumstances and conditions under which they will become mothers and, indeed, whether they will become mothers at all. Although there is a widespread belief that the desire for children is either an inborn or an early acquired trait. The state, the community, and the family have always asserted an interest in women's fertility and have expressed that interest through rules and restrictions on sexuality as well as contraception, abortion, and, in some cases, infanticide. Thus, persons outside the immediate family have always intruded on the so-called natural and private consideration of people to become parents, or more particularly, of women to become mothers.

Gerson's study further shows that it is the family situations of women that determine their personal and collective views on family and community roles.[103] Those women who are most economically dependent on men profess the most traditional views. Among women who do not work for pay or who work outside the home in dead-end jobs but whose husbands are good providers, motherhood is primary. Their positions on issues such as abortion, equal rights for women, affirmative action progress, or publicly provided day care follow their own choices and situations, a finding that confirms the research of Luker on abortion activists on both sides of the issue.

THE EFFECTS OF MATERNAL EMPLOYMENT ON CHILDREN

Another consequence of the movement of women into the labor force is the concern about the effects of maternal employment on children. Most studies of this issue, it should be noted, ignore the effect of paternal employment on children. This is not surprising because the assumptions are (1) that if women are not minding the home, *no one* is, and (2) that it does not matter whether fathers spend much or little time in the home as long as they are consistent breadwinners and have a regular attachment to the family. Whether these underlying assumptions are justified or not, a brief review of some studies indicates the inconsistency of findings and calls attention to the problems of viewing them without attention to context.

Woods states that full-time work by mothers is better for children than part-time work[104]; Hoffman claims the opposite[105]; and, according to Howell, there are "almost no constant differences" between children of employed and nonemployed mothers.[106] Hoffman has noted that, as children develop through adolescence, positive outcomes accompany maternal employment. For example, girls are felt to develop a greater sense of independence, are less likely to accept traditional sex roles, are less fearful and more outgoing and ambitious, and have higher self-esteem.[107]

Other findings do not indicate agreement on these points. Van Vliet, for example, has found less traditional sex roles and attitudes among the daughters of employed mothers but also found them to be less independent and to have lower feelings of self-esteem and control.[108] Hoffman raises the question of whether older children run more risk of delinquency if they are less supervised at home after school, but the evidence is scant.[109] In contrast, Hansson and colleagues note that although being home alone offers the child an opportunity for promiscuity and mischief, the experience of being home alone often leads the child to an increased sense of self-discipline and responsibility.[110] Gold and Andres believe that employed mothers are less restrictive with their children and that children in these families often have more contact with their fathers (which they feel adds to the child's positive sense of nontraditional roles).[111]

Quite a bit has been written on the effect that maternal employment may have on a child's achievement. Until fairly recently, it was believed that a mother's employment had a small but consistently negative effect on the child's reading and mathematical achievement, and that this effect was cumulative and proportional to the mother's time spent working.[112] However, Heyns and Catsambis argue that this research is based on faulty methodology, and they pose an alternative analysis of the data.[113] They conclude:

> There do seem to be patterns of employment that are consistently related to children's achievement, irrespective of background factors. In particular, when other family characteristics are controlled, children whose mothers work briefly during only one period, or who decrease their commitment to work over time, are one to two percentage points behind children whose mothers never worked. For women who are eager to increase their hours or loath to leave the labor force, these results clearly suggest that their children will not be adversely affected. The cumulative negative effect of mother's employment hypothesized by Milne *et al.* seems to be a figment of a psychologist's nightmare.[114]

Michelson summarizes the literature on the effects of maternal employment in this way: "While there are many concerns and claims about how children may encounter negative outcomes as a consequence of maternal employment, the literature as a whole does not support these or very many of the hypothesized positive outcomes."[115] As Skinner put it:

> There is no evidence to suggest that the dual-career lifestyle, in and of itself, is stressful for children. What may be more significant for the children is the degree of stress experienced by the parents which may indirectly affect the children.[116]

Few researchers interview children, and few data indicate the attitudes of children in different social contexts. For example, it is probable that children who expect their mothers to work do not regard their time away from the home as unusual, and therefore do not feel deprived. Goode hypothesized that, as more mothers work, resistance of children will decrease.[117] Of course, in the past as in the present, women in poor families worked and children (and other family members) did not regard it unusual or detrimental. It was seen, rather, as a normal contribution to the family.

Although much of the discussion about women's employment today centers on the problems this creates for children, many other latent concerns have to do with women's growing independence and the disruption of the middle class life pattern that has set the norm for family life more generally. We might well ask to what extent our attitudes toward child care, and the consequences for children of mothers' employment, are class bound and time bound.

Through history many patterns of child care have reflected the living patterns of Americans. Children were certainly tended more by kin and other members of the community when small-town life was characteristic of the American way of life and in places where people were rooted in community and not affected by the mobility inflicted by expanding corporations that expected its managers to move. Models of child care tend to be predicated on the middle-class mobile families rather than working-class settled families whose preference is for work lodged in their communities. Of course, Americans, more than other people, have tended to be mobile, creating several different patterns of child care. For those who were rooted in community-based work, kin shared child care. For those who were mobile, child care became more focused on individual mothers. There are some notable exceptions to this. Among mobile black families, child care was often shared by grandparents and other family members who took in children whose parents needed to travel far from home to obtain employment.

The social changes resulting from mother's employment are difficult to disentangle from other social changes, and few researchers attempt to do so. In the discussions on child care, few ask the question, what are the optimum social arrangements for child care? Not only have there been changes in the work force behavior of mothers, but also lower fertility has meant that children have fewer siblings. Many children also have fewer other relatives around, such as grandparents, uncles, aunts, and cousins. In addition, they also have fewer informal relationships with people such as shopkeepers, occasional home workers, farm workers, the policeman on the corner, the family doctor, and so on. Fewer diffuse ties probably make for more intense mother–child ties.

Yet nontraditional ties have increased as a result of divorce and remarriage. Many young people now acquire half-sisters and half-brothers, step-fathers and step-mothers, and even step-grandparents. Ironically, the increase in divorce has altered the roles of some grandparents in that they are reassuming the functional role that was more widespread a few generations ago.[118] Furthermore, both mothers and children have acquired diffuse ties created by their involvement with formal organizations (such as with social workers). Thus, more non-kin people perform kinlike services. Many people object to certain of these ties without understanding their consequences. Certainly, the new diffuse relationships are considerably different from the ones of the past. New step family ties are not institutionalized and there are no established norms regarding "proper" behavior in them. Some of the more formal ties are centered in bureaucratized settings without linkages into the community.

Another question has to do with the zero-sum perspective that assumes a mother's well-being is achieved at some cost to the child's well-being. Here, the common referent is to the mother's interest in and commitment to a demanding but satisfying job. Of course, there is a zero-sum dimension to the total number of hours in a day and a week, but mothers who can share child care with fathers, other relatives, friends, paid caretakers and teachers in school and after-school programs may even improve their children's well-being.

Are women who are interested in their careers less interested in their children than full-time mothers? There is no evidence to support this view. In fact, there is a great deal of anecdotal evidence that middle-class, career-oriented mothers are even more invested in the intellectual and psychic development of their children and pay more attention to their supervision (even if some of it is delegated). The mother need not be on board, so to speak, for the child to know she has arranged for music and sports lessons, for medical checkups and birthday parties. In fact, the same mothers who focus a great deal of attention on children are often placed in the double bind of being faulted for too much concern and too much input into their children's development. The no-win situation with regard to child care is not unlike what women face in the occupational world where they are "damned if they do and damned if they don't" commit themselves to work.[119]

As I pointed out elsewhere,[120] standards of child care and child involvement may differ considerably by class and social circle. The middle class is often more affected by trends in psychology and distinct ideological positions than the working class, but the working class, too, becomes fixed on cultural models that are reinforced by the media; the working class is also motivated by a propensity to emulate the middle class. As pointed out earlier, a legacy of the psychoanalytic model has been a strong cultural emphasis on the mother–child bond. Dr. Spock's famous book, *The Commonsense Book of Baby and Childcare*, stressed the importance of the mother's staying home during the child's early years, a position he altered in the book's later editions.[121] Some regard child care by a person other than the mother to be an indicator of a breakdown in the "family." Both working-class and middle-class men derive social standing when their wives are full-time mothers, and they often rationalize their preference by referring to psychological benefits. In a study of lawyers, I found that feminist lawyers who tended to be ideological about the rights of the poor and other matters were also ideological with regard to the importance of mothering. As a result, they often suffered more conflict about the work-versus-home issue than lawyers who worked in corporate settings in which these ideological commitments were not the subject of constant intense discussion.[122]

Yet another interesting issue concerning child care is the way in which it reinforces gender norms. If women were not bound to child care, they could live lives much more like those of men and thus become more *like* men with regard to the accumulation of resources and power. Most societies expend considerable effort to maintain gender distinctions[123] and perpetuate gender inequality. Few decisionmakers dare question whether child care is good for women; cultural norms simply make the assumption. It is doubtful, however, whether formal child care arrangements would cause a breakdown in gender norms. For one thing, child care workers would probably continue to be women, reinforcing the notion that child care is woman's work. For another, even formal arrangements that *help* women manage child care and work (such as the provision of child care leave) probably also reinforce the definition of women as child caretakers. Cultural norms still determine that women will take child care leave more than men, and because of the pay inequity in the labor force, there is also an economic motivation for a woman rather than her husband to forego pay. I learned during a recent trip to Scandinavia that formal child care seems to reinforce gender segregation in the workforce, because employers do not seem eager to hire women of childbearing age for responsible, high-paying jobs because of the generous leave time (11 months in Finland) they may have from work.

CONCLUSION

Changes in the lives of mothers have occurred in a social context in which there have been changes in norms regarding women's equality, men's responsibilities in the family, changing economic pressures, and expectations regarding living standards. As with other social changes, attitudes and behavior are not consistent. For example, the steady increase in mothers' labor force participation, while meeting more approval than was the case in prior times, is still regarded as less than ideal by many, including policymakers who disagree on the extent to which there should be government intervention to ease the burden of working mothers.

Yet certain structural changes seem clear-cut no matter what the attitudes of families or policymakers. As we have seen, women are increasing their participation in the labor force, and they are remaining attached to it with a commitment less diminished by the presence of small children in the home. This has also increased women's power in the home and in the greater society, especially for those whose work provides financial independence and personal autonomy.

Changes in norms also have contributed to the changing lives of women, but they are not clear-cut. They support women's investment in their human capital through longer and higher education and training. Although we have not referred here to women's growing political participation and their representation in government (at the local and state levels, in particular), women certainly have a much greater sense of political efficacy and actual power in setting up the political agenda. We can expect greater emphasis on "women's issues" as a result, and further discussion in public. Of course, women do not speak with one voice, and their political participation can be found across all sectors of the spectrum. However, concerns about motherhood and the care of children will undoubtedly become an important focus in public forums.

Norms supporting early marriage also have changed, as has the view of ideal family size. Part of this change is due to the economic costs of raising a child. Another part is due to the greater value placed on women's economic contributions and on the expectation that women have the capacity to obtain higher returns for their labor force participation.

One could argue that as women become more attached to the labor force, given the inadequacy of child care provisions, they may become less interested in mothering and less resigned to its inevitability. It seems doubtful that many women will decide against motherhood altogether; instead, motherhood may assume a more measured place in women's lives, and most women will expect to combine motherhood and employment in their lives. They are less fearful of negative effects on children, a view supported by research that shows the consequences for children are not harmful. Mothering remains a powerful source of affirmation for women who have yet to assume the privileges and options of men in creating their future. It provides one domain in which a woman may exercise authority no matter what her class.

But men also fulfill the norms of maturity and authority when they become fathers. We may find that men want to be fathers as much as women want to be mothers. As men become more articulate about their interest in procreation, they may also be prepared to take a more active parental role as an inducement for women to collaborate in parenthood.

However, it would be foolish to regard procreation as rooted only in private decisions. Policymakers typically express concern when middle- and upper-class women do not produce more members. Hence, we may see more social investment in providing care for women contemplating later pregnancies and more social approval for women with large investments in careers who drop out of the labor force, or take time out from it, to care for children. (This decision is often made when women face a ceiling on their opportunities in the work world and become discouraged in their dreams of achievement.)

It is unrealistic to expect that women will withdraw en masse from the labor market as a response to the stress, because families need their income and women have demonstrated growing commitment to the labor force. And, as we have seen, there are other solutions to the "overload" experienced from multiple roles. Mothers are now overloaded because they have the sole responsibility for child care that could be assumed by other family members if firms and schools were to make reasonable adjustments. As pointed out earlier, mothers have always engaged in market activities while fulfilling family responsibilities, and they have done so with social approval, as long as the market activity was not a source of women's independence. Given the changes that have occurred in women's consciousness and situation, it would be wise for policymakers to acknowledge their changed circumstances and to make adjustments that would be supportive of families in which the caretakers of children were also wage-earners.

We need to think creatively about how to treat the family as a system, and not only a mother–child dyad or a mother–father–child triad. Furthermore, the community context needs to be identified. Community influences may be helpful to the family or may be pernicious. It is important to strengthen positive family–community ties and make the community a resource for families. The workplace and family should be considered an interactive unit. For example, the schedules for the work day, the school day, and holidays should be coordinated to create a better fit, or institutional provision should be made for discrepancies such as vacation programs for children in schools or time-off provisions for parents at work to coincide with school events.

Thinking grandly, a national service program (similar to the National Guard) might be considered to incorporate education for citizenship and community and family responsibility for boys and girls, young men and women. Less grandly, such themes could be incorporated into school curricula or summer programs. Because the family can no longer be responsible for many child care services, and perhaps no longer *should* be responsible (because children may be better served by alternative measures), we ought to direct our attention to a range or policies and programs that would meet diverse needs. Briefly stated, they might include tax benefits and other incentives for employers to provide child care facilities or assistance; provision of public facilities (such as schools) and trained personnel for after-school care and other dependent care; incentives for industry to provide flexibility for fathers and mothers to help them deal with family demands; tax incentives and regulations for new multiple unit residences to provide space for child care and family activities on the premises.

Above all, what we need from government is symbolic leadership that helps to legitimate the role of the employed mother, and, in so doing, weaken the contradictory norms that make life for working women and their families more difficult. This symbolic role may be more important than the specifics of any programs enacted. An expression of concern and support by government leaders is critical to the health of the new dual-earner American family.

The support of the Russell Sage Foundation in the preparation of this paper is acknowledged with thanks.

Notes

1. William J. Goode, *The Family*, 2nd ed. (Englewood Cliffs, N.J.: Prentice-Hall, 1982), xiii.

2. Family change in the United States has been a long-term process. In The New American Grandparent: A Place in the Family, A Life Apart (New York: Basic Books, 1986) Andrew Cherlin and Frank F. Furstenberg, Jr. point out that, according to the still incomplete historical record (the subdiscipline of family history is only about twenty years old), the change may have been discontinuous, occurring in great bursts and then subsiding for a time.

3. William J. Goode, *World Revolution and Family Patterns* (Glencoe, Ill.: Free Press, 1963).

4. The vision of an ideal family living in a large household is played out in the fantasies provided by popular prime-time television programs such as "Dallas," "Dynasty," "The Colbys," and "Falcon Crest." In each, a family composed of parents, children and their spouses, grandchildren, and even estranged spouses live in a grand household. Although relationships are always complicated and filled with the stress necessary for dramatic interest, the family ties are regarded as important and enduring. These programs are also popular in other parts of the world where they are shown—throughout Europe and even in the Third World.

5. Christopher Lasch, *Haven in a Heartless World: The Family Besieged* (New York: Basic Books, 1977).

6. Judith Stacey, "The New Conservative Feminism," *Feminist Studies* 9, no. 3 (Fall 1983): 559–83.

7. Mirra Komarovsky, "Cultural Contradictions and Sex Roles," *American Journal of Sociology* 52 (1946):184–89.

8. Talcott Parsons, "The Kinship System of the Contemporary United States," in Talcott Parsons, ed., *Essays in Sociological Theory*, rev. ed. (Glencoe, Ill.: Free Press, 1954):177–196.

9. Marion Levy, Jr. and Lloyd Fullers, in "The Family: Some Comparative Considerations," *American Anthropologist* 61, no. 4 (August 1959): 647–51, refuted Parson's assertion of the ubiquity of the nuclear family on the basis of Levy's *The Family Revolution of Modern China* (Cambridge: Harvard University Press, 1949), a study of the Chinese family and research on other societies that did not conform to the model, such as the Nayar (Kathleen E. Gough, "Changing Kinship Usages in the Setting of Political and Economic Change among the Nayars of Malabar," *Journal of*

the Royal Anthropological Institute 82, pt. 1 [1952]:71–88) and Hopi (Fred Eggan, *Social Organization of the Western Pueblos* [Chicago: University, 1950]).

10. Talcott Parsons, "The Kinship System": 177–196. According to the U.S. Census Bureau, in 1960 59.21 percent of the total number of married couples had at least one child under 18 years of age living with them.

11. Betty Friedan, *The Feminine Mystique* (New York: W. W. Norton and Co., 1963).

12. These writings included the journals *Aphra*, *Off Our Backs*, *Up From Under*, *Notes from the Second Year* (New York: Radical Feminists, 1969); Kate Millet's book *Sexual Politics* (Garden City, N.Y.: Doubleday and Co., 1970); Shulamith Firestone's *The Dialectic of Sex* (New York: Bantam Books, 1972); Gayle Rubin's article "The Traffic in Women: Notes on the 'Political Economy' of Sex," Rayna R. Reiter, ed., *Toward an Anthropology of Women* (New York: Monthly Review Press, 1975):157–210; and Jeanne Arrow's " 'Dangers in the Pro-woman Line and Consciousness-Raising' Ideas of the Feminists," mimeo, November 1969, reprinted in Cynthia Epstein and W. Goode, eds., *The Other Half: Roads to Women's Equality* (Englewood Cliffs, N.J.: Prentice-Hall, 1971):203–207. "Equality Between the Sexes: A Immodest Proposal," *Daedalus* (Spring 1964):607–52, although not reported as part of the "radical" literature, was an important theoretical analysis of gender roles and included a prescription for change.

13. Barrie Thorne, "Feminist Rethinking of the Family: An Overview," in Barrie Thorne and Marilyn Yalom, eds., *Rethinking the Family: Some Feminist Questions* (New York and London: Longman, 1982), 5.

14. Ibid.

15. Jane F. Collier, Michelle Z. Rosaldo, and Sylvia Yanagisako, "Is There a Family? New Anthropological Views," in Thorne and Yalom, eds., *Rethinking the Family*: 25–39.

16. Rayna Rapp, "Family and Class in Contemporary America: Notes Toward and Understanding of Ideology," *Science and Society* 42 (Fall 1978):278–300.

17. Jessie Bernard, *The Future of Marriage* (New York: World, 1972); and Constantina Safilios-Rothschild, *Women and Social Policy* (Englewood Cliffs, N.J.: Prentice-Hall, 1974).

18. Sylvia Ann Hewlett, *A Lesser Life: The Myth of Women's Liberation in America* (New York: Morrow, 1986).

19. Grace K. Baruch, Rosalind Barnett, and Caryl Rivers, *Lifeprints: New Patterns of Love and Work for Today's Woman* (New York: McGraw Hill, 1983); Rosalind C. Barnett and Grace K. Baruch, "Determinants of Fathers' Participation in Family Work," *Journal of Marriage and the Family* 49 (February 1987):29–40; Faye J. Crosby, *Relative Deprivation and Working Women* (New York: Oxford University Press, 1987); and Cynthia Fuchs Epstein, *Women in Law* (New York: Basic Books, 1981).

20. Lewis Coser and Rose Laub Coser, "The Housewife and Her 'Greedy Family,' " in Coser and Coser, eds., *Greedy Institutions: Patterns of Undivided Commitment* (New York: Free Press, 1974):89–100.

21. Susan M. Strasser, *Never Done: A History of American Housework* (New York: Pantheon Books, 1982); Ruth Schwartz Cowan, *More Work for Mother* (New York: Basic Books, 1983); and Alice Kessler-Harris, *Women Have Always Worked: A Historical Overview* (Old Westbury: Feminist Press, 1981).

22. Kessler-Harris, *Women Have Always Worked*.

23. In l980, 60 percent of all women between the ages of 16 to 64 were employed; they made up 42.8 percent of the labor force.

24. Susan Moller Okin, *Women in Western Political Thought* (Princeton, N.J.: Princeton University Press, 1979).

25. Albie Sachs and Joan Hoff-Wilson, *Sexism and the Law* (New York: Free Press, 1978).

26. Robert K. Merton, *Social Theory and Social Structure* (Glencoe, Ill.: Free Press, 1957).

27. See *More Work for Mother.*

28. Cynthia Fuchs Epstein, "Women and Professional Careers: The Case of the Woman Lawyer" Ph.D. dissertation, Columbia University, 1968; idem, *Woman's Place: Options and Limits in Professional Careers* (Berkeley: University of California Press, 1970); idem, *Women in Law.*

29. Merton, *Social Theory and Social Structure*; and Everett C. Hughes, "Dilemmas and Contradictions of Status," *American Journal of Sociology* 50 (March 1945): 353–59.

30. Epstein, *Women's Place.*

31. Hughes, "Dilemmas and Contradiction of Status."

32. Merton, *Social Theory and Social Structure.*

33. William J. Goode, "A Theory of Role Strain," *American Sociological Review* 25 (1960): 483–96.

34. Epstein, *Women's Place.*

35. Ibid.; idem; "Separate And Unequal: Notes on Women's Achievement," *Social Policy* 6, no. 5 (March/April 1976):17–23.

36. Robert Karasek, "Job Demands, Job Decision Latitude, and Mental Strain: Implications for Job Redesign," *Administrative Science Quarterly* 24 (1979):285–307.

37. S. Haynes and M. Feinleib, "Women, Work and Coronary Heart Disease: Prospective Findings from the Framingham Heart Study," *American Journal of Public Health* 70, no. 2 (1980):133–44.

38. Robert Kahn, *Work and Health* (New York: John Wiley, 1981); and P. Warr, "Psychological Aspects of Employment and Unemployment," *Psychological Medicine* 12(1982):7–11.

39. W. R. Gove and M. R. Geerkin, "The Effect of Children and Employment on the Mental Health of Married Men and Women," *Social Forces* 56(1977):66–76; and R. C. Kessler and J. McRae, Jr. "The Effect of Wives' Employment," *American Sociological Review* 47, no. 2 (1982):216–26.

40. Faye J. Crosby, *Relative Deprivation and Working Women* (New York: Oxford University Press, 1982).

41. Epstein, *Women in Law.*

42. Epstein, *Women's Place.*

43. Harriet Zuckerman and Jonathan Cole, "Women in American Science" *Minerva* 13, no. 1 (January 1975):82–102; Mary Roth Walsh, *Doctors Wanted—No Women Need Apply: Sexual Barriers in the Medical Profession* (New Haven: Yale University Press, 1977); Epstein, Women and Law; and Judith Lorber, *Women Physicians: Careers, Status and Power* (New York: Methuen, Inc., 1984).

44. Baruch, Barnett and Rivers, Lifeprints.

45. Baruch, Barnett, and Rivers draw on Ilfeld's "Sex Differences in Psychiatric Symptomatology," paper presented at meeting of the American Psychological Association, 1977.

46. Brigid O'Farrell and Sharon Harlan, "Job Integration Strategies: Today's Programs and Tomorrow's Needs," in Barbara F. Reskin, ed., *Sex Segregation in the Workplace: Trends, Explanations, Remedies* (Washington D.C.: National Academy Press, 1984):267–91.

47. Rosalind C. Barnett and Grace K. Baruch. "Mothers' Participation in Childcare: Patterns and Consequences," in Faye Croby, ed., *Spouse, Parent, Worker: On Gender and Multiple Roles* (New Haven: Yale University Press, 1987): 91–106.

48. Melvin Kohn and Carmi Shooler, "The Reciprocal Effects of the Substantive Complexity of Work and Intellectual Flexibility: A Longitudinal Assessment," *American Journal of Sociology* 84 (July 1978):24–52.

49. Judith Thomas, "Co-Parenting and Careers: Divorced Mothers Discover Advantages in Dual Households," paper presented at the Eastern Sociological Society, March 1983.

50. Coser and Coser, "The Housewife and Her 'Greedy Family.' "

51. Epstein, *Woman's Place.*

52. Stephen R. Marks, "Multiple Roles and Role Strain: Some Notes on Human Energy, Time and Commitment," *American Sociological Review* 42, no. 6 (December 1977):921–36.

53. Sam Sieber, "Toward a Theory of Role Accumulation," *American Sociological Review* 39 (August 1974):567–78.

54. Rose Laub Coser, "The Complexity of Roles as a Seedbed of Individual Autonomy," in Lewis Coser, ed., *The Idea of Social Structure* (New York: Harcourt Brace Jovanovich, 1975).

55. Peggy Thoits, "Multiple Identities and Psychological Well-Being: A Reformulation and Test of the Social Isolation Hypothesis," *American Sociological Review* 48 (April 1983):174–87.

56. Robert O. Blood and Donald M. Wolfe, *Husbands and Wives: The Dynamics of Married Living* (Glencoe, Ill.: Free Press, 1960); John Scanzoni, "A Historical Perspective on Husband-Wife Bargaining Power and Marital Dissolution," in A. Levinger and O. C. Mobs, eds., *Divorce and Separation* (New York: Basic Books, 1975); and Gerald W. McDonald, "Family Power: The Assessment of a Decade of Theory and Research, 1970–79," *Journal of Marriage and the Family* 42, no. 4 (November 1980):841–54.

57. Rose Laub Coser, "Women at Work: Power and Exchange in the Family," paper presented at the Eightieth Annual Meeting of the American Sociological Association, Washington, D.C. August 26–30, 1985.

58. Thomas J. Espenshade, "The Recent Decline of American Marriage: Blacks and Whites in Comparative Perspective," in Kingsley Davis, ed., *Contemporary Marriage* (New York: Russell Sage Foundation): 53–90.

59. William C. Johnson and Dwight L. Johnson. "America's Black Population: 1970 to 1982, A Statistical View," U.S. Bureau of the Census, Special Publication, PIO/POP-83-1, 1983.

60. UPDATE, Congressional Caucus for Women's Issues, 7, no. 4 (May 1987), 4.

61. Ann Oakley, *The Sociology of Housework* (London: Martin Robinson, 1974).

62. Constantina Safilios-Rothschild, "Women and Work," in A. H. Stromberg and S. Harkess, eds., *Women Working* (Palo Alto, Calif.: Mayfield Publishing Company, 1978.)

63. Many men "hang around" at the workplace, socializing with co-workers or engaging in union activities. However, this is generally regarded as work.

64. Eugen Lupri and Gladys Symons, "The Emerging Symmetrical Family, Fact or Fiction?" Paper presented at Annual Meeting of the Pacific Sociological Association in Portland, Oregon, March 20, 1981.

65. V. Gecas, "The Socialization and Child Care Roles," in F. I. Nye, ed., *Role Structures and Analogies of the Family* (Beverly Hills: Sage, 1976):35–59; and J. A. Ericksen, W. L. Yancey, and E. P. Erickson, "The Division of Family Roles," *Journal of Marriage and the Family* 41(1979):301–13.

66. See Joanne Miller and Howard H. Garrison, "Sex Roles: The Division of Labor at Home and in the Workplace," *Annual Review of Sociology* 8 (1982):237–62 for a review of sources on this subject.

67. Rosalind C. Barnett and Grace K. Baruch, "Determinants of Fathers' Participation in Family Work," *Journal of Marriage and the Family,* 49 (February 1987):29–40.

68. Barrie Thorne, "Feminist Rethinking of the Family: An Overview," in Thorne and Yalom, eds., *Rethinking the Family:* 1–24.

69. Pat Mainardi, "The Politics of Housework" in P. Morgan, ed., *Sisterhood Is Powerful* (New York: Vintage, 1970):447–5.

70. S. K. Araji, "Husbands' and Wives' Attitude-Behavior Congruences on Family Roles," *Journal of Marriage and the Family* 39(1977):309–20.

71. W. L. Slocum and F. I. Nye, "Provider and Housekeeper Roles," in F. I. Nye, ed., *Role Structure and Analysis of the Family* (Beverly Hills: Sage Publications, 1976): 81-99; B. Duncan and O. D. Duncan, with J. A. McRea, Jr., *Sex Typing and Social Roles: A Research Report* (New York: Academic Press, 1978); S. F. Berk and A. Shih, "Contributions to Household Labor: Comparing Wives' and Husbands' Reports," in S. F. Berk, ed., *Women and Household Labor,* (Beverly Hills: Sage Publications, 1980): 191–227; and Arlie Russell Hochschild, "Housework and Gender Strategies for Getting Out of It," paper given at the American Sociological Association, University of California, Berkeley, August 26–30, 1985.

72. Oakley, *The Sociology of Housework;* Joanne Miller and Howard H. Garrison, "Sex Roles: The Division of Labor at Home and in the Workplace," *Annual Review of Sociology* 8 (1982): 237–62; Hochschild, "Housework and Gender Strategies for Getting-Out of It."

73. G. Farkas, "Education, Wage Rates and the Division of Labor Between Husband and Wife," *Journal of Marriage and the Family* 38(1976):473–83.

74. Ericksen et al., "The Diviation of Family Roles."

75. Epstein, *Women in Law.*

76. Farkas, "Education, Wage Rates and The Division of Labor"; and Eriksen et al., "The Division of Family Roles."

77. R. C. Cronkite, "The Determinants of Spouses' Normative Preferences for Family Roles," *Journal of Marriage and Family,* 39(1977):575–85.

78. Grace K. Baruch and Rosalind C. Barnett, "Role Quality and Psychological Well-Being," in Faye J. Crosby, ed., *Spouse, Parent, Worker: On Gender and Multiple Roles* (New Haven and London: Yale University Press, 1987).

79. Sarah Fenstermaker Berk, *The Gender Factory* (New York: Plenum Press, 1985).

80. Christine E. Bose, "Social Status of the Homemaker," in Berk, ed. *Women and Household Labor.*

81. Barbara Ehrenreich and Deirdre English, *For Her Own Good: 150 Years of Experts' Advice to Women* (New York: Doubleday and Co. 1978).

82. David Levy, *Maternal Overprotection* (New York: Columbia University Press, 1943).

83. Theodore Lidz, *The Origin and Treatment of Schizophrenic Disorders* (New York Basic Books, 1965); G. Bateson and D. Jackson, "Toward a Theory of Schizophrenia" in J. G. Howells, ed., *Theory and Practice of Family Psychiatry* (New York: Brunner/Mazel, 1971):745–64.

84. Paula Caplan and Ian Hall-McCorquodale, "Mother-Blaming in Major Clinical Journals," *American Journal of Orthopsychiatry* 55, no. 3 (July 1985):345–613.

85. Dorothy Dinnerstein, *The Mermaid and the Minotaur: Sexual Arrangements and Human Malaise* (New York: Harper and Row, 1976); and Jane Flax, "The Conflict Between Nurturance and Autonomy in Mother-Daughter Relationships and Within Feminism," *Feminist Studies* (June 2, 1978):171–89.

86. Nancy Chodorow and Susan Contratto, "The Fantasy of the Perfect Mother," in Thorne and Yalom, eds., *Rethinking the Family:* 34–75.

87. Ibid., 65.

88. David Spiegel, "Mothering, Fathering and Mental Illness," in Thorne and Yalom, eds., *Rethinking the Family.*

89. Philip Wylie, *Generation of Vipers* (New York: Farrar, Rinehart, 1942).

90. Louis Wladis Hoffman, "Mother's Enjoyment of Work and Effects on the Child," *Child Development* 32 (March 1961):187–97; S. R. Orden and N. N. Bradburn, "Working Wives and Marriage Happiness," *American Journal of Sociology* 78(January 1969):853–72; Constantina Safilios-Rothschild, *Women and Social Policy* (Englewood Cliffs, N.J.: Prentice-Hall, 1974); Lotte Bailyn, "Career and Family Orientation of Husbands and Wives in Relation to Marital Happiness," *Human Relations* 22(1970):97–113; Rosabeth Moss Kanter, *Work and Family in the United States: A Critical Review and Agenda for Research and Policy* (New York: Russell Sage Foundation, 1977).

91. Helene Deutsch, *The Psychology of Women: A Psychoanalytical Interpretation* (London: Research Books, 1947).

92. Alice Rossi, "The Biosocial Basis of Parenting," *Daedalus* 106(1977): 1–31.

93. Nancy Chodorow, *The Reproduction of Mothering: Psychoanalysis and the Sociology of Gender* (Berkeley: University of California Press, 1978).

94. Sylvia Ann Hewlett, *A Lesser Life: The Myth of Women's Liberation in America* (New York: Morrow, 1986).

95. Judith Lorber, Rose Laub Coser, Alice R. Rossi, and Nancy Chodorow, "On the Reproduction of Mothering: A Methodological Debate," *Signs* 6, no. 3 (1981).

96. Jessie Bernard, *Women and the Public Interest* (Chicago and New York: Aldine, Atherton, 1971).

97. H. Medick and David W. Sabean, "Interest and Emotion in Family Studies: A Critique of Social History and Anthropology," in Medick and Sabean, eds., *Interest and Emotion* (New York: Cambridge University Press, 1984).

98. Kathleen Gerson, *Hard Choices: How Women Decide About Work, Career and Motherhood* (Berkeley: University of California Press, 1985).

99. Elizabeth Badinter, *Mother Love: Myth and Reality* (New York: Macmillan, 1981).

100. Goode, *World Revolution and Family Patterns.*

101. Joan Huber and Glenna Spitze, *Sex Stratification: Child in Housework and Jobs* (New York: Academic Press, 1983).

102. Kristen Luker, discussion, session on "A Social Issue: Reflections on Kristen Luker's Abortion and the Politics of Motherhood," *American Sociological Association Convention*, Washington, D.C., August 26–30, 1985.

103. Kathleen Gerson, "Emerging Social Divisions Among Women: Implications for Welfare State Policies," remarks prepared for a panel discussion of "A Social Issue in U.S. Politics: Reflections on Kristin Luker's Abortion and the Politics of Motherhood," American Sociological Association Convention, Washington, D.C., August 26–30, 1985.

104. M. Woods, "The Unsupervised Child of the Working Mother," *Developmental Psychology* 6(1972):14–25.

105. Lois Hoffman, "Effects of Maternal Employment on the Child—A Review of the Research," *Developmental Psychology* 10 (1974):204–28.

106. Mary Howell, "The Effects of Maternal Employment on the Child," *Pediatrics* 52, no. 3 (September 1973):327–43.

107. Hoffman, "Effects of Maternal Employment on the Child."

108. Willem Van Vliet, "Use, Evaluation and Knowledge of City and Suburban Environment by Children of Employed and Non-employed Mothers," unpublished Ph.D. dissertation, University of Toronto, 1980.

109. Hoffman, "Effects of Maternal Employment on the Child."

110. Robert O. Hansson, Mary E. O'Connor, Warren H. Jones, T. Jean Blocker, "Maternal Employment and Adolescent Sexual Behavior," *Journal of Youth and Adolescence* 10 (February 1981):55–60.

111. D. Gold and D. Andres, "Comparisons of Adolescent Children with Employed and Non-employed Mothers," *Merrill-Palmer Quarterly of Behavior and Development* 24, no.4 (1978):243–54.

112. Ann M. Milne, David E. Meyers, Alvin S. Rosenthal and Alan Ginsburg, "Single Parents, Working Mothers, and the Educational Achievements of School Children," *Sociology of Education* 59(July 1986):125–39.

113. Barbara Heyns and Sophia Catsambis, "Mothers' Employment and Children's Achievement: A Critique," *Sociology of Education* 59 (July 1986):140–51.

114. Ibid., 109.

115. William Michelson, *From Sun to Sun: Daily Obligations and Community Structure in the Lives of Employed Women and Their Families* (Totowa, N.J.: Rowman and Allenhelf, 1985), 103.

116. Denise Skinner, "Dual-Career Families: Strains of Sharing," in Hamilton I. McCubbin and Charles R. Figley, eds., *Stress and the Family*, vol. 1 (New York: Bruner/Mazel, 1983), 268.

117. William J. Goode, "Individual Investments in Family Relationships Over the Coming Decades," *Tocqueville Review* 6 no. 1, (Spring–Summer, 1984):51–83.

118. Andrew Cherlin and Frank F. Furstenberg, Jr., *The New American Grandparent: A Place in the Family, A Life Apart* (New York: Basic Books, 1986).

119. Epstein, *Women's Place.*

120. Epstein, *Women in Law.*

121. Benjamin Spock, *The Commonsense Book of Baby and Child care* (New York: Pocket Books, 1946).

122. Epstein, *Women in Law.*

123. Cynthia Fuchs Epstein, *Deceptive Distinctions: Theory and Research on Sex, Gender and the Social Order* (New York: Russell Sage Foundation and Yale University Press, forthcoming 1988).

Chapter Five

GOOD DADS–BAD DADS: TWO FACES OF FATHERHOOD

Frank F. Furstenberg, Jr.

Bill Cosby's bestselling *Fatherhood* was no fluke. It is one of a growing list of volumes on the rewards of paternity with titles like *The Father's Book, The Nurturing Father,* and *The Wonderful Father Book.* Treatises on how to be a good dad are by no means unprecedented but the popularity and profusion of father self-help books in the 1980s are. There is no question about it: fatherhood is in vogue. Men enter fatherhood consciously and perform their fatherly duties self-consciously.

Television, magazines, and movies herald the coming of the modern father—the nurturant, caring, and emotionally attuned parent. Cosby is the prototype. No longer confined to their traditional task of being the good provider, men have broken the mold. The new father is androgynous; he is a full partner in parenthood. Today's father is at least as adept at changing diapers as changing tires.

There is another side to fatherhood, a darker side. More fathers than ever before are absent from the home. A growing proportion of men fathering children deny paternity or shirk their paternal obligations. This darker side of fatherhood has also entered our cultural consciousness through the mass media. We are bombarded with research data detailing the rising number of single mothers, inadequately supported by the men who fathered their children. A TV documentary on the breakdown in the black family, hosted by Bill Moyers, presents a young father boasting about the number of women he has impregnated. The nation is outraged. Deadbeat fathers—men who refuse to support their children—have become a political issue. The level of child support is so low that federal and state laws have been enacted to try to enforce paternal obligations.

Reconciling or at least making sense of these seemingly conflicting trends is the aim of this chapter. The simultaneous appearance of the good father and the bad father are two sides of the same cultural complex. Both patterns can be traced to the declining division of labor in the family. To advance this argument, the first section of this chapter briefly recounts the historical change in the role of fathers. The second part examines varied sources of data that have mapped recent trends in the attitudes and behavior of fathers and points out some of the consequences of change. This examination is intended to uncover some indications of future trends in the paternal role. Is the pattern of polarization that has yielded two distinct paternal styles likely to continue? Answering this question involves considering how current public and private policies affect the distribution of paternal styles. The concluding section speculates about how some of these policies could shape the future of fatherhood.

Lest the reader expect more from this ambitious agenda than will be forthcoming, let me emphasize that this chapter primarily summarizes and interprets existing research. Evidence on fatherhood, though far more abundant now than a few years ago, is still sparse, especially when it comes to trend data (Lewis 1986; Parke and Tinsley 1984; Stein 1984). In any event, this chapter is not intended to be a review of existing research on fathers; several excellent reviews and compilations of reviews have already summarized the fragmentary literature (Lamb 1987; Lewis and Sussman 1986; Parke and Tinsley 1984). I draw on these reviews and certain seminal studies to present an impression of the changing character of fatherhood and to render a sociological reading of present trends and possible futures. On this latter matter, I am unabashedly, but I hope not recklessly, speculative.

A BRIEF HISTORY OF FATHERHOOD IN AMERICA

John Demos (1986) begins his recent essay on the social history of fatherhood by commenting, "Fatherhood has a very long history, but virtually no historians." Apparently, family historians and feminist scholars have written much about patriarchy while largely ignoring the role of the patriarch (Bloom-Feshbach 1981). Relying heavily on the work of several of his students, Demos briefly outlines the changing role of fathers over the past several centuries.

The story that Demos tells sounds familiar to readers acquainted with other features of family history. The pattern of change has not been completely linear, and much of the action has occurred in the twentieth century (Filene 1986; Parke and Tinsley 1984). After all, the changing role of fathers is part and parcel of a larger configuration of changes in the American family. (For a succinct summary of these changes, see Cherlin 1981; Thornton and Freedman 1983.)

Fathers played a dominant role in the lives of their children in the Colonial period. Fathers assumed a broad range of responsibilities, defining and supervising the children's development. Domestic control largely resided in the hands of men; wives were expected to defer to their husbands on matters of child rearing. According to E. Anthony Rotundo (1985, p. 9), a student of Demos, who has surveyed the history of fatherhood:

> Colonial fathers often showed a keen interest in the infants and toddlers of the household, but it was the mothers who fed the little ones, cared for them, and established intimate bonds with them. When children reached an age where they could understand what their parents told them (probably around age three) the lines of parent-child connection changed. Fathers began to tutor all their children in moral values at this point.

A father's moral role persisted throughout childhood, indeed into adult life; his influence was pervasive, usually exceeding the mother's responsibilities over the child. This was especially true for sons. Demos illustrates this point by noting that typically sons, when serving as apprentices, would write to their fathers, asking only to be remembered to their mothers. Both Demos and Rotundo argue that the dominant position of fathers can be traced to their economic role as landowners. (See also Greven 1970.)

At least one source of the erosion of paternal control over children was a shortage of land in New England and the shift away from an agrarian to an industrial mode of production in the beginning of the nineteenth century. However, European scholars argue that from the late eighteenth century, and perhaps earlier, an increase of affective ties within the family reshaped the nature of parenthood and parent-child relations (Shorter 1975; Stone 1979). A general decline of patriarchy, indeed, of parental authority, initiated the emergence of modern fatherhood. As men's economic roles increasingly drew them outside the home and into the marketplace, women extended their sphere of domestic influence (Filene 1986; Lasch 1977).

In a wonderfully provocative essay on the rise and fall of the "good provider" role, Jessie Bernard (1981) provides a similar account of the shift in the balance of power within the family. She observes that by the time that Tocqueville visited America in the 1830s, the nineteenth century pattern of a sharp family and parental division of labor was plainly evident. Tocqueville (1840, p. 212) portrays, as did scores of other foreign travelers (Furstenberg 1966), the contours of the modern nuclear family when he wrote that the public responsibility of men "obliges a wife to confine herself to the house, in order to watch in person and very closely over the details of domestic economy."

The spatial separation of work and home, the hallmark of an urbanized and industrialized economy, was revising both marriage and parent roles. For fathers, it meant the beginning of an almost exclusive emphasis on economic responsibilities, which curtailed the men's day-to-day contact with their children. Demos (p.51) tells us that the consequences of the uncoupling of work and family life for men cannot be exaggerated. "Certain key elements of pre-modern fatherhood dwindled and disappeared (e.g., father as pedagogue, father as moral overseer, father as companion), while others were transformed (father as psychologist, father as example)."

Rotundo reports that men still continued to act as disciplinarians in the family, but their removal from the home meant that they "stood outside the strongest currents of feeling that flowed between generations in a family." The father as "instrumental leader," as he was later dubbed by sociologists, derived his status from the outside world, that is from his position in the marketplace. A man's occupational standing established his authority in the home and his worthiness as a husband and father. This movement from ascription to achievement, which occurred throughout the nineteenth century, signaled a profound erosion in the role of fathers. And this transformation is one source of the good father–bad father complex that becomes more evident in the twentieth century.

The strength of the evidence for this historical account is not great, however. True, as Demos and Rotundo observe, the nineteenth-century advice books reveal a growing tendency to speak to mothers exclusively about child-rearing matters, apparently acknowledging the shrinking role of fathers. A more convincing bit of evidence is provided by changing custody practices. Until the middle of the nineteenth century, custody following marital disruption was typically awarded to fathers, who, after all, were assumed to maintain control over marital property (of which the children were a part). By the end of the century, with the growth of family specialization, children increasingly remained with their mothers when marriages dissolved. Early in the twentieth century, the practice of granting custody to mothers was enshrined in the doctrine of "the tender years," which holds that the children's interests are best served when they are raised by their mothers, who ordinarily possess superior parental skills.

Yet, it is easy to overdraw the picture of change. Most available evidence is derived from the middle class. Then, too, accounts of family life in the nineteenth century, not to mention earlier times, are so sketchy that it is difficult to tell how much confidence to place in the existing evidence. As Demos points out, fathers retained considerable authority throughout the nineteenth century, while some may even have increased their affective involvement in child rearing. We should, therefore, assume only that a change occurred in the modal family type, or perhaps in the degree of cultural support for a more detached and distant style of child rearing. But as is true today, some fathers were unwilling to cede so much of the supervision of their offspring to their wives and became involved in the day-to-day upbringing of their children. It seems likely, however, that the number of these actively involved fathers may well have declined in the nineteenth century (Filene 1986). Jessie Bernard, among others, has contended that the more restrictive role of fathers ("good providers") accompanies the development of the privatized nuclear family, the "haven in a heartless world" (cf. Lasch 1977).

The image of the father as good provider remained securely in place—except, perhaps, during the Depression years, when many men could not make good on their end of the bargain (Benson 1968)—until the middle of the twentieth century. The Great Depression literature contains abundant evidence that the strict division of labor was necessarily violated, as women frequently were forced or permitted to assume a more dominant economic role and men occasionally were compelled to pick up domestic tasks in the wake of these changes (Komarovsky 1940). Women's economic roles were also expanded during the war years, as they demonstrated a capacity to fill positions in the job market. Despite these changes, there is little reason to believe that the legitimacy of the existing domestic order was seriously challenged until the 1960s. Indeed, the early post-World War II era appeared to restore the so-called traditional family by strengthening the gender-based division of labor in the family. Perhaps, participation in war enhanced the relative position of males in society and undermined gender stratification within the family. In any event, the post-war period appears to have been the heyday of the nuclear family.

Yet it was becoming clear that discontents on the part of both sexes were producing fault lines in this family form. Feminist scholars have made a strong case that the domestic accord regulating the division of labor within the family was problematic even before Betty Frieden's proclamation of grievances in 1963 issued in *The Feminine Mystique.* Barbara Ehrenreich (1983), in a fascinating cultural account of the changing male role, forcefully argues that concurrent with, if not prior to, the reawakening of feminist consciousness, men were experiencing their own resentments about the burdens of the good-provider role. She contends that in the 1950s men gradually began to retreat from the breadwinning role because they felt imprisoned both socially and emotionally by the sharply delineated masculine role. (See also Filene 1986.) So men had an independent interest in shucking the exclusive responsibilities of providing for their families. Ehrenreich (1983, p. 116) writes:

> The promise of feminism—that there might be a future in which no adult person was either a "dependent creature" or an overburdened breadwinner—came at a time when the ideological supports for male conformity were already crumbling.

What followed, Ehrenreich argues, was a male revolt that occurred in tandem with the feminist revolution of the 1970s. Both movements helped reorder domestic life, producing a family form singularly different from the traditional model that had emerged in the nineteenth century. The collapse of the breadwinner role and the simultaneous entrance of women into the labor force are twin products of twin discontents, according to Ehrenreich.

Ehrenreich gives far more weight to cultural discontents than do economists, who argue that it was the economic expansion of service jobs and the growth of wage rates for female employment that ultimately drew women into the labor force. Similarly, demographers and sociologists might provide other accounts for the disintegration of the strict, gender-based division of labor in the family. Declining fertility and high rates of divorce figured into changing opportunities or requirements for women to assume a larger economic role. And economists, demographers, and sociologists all might argue that rising educational levels of women made work outside the home more attractive than full-time mothering.

It is probably not useful to try to separate the cultural from the structural determinants of family change. They are really part and parcel of the events in the 1960s and 1970s that transformed the family. The decline of the good-provider role and of the father as instrumental leader came about when ideology and social structural change converged. The changes in the family that took place during the past two decades were, in effect, sociologically "overdetermined."

The cultural and structural accounts of change strike a common theme: the strict division of labor in the family that predominated for a century or more was precarious from the start. This family arrangement lasted for a time because gender roles were clear and men and women were mutually dependent, owing to their trained incapacity to share tasks. But its demise was predetermined because it set such rigid conditions for successful performance. Ultimately, neither men nor women were willing to uphold their end of the bargain. Women insisted on a larger role in the outside world, and men, it seems, demanded a larger role inside the family. Or, did they? On this point the evidence is much less clear-cut and consistent.

The next section of this chapter examines in greater detail the experiences of men over the past decade as they have presumably relinquished their responsibilites as sole providers and presumably taken up more of the slack in the home.

MEN IN THE HOME: CURRENT PATTERNS OF FATHERING

Our consideration of fathers in the home begins on a discordant note. There are two sides to male liberation. As men have escaped from the excessive burdens of the good provider role, they have been freed to participate more fully in the family. They have also been freed from family responsibilities altogether. This contradiction emerges directly from the history of fatherhood just reviewed.

The "flight from commitment," as Barbara Ehrenreich describes the process of male liberation, is the inevitable process of the breakdown of the gender bargain that prevailed until the middle of the twentieth century. Ehrenreich (1983, p. 181), citing statistics of the rising reluctance of males to enter and maintain marital arrangements, is deeply skeptical about men's willingness to support women:

> If we accept the male revolt as a historical fait accompli and begin to act on its economic consequences for women—which I have argued that we must do—are we not in some way giving up on men . . . ? Are we acquiescing to a future in which men will always be transients in the lives of women and never fully members of the human family?

Hedging just a bit on the answer to this unsettling question, Ehrenreich concludes that in all probability men will not change and that women must rely on the their own economic power with the support of an expanded welfare state.

Jessie Bernard, analyzing the changing role of the good-provider, arrives at a similar conclusion, although she is less prepared to abandon the possibility that men may find a way back into the family. The good-provider role is on its way out, she tells us, but "its legitimate successor has not yet appeared on the scene." She compares the reconstruction of gender and family roles to the deprogramming of a cult member. It has been far easier to convince husbands to share economic responsibilities with their wives than to assume domestic and child care responsibilities.

Historians Demos and Rotundo, in their individual assessments of the future of fatherhood, express similar apprehensions. Rotundo, in particular, is alarmed about the growing trend toward fathers' absence from families and the apparent unwillingness, when living apart from their children, to assume economic responsibility for their support. Rotundo comments, "Although this failure (of divorced fathers to pay child support) represents a dramatic defiance of the ideas of Modern Fatherhood, it is, consistent with an extreme strain of male individualism that reacts to family responsibility as a quiet form of tyranny." He, too, questions whether androgynous fatherhood will emerge as the predominant pattern, even in the middle class where it has been championed, at least in some quarters. In sum, Rotundo expresses many of the same doubts that were voiced by feminists like Ehrenreich and Bernard about the willingness of males to remain involved in the family, now that the gender-based division of labor is no longer in place.

Let us have a closer look at the evidence they find so disturbing—the retreat from paternal obligations. Then we shall turn to the data on the other side: are fathers becoming more involved and, if so, what are the likely consequences for their spouses and their offspring?

In drawing any conclusions about trends in paternal involvement, we must be aware that the time we choose to begin our examination will to some extent affect the results. Most comparisons of demographic changes in the family begin in the 1950s and 1960s, in part because data from that period are abundant and the contrasts are almost invariably dramatic. Yet it is important to recognize, as Cherlin (1981) and others have pointed out, that comparisons between today and the baby boom era invariably exaggerate the amount of change. Even taking into account this tendency to magnify the patterns of change, it is hard to dispute that in some important respects, fathers do indeed seem to be receding from the family.

Eggebeen and Uhlenberg (1985), two demographers, have provided a descriptive overview of the declining involvement of men in families during the period from 1960 to 1980. Using data from the decennial censuses in 1960 and 1970 and the 1980 Current Population Survey, they calculate the amount of time men spend in family environments living with children. Later marriage, a decline in fertility, and increasing rates of marital dissolution all have contributed to a sharp decline—43 percent between 1960 and 1980—in the average number of years that men between ages 20 to 49 spend in families where young children live (falling from 12.34 years on average in 1960 to just 7.0 in 1980).

The decline is most evident for more educated males and is much sharper for blacks than whites. Eggebeen and Uhlenberg interpret these results to mean that the opportunity costs for entering fatherhood may be growing as the social pressure for men to become parents declines. In short, fatherhood is becoming a more voluntary role that requires a greater degree of personal and economic sacrifice.

An interesting corollary of this observation is that as fewer men assume the role, those who do will be selected among the most committed and dedicated. If this is true, one might expect to find that fathers today are fulfilling their paternal obligations more, not less, conscientiously. Fathers may be becoming a more differentiated population, with only more highly committed males entering their ranks.

This reassuring observation is, however, not entirely consistent with much of the available evidence on the entrance to fatherhood. Trends on the resolution of premarital pregnancies show a growing proportion of couples electing not to marry (O'Connell and Rogers 1984). Of course, women may be less eager than formerly to enter marriage. Social pressure and pressure from sexual partners have both declined, freeing males from entering marriage in order to make "honest women" of their partners or to "give their child a name." This more elective response to unplanned parenthood has been accompanied by a widespread reluctance of unmarried males to assume economic responsibility for their offspring. Data are unavailable to document whether or not the proportion of unmarried men who contribute to the support of their children has decreased during the past several decades, but most experts would probably agree that it has.

First, many males today do not report their children in social surveys. Fertility histories from males are notoriously unreliable because many men simply "forget" children living outside the household. My own study of unmarried youth in Baltimore showed strikingly higher reports of offspring among females than males, and recent reports indicate that many males are simply reluctant to acknowledge children they do not see or support.

Of course, it is possible to argue that such findings are not discrepant with a trend toward a more voluntaristic notion of parenthood. After all, men are increasingly selective in their willingness to assume the responsibilities of parenthood. But once they do, they may be counted on for support. Not so. A growing body of evidence suggests that adherence to child support is very undependable, even among men who are under a court agreement.

More than half of all men required to pay child support do not fully comply. Moreover, a substantial number of males leave marriage without a child support agreement. In all, only a third of all children living in fatherless homes receive paternal assistance. Among those receiving economic aid, the level is usually so low that it only rarely lifts children out of poverty. The average amount of child support paid to divorced women was $2,220 in 1981 (this figure excludes women due but not receiving support). The amount of child support measured in real dollars actually dropped from 1979 to 1981 (Weitzman 1985, ch.9). Several studies show that divorced men typically spend a much lower proportion of their postmarital income on child support than do their ex-wives. According to Weitzman (p. 295):

> Most fathers could comply with court orders and live quite well after doing so. Every study of men's ability to pay arrives at the same conclusion: the money is there. Indeed, there is normally enough to permit payment of significantly higher awards than are currently being made.

Many authorities believe that the main reason why men do not pay child support is limited enforcement. In 1984, Congress enacted legislation empowering and encouraging states to adopt stricter provisions for collecting child support. It is still too soon to tell whether the new procedures will significantly alter the level of compliance.

My own hunch is that the issue cannot be solved merely by stricter enforcement measures, although they are certainly a step in the right direction. The more intractable problem stems from the fact that many, if not most, noncustodial fathers are only weakly attached to their children. Data from the 1981 National Survey of Children revealed some alarming statistics on the amount of contact between noncustodial fathers and their offspring (who were between the ages of 11 and 16 at the time of the interview). Close to half of all children in mother-headed households had not seen their biological father during the 12 months preceding the survey, and another sixth of the sample had seen him only once or twice in the past year. And, only a sixth of the children saw their fathers as often as once a week on the average (Furstenberg et al. 1983).

Contact between children and their noncustodial fathers drops off sharply with the length of time since separation. Only about a third of the children in marriages that broke up 10 years earlier have seen their fathers in the past year. The provision of child support is closely related to the amount of contact maintained, which, in turn, is strongly associated with men's socioeconomic position. Less educated and lower income males are less likely to remain connected to their children than those with more resources. Significantly, the figures for support by and contact with never-married fathers are almost as high as the figures for men who were wed to the mothers. It appears, then, that matrimony confers little advantage in maintaining bonds between noncustodial fathers and their offspring.

In general, these figures, along with the child support statistics, provide a dismal picture of the commitment of fathers to their children—at least to those not living in the home. Of course, we cannot completely dismiss the accounts of some noncustodial fathers who report that they are, in effect, "locked out" of a relationship with their offspring by their former wives, who resist their efforts to play a larger role in child rearing. Such men often say they are unwilling to provide child support when they are not permitted to see their offspring regularly.

Some of these responses, no doubt, are credible. More often, it seems, custodial mothers complain that they cannot interest their former husbands in seeing their children. In the National Survey of Children, 75 percent of the women stated that they thought that the children's fathers were too little involved in child care responsibilities, and most stated that they wished the fathers would play a larger role in the children's upbringing.

Having sifted through evidence from this survey and from a smaller and more qualitative study I carried out with Graham Spanier in Central Pennsylvania, the women's accounts are generally more accurate (Furstenberg and Spanier 1984). Fathers typically are unwilling or unable to remain involved with their children in the aftermath of divorce. Instead, men often assume child-rearing responsibilities in a new household after remarriage. This curious arrangement resembles a pattern of "child swapping," whereby many men relinquish the support of biological children from a first marriage in favor of biological or stepchildren in a successive union.

Interestingly, children in stepfamilies report roughly comparable levels of interaction with parents as children in families with two biological parents. Although they are less content with their stepfather's attentions, most acknowledge that their stepfathers are indeed involved in their upbringing—almost as involved as biological fathers in never- divorced families (Furstenberg 1987). It seems, then, that fatherhood is a transient status for many men. Paternal obligations are dictated largely by residence. This is not to say that some men do not maintain enduring ties with biological children when they move apart, especially with sons (Morgan, Lye and Condran 1987), but a substantial number seem to give equal or greater allegiance to their stepchildren.

This picture of men migrating from one family to the next modifies to some extent the proposition that a growing number of men are retreating from fatherhood. Just as they return to marriage, many men who have abandoned their biological children ultimately assume paternal responsibilites for a new set of offspring. Over their life course, most men will spend time raising children, if not their own, then someone else's. Yet it is clear that, from the children's point of view, this more transient notion of fatherhood may be less secure and satisfying.

Current estimates reveal that more than half of all children growing up today will spend at least part of their childhood in a single-parent household, usually headed by a woman. For many of these children, contact with and support from their biological fathers will be sporadic, at best. Although most will, in time acquire stepfathers, these men will often be imperfect surrogates for missing biological fathers. They will be less constant in their attentions and, at least from the children's perspective, less often role models for adulthood. Researchers are divided over the issue of how much permanent emotional damage to children is created by marital disruption, but virtually all studies show that spells of paternal absence inevitably place children at a severe economic disadvantage in later life.

Unquestionably, then, the dark side of fatherhood, which I discussed at the beginning of this chapter, casts a large shadow over the sanguine reports of a rising interest in fatherhood. In the breakdown of the good-provider role, a large number of men, in Jessie Bernard's words, have become "role rejectors," men who retreat from family obligations. As she observes, the retreat from fatherhood is not new. Family desertion has always occurred and appeared to be common during the Depression. Then and now, a disproportionate share of the role rejectors are drawn from the ranks of the economically disadvantaged. What may be new is the number of middle-class men who are reneging on their paternal obligations—men who presumably have the resources but not the commitment to perform their fatherly responsibilities. In the concluding section of this chapter, I return to a consideration of what can or should be done to bolster the involvement of these derelict dads.

Despite the ominous rise in the number of transient fathers, it is impossible not to acknowledge that the decline of the good-provider role has, as so many observers have claimed, also brought about a more felicitous trend—the expansion of fatherhood to permit greater emotional involvement in child care. When I asked my barber, a father of two young children, whether he thought that dads were different today, he said, "They've got to be. They are there right at the beginning, don't you think?" he replied with a question back to me, the expert. When I asked him to elaborate he said, "You are right there when the baby is born. That's got to make a difference, don't you think?" he repeated.

I have not collected any statistics on the presence of men in childbirth classes and the delivery room, but I suspect that my barber is correct. Making childbirth and early infant care an important event for fathers conveys a powerful symbolic message: men are no longer on the outside, looking in; they are now part of the birth process. Whether that early contact has enduring "bonding effects," as some have argued, is a much less interesting and important question than the general impact of permitting, indeed expecting, fathers to be involved (Parke and Tinsley 1984). Unquestionably, as a number of leading developmental psychologists have observed, the shifting emphasis on paternal participation in early child care has created opportunities for a new and expanded definition of fatherhood (Lamb 1987).

The burgeoning developmental literature on fatherhood has focused largely on the consequences of new role responsibilities, especially during infancy and early childhood, for children's relations to their fathers and for their cognitive and emotional gains. Because this research is not central to the theme of this chapter, I merely note in passing that the seemingly obvious proposition that fathers' involvement in child care consistently and substantially benefits the child has not been well established. Existing evidence suggests that the relationship between paternal involvement and children's well-being is mediated by a number of conditions—the mother's attitude toward paternal participation, her ability to collaborate with the father, the father's skill in establishing a warm relationship to his offspring, and the child's needs, among others.

The fact that increasing paternal involvement in child care does not automatically result in improved outcomes for children is not altogether surprising, especially to skeptics of simplistic proposals to enhance family functioning. Nonetheless this discovery has disappointed some of the proponents of the new fatherhood movement (Lamb 1982).

Fathers, it seems, neither matter so much emotionally as some wishful observers claim, nor so little as other skeptics contend. When fathers are strongly committed to playing a major role in their children's upbringing their impact can be large, especially when mothers are a less conspicuous presence in the family. Ordinarily, this is not what happens: mothers are the preeminent figures, and the added impact of paternal involvement in shaping the child's emotional development seems rather small.

But a growing body of research indicates that in certain circumstances fathers do play a central role in child rearing, a role that greatly benefits the cognitive and emotional development of young children. Despite some people's reservations (Rossi 1985), fathers, it seems, can be perfectly capable caretakers of young infants. The notion that mothers possess special or unique talents for child care has not been substantiated (Russell 1986). Fathers do characteristically perform child care duties differently, according to Michael Lamb and others who have investigated infant care by men. In particular, fathers tend to engage in more play and roughhousing. Yet Lamb (1987, p. 13) observes that the emotional tone of the paternal relationship is what matters: "As far as influence on children is concerned, there seems to be little about the gender of the parent that is distinctively important. The characteristics of the father as a parent rather than the characteristics of the father as a man appear to influence child development."

Moreover, it is likely that active paternal participation has broader consequences for family functioning. Lois Hoffman (1983), for example, has assembled evidence showing that greater involvement by fathers in household and child care duties reduces the role strain experienced by working mothers. On the basis of fragmentary data, Hoffman speculates that easing the burdens of employed wives enhances marital well-being, which, in turn, contributes to children's adjustment. If fathers assumed an equal parental role, children would be less likely to acquire gender conceptions that restrict the future family performance of males and occupational performance of females. More immediately, however, conjugal bonds might be strengthened when couples share parental tasks.

Hoffman's assessment of the possible benefits of greater paternal participation is not uniformly rosy, however. She notes that the expansion of fatherhood can and has encroached on the prerogatives of women in the home. A breakdown of the traditional division of labor can erode women's power, create greater conflict when parents do not share similar definitions of desirable parental behavior, and dilute the satisfactions of motherhood for women. Hoffman also observes that as men become more competent parents, they may be more willing to divorce, knowing that they have the skills to claim custodial rights. I arrived at a similar conclusion in a study of divorce and remarriage in Central Pennsylvania. When fathers assumed a more active parental role before divorce, the possibility of postmarital conflict over rights and responsibilities for the children tended to increase.

On balance neither I nor, probably, Hoffman would claim that the costs of greater paternal participation outweigh the potential benefits for children. Most women are only too happy to see their husbands play a greater role in child care and would gladly yield territory in the home to increase their power outside the household. The greater involvement of men in child care probably does more to contribute to marital contentment than it does to increase the risk of conflict and divorce.

What is more open to serious question is the extent to which fathers today actually involve themselves in child care. Here again I turned to my barber for an opinion. How much child care does he, as a liberated father, actually do? "Well, I give my wife some relief, but she naturally does most of it," he volunteered. "I really don't have that much time to help out." He is not unique. The preponderance of data from a variety of sources indicates that most fathers still do very little child care, especially when their children are very young.

The extent to which fathers' roles have changed in recent years cannot easily be measured, for researchers simply did not think to ask about paternal involvement in child care even a decade or so ago. This fact itself might be taken as an index of change. Yet it is possible that fathers in the recent past did more than they got credit for and today do less than we like to think. The consensus of most scholars who have studied the question of role change is that modest change has taken place in both the attitude and the behavior of fathers. The change that has occurred is linked to a general shift in less gender-specific family roles (Thornton and Freedman 1983; Stein 1984). Recent data from the Virginia Slims Survey of American

Women, times-series data on women's issues collected by Roper, reveal similar shifts on a range of gender-related attitudes, although limited information was collected specifically on paternal obligations. From 1974 to 1985, women significantly increased (from 46 to 57 percent) their preference for a marriage in which husband and wife shared responsibility for work, household duties, and child care more equitably. Similarly, the Virginia Slims Survey recorded a sharp rise in wives desire to be paid by their husbands for household work (1985 Virginia Slims American Women's Opinion Poll). Although men were not asked these specific questions, their opinions on other related matters indicated that they, too, had greatly increased their support for more egalitarian marriages.

Whether these attitudinal changes are matched by parallel shifts in behavior is doubtful, though clearly some realignment of marital and child care roles has taken place. Joseph Pleck (1985), who has done the most extensive research on the question, concludes that most of these changes have been relatively modest.

The most recent data on changing patterns of paternal involvement were assembled by Juster and Stafford (1985) of the Institute for Survey Research at the University of Michigan. Juster, in a brief analysis of time spent in family activities, traces changes from 1975 to 1981. Using time diaries, he is able to show that men decreased hours spent at work in favor of home activities while women followed the opposite course. This change was especially marked for younger people. Further evidence of domestic change could be seen in the amount of time men spent in "female" types of activities—household duties that have traditionally been performed by women. Between the mid-1970s and the early 1980s, a distinct realignment in roles occurred, with women relegating more domestic tasks to men. This is further evidence of a movement toward greater equality between the sexes, a movement that Juster believes is likely to accelerate in years to come.

Unfortunately, Juster does not break out the data on child care separately or analyze the changes by the presence or absence of children in the home. Pleck's analysis of time diaries reveals that fathers spend substantially more time in domestic and child care duties in households when mothers are employed, but the men still fall far short of assuming an equal load. Moreover, men in families with young children do less than those in households with no children or older offspring. Clearly, these analyses confound a number of related variables—age, cohort, the number and age of children, and the labor force status of mothers. Unless these separate components of paternal participation in child care are disentangled, it is difficult to get a clear picture of the magnitude of the changes in patterns of child care by men and women.

Lamb and Pleck draw interesting distinctions in paternal child care that involves time spent interacting, time spent being available (being the parent on duty), and time spent being responsible, that is making child care arrangements. Apparently, much of the increase in paternal activity has been in the first realm—fathers as babysitters. The least change has occurred in the sphere as father as orchestrator of the child's activities. In this respect, it appears that fathers are still pinch hitters or part-time players rather than regulars.

Evidence from studies of father's role after divorce or separation shows much the same pattern. Fathers are even more marginal. Despite the considerable attention given to joint-custody arrangements in the mass media, in fact, such agreements are rare and often short-lived. Typically, fathers, even when they remain on the scene, play a recreational rather than instrumental role in their children's lives.

In conclusion, evidence of change is compelling, and some researchers believe that the pace of change may be picking up. But fathers, except in rare circumstances, have not yet become equal partners in parenthood. This is not to say that androgynous fatherhood could not happen, only that it has not happened and is not likely to happen in the near future.

Michael Lamb, Joseph Pleck, and their colleagues have analyzed some of the sources of resistance to change. They mention four in particular: motivation, skills and self-confidence, social support, and institutional practices. Motivation represents the willingness of men to change. (William Goode [1982] has written most cogently on the subtle barriers to changing male prerogatives.) Clearly, further change requires a growing number of men to accept an expanded family role. Unless they acquire the skills to assume a greater scope of parental responsibilities, they are likely to confine their attentions to traditional male tasks. The restructuring of the father role requires support and encouragement from wives. Presumably, some wives are reluctant to give up maternal prerogatives. Finally, a number of institutional practices contribute to the maintenance of the status quo by denying fathers the resources to assume a greater share of child care responsibilities. Entrenched social practices continue to convey the message that parenting is mainly women's work.

Lamb argues that unless there is movement on all four of these fronts, fathers are likely to continue to play a relatively marginal role in the family. Clearly, however, these four components overlap and are interconnected. Although Lamb conceives of them as hierarchical, they are probably better thought of as isomorphic. Change in any one will have ramifications for the others. Shifts at the personal and interpersonal level are likely to create social and political demands for widening opportunities for fathers to become active caretakers, just as changes in women's attitudes and the views of men have created change in the marketplace. But political and economic change—sometimes loosely referred to as structural change—can, by the same token, drastically alter personal and interpersonal expectations. In the next and concluding section, which explores the link between public policy and change in paternal practices, I assume that change may be instituted in a variety of ways. I am primarily interested in the prospects for change, ways that change could come about, and some possible consequences for the future of the family.

PUBLIC POLICY AND PATERNAL PRACTICES

Up to now, I have largely avoided the political question of whether the breakdown of the good-provider role was desirable. But I cannot entirely ignore this issue if I am going to discuss the potential effects of future policy initiatives to further equalize parental responsibilities. After all, many people wish to restore the gender-based division of labor that served as the mainspring of the nuclear family until the middle part of this century.

I suppose that if I believed that the costs involved in this transformation of family form greatly exceeded the benefits derived, I would be obligated to try, at least, to imagine ways of returning to the status quo ante. Some costs may exist, especially for children, who have probably been somewhat ill-served by the rapidity of change. This is not to say that children, girls particularly, have not benefited from the collapse of the gender-based division of labor. But we have not managed to protect children as well as we might have if we regarded their welfare as a collective, rather than merely family-based, obligation.

Change has not been cost-free for women, either. Restrictions on divorce provided social and material protections for women, albeit of a paternalist type. Certainly, the declining economic circumstances of divorced women constitute a serious penalty in the quest for equality. Furthermore, as women have entered the marketplace, they have become susceptible to greater occupational stress, leading in some instances to an increase of mental and physical maladies. Finally, some people have argued that the sexual liberation has placed women at greater, not lesser, risk of sexual exploitation by men. Rises in venereal diseases, pregnancy, abortion, and possibly sexual abuse and rape could be seen as adverse side effects of freer sexual relations.

Yet if one examines the sentiments of both men and women, admittedly imperfectly captured in public opinion surveys, most Americans, men and women alike, seem to endorse the changes that have occurred in recent decades. When asked whether they favored or opposed most of the efforts to strengthen and change women's status in society, only 40 percent of women and 44 percent of men were supportive in 1970. Today, 73 percent of women and 69 percent of men sanction continued efforts to improve the status of women. Both men and women anticipate further changes in women's roles, while only a tiny minority believe that traditional roles will be restored. Most important of all, the vast majority of women believe that they have gained respect in the process (1985 Virginia Slims). Possibly these sentiments should be counted as mere rationalizations, but I am inclined to interpret them as strong support for changes that have occurred. Even after experiencing the costs associated with family change, most Americans desire continued movement toward gender equality.

In any event, it is difficult to imagine a scenario that would restore the family form common a generation ago. The collapse of the good-provider role resulted from a combination of economic changes and ideological discontents. What is the possibility of reversing these changes? Engineering the withdrawal of women from the labor force and persuading men to pick up the economic slack would be somewhat like putting Humpty Dumpty together again.

Indeed, there is every reason to believe that we are in for more change of the type that we have seen. The proportion of working mothers with young children continues to climb, putting more pressure on fathers to shoulder more of the child care. Men's attitudes and behavior, whether willingly or grudgingly, may well fall into line, as they are increasingly pressured by their partners and society at large to help out more (Goode 1982). Open support for patriarchical privilege has receded in the middle class and may be on the wane in the working class as well. It is unacceptable to make sexist comments in public arenas and unfashionable to do so in private circles. Sexism, like racism, has been forced underground.

Proponents of change have called for a variety of policies that might hasten the process of accommodation to the new family order: parent education to prepare men for future paternal roles, paternity leave to allow them to accept a fuller measure of care for infants, and flex time to enable them to invest more time in child-rearing and domestic duties.

The limited evidence for the efficacy of such programs does not persuade me that any of these measures is likely to substantially increase the level of paternal involvement. Parent education classes may enhance the motivation and skills of young men who want to assume a larger paternal role, but they are not likely to produce many converts to the cause. They are somewhat like watered-down job training programs, which have had little or no effect in increasing occupational prospects. In Sweden, where paternity leave has been available for a number of years, only a small fraction of fathers use the benefit. There is little evidence that Swedish men, who are also exposed to more parent education, have developed more egalitarian child care patterns than American fathers. Finally, experiments to implement more flexible work schedules seem to have had a negligible effect on the participation of fathers in child care.

I do not dismiss these programs out of hand; they may not have had a full and fair chance to show effects. There is some evidence that many parents manage to get by with no outside day care when husbands and wives are able to work separate shifts (Presser and Cain 1983). Possibly, as some have argued, flex-time programs do not go far enough. The same can be said for measures such as education in parenthood or paternity leave. Besides, it might be argued that these provisions convey an important symbolic message to men that they have the right and the obligation to become more involved. Thus, these programs may have important indirect effects on men by changing the normative climate in society at large rather than by directly affecting the men who participate in them.

General family support services such as day care or preschool programs, which relieve the burden of child care for both employed parents, may do as much to foster paternal involvement as do categorical programs directed at fathers alone. Specialized programs can serve only a limited number of fathers—probably, largely the men who are already ideologically receptive. Systems designed to assist parents, regardless of gender, draw from a larger base and attract more public support. Thus, the arena for change may be played out in Parent-Teacher Associations, church groups, professional organizations, and the like. The degree to which these groups welcome or resist gender change within the family is a sensitive barometer to the transformation of family roles.

Enticing fathers in two-parent families to assume a greater share of child care responsibilities may be much less difficult than gaining their involvement when childbearing occurs out-of-wedlock, or retaining their involvement after marriages break up. As we saw earlier, some feminists are prepared to give up on men and turn to a more benign and generous welfare system for support. Building an economic support system that further weakens paternal obligation is questionable policy on several grounds. First, it is not clear how generous we are prepared to be in providing for the children of single mothers. And even if we raise the economic situation of female heads of families, their children are not going to be on a par with children in two-parent families. Furthermore, policies that let men off the hook are bound to contribute further to the retreat of men from the family. That is bad for women, bad for children, and bad for men as well. It is difficult to argue that black women, children, or even men, for that matter, have benefited from the retreat of males from participation in family life. Everyone seems to have lost as the ability of black males to contribute economically has been eroded over the past two decades. Some might say that the same trends are beginning to occur among poorer whites, as males increasingly offer little economic support to women and children. The rising rates of nonmarital childbearing among young white women may be an ominous harbinger.

As mentioned, vigorous efforts have recently been made to increase the contribution of males to children they have fathered but are not living with. This hard-line policy is intended to make men feel responsible for their children, but whether a more aggressive approach to the collection of child support produces a greater sense of paternal obligation remains to be seen.

The "stick" approach is worth trying, but should we not also be conjuring up a few carrots—programs designed to create incentives to paternal participation? In a recent article in the Public Interest, Vinovskis and Chase-Lansdale (1987) question whether teenage marriages ought to be discouraged. Citing a mixed bag of evidence, they assert that at least some fathers are capable of supporting their children and young mothers might do better if they were to enter marriage—even if the likelihood of the marriage's survival is low. Without discussing the validity of their claim, it is discouraging to discover that the authors of this provocative thesis suggest no policies for encouraging men to enter marriage other than to say that social scientists have been overly pessimistic about the merits of matrimony. Can we not conceive of ways to make marriage more attractive and to discourage single parenthood?

Previously I have argued, along with Wilson (Wilson and Neckerman 1985) and many others, that marriage is increasingly inaccessible to many low-income youth because males simply do not have the economic prospects to provide females with an incentive for entering marriage. The income-maintenance experiments notwithstanding, I am also persuaded that for many low-income couples, unemployment and poor future earnings weaken conjugal bonds and contribute to the especially high rates of marital instability among poorer Americans. Despite the demise of the good-provider role, men are more likely to move out of a marriage to which they do not contribute and women are less likely to want them to remain even if men are so inclined.

This situation probably could not be immediately remedied even if the unemployment rates were to return to the 1960s levels. With the breakdown of the division of labor within marriage, the value of men's economic contributions probably counts for less today than it once did, and the emotional exchange probably counts for more. Yet material contributions still matter, and a healthier economy would probably reduce, or at least slow down, the retreat from marriage and make remarriage more attractive, especially among disadvantaged populations.

There are probably other ways of making marriage more economically appealing to couples. Eliminating the residual marriage penalty and creating tax incentives for marriage, especially for poor people with children, might have some modest effects by at least reducing the disincentives to marrying. It might also be feasible to devise a program of family assistance linked to Social Security payments. Couples who contribute to the support of children might receive added payments during retirement. Although such a plan might not directly hold couples together, it would certainly encourage fathers to contribute to child support. It might be possible to provide bonus payments to households with two earners or two parents, or both.

Such programs are costly, and, judging from efforts designed to promote pronatalist policies, we should not look for large effects on nuptial behavior from incentive schemes. In some instances, though, even modest results might be cost-effective, given the very real price tag to society associated with single parenthood and the absence of child support. Moreover, as I have contended throughout this chapter, programs tailored to promote paternal involvement bolster the norm that it is desirable for men to participate in the family and support their offspring. As such they may produce indirect effects consistent with the aim of increasing paternal participation in the family.

Finally, it is reasonable to suppose that marital stability may be enhanced, at least slightly, by the diffusion of cultural norms permitting and promoting more child care involvement among fathers. Scattered evidence from a variety of studies, as I mentioned earlier, reveals that marital stress is relieved when men assume a larger burden of child care. Also, greater emotional investment in children by men appears to increase marital stability, reducing the risk that fathers will withdraw from the family (cf. Morgan, Lye, and Condran 1987).

CONCLUSION

Ordinarily it is difficult to predict future family trends. Forecasting changes in the father role is extremely hazardous, as we are witnessing a confluence of conflicting trends. About one thing we can be fairly certain—further attenuation of the good-provider role is likely to take place as fewer women count on their husbands to provide economic support without women's aid and fewer men expect women to manage the household and children without men's assistance. Whether the gender-based division of labor that characterized families until the middle of the twentieth century will disappear altogether is highly questionable. But if I am correct that the breakdown of the good-provider role for men is ultimately responsible for the rise of the good dad–bad dad complex, the bifurcation of fatherhood could continue unabated, creating both more fathers that are closely involved with their children and more that are derelict. Even if two discrete male populations are formed, men, as noted earlier, may migrate from one category to the other during their lifetime.

Some of the conditions that might reduce the number of men who are retreating from fatherhood involve normative shifts that encourage greater participation of fathers in child rearing; these shifts are not easily susceptible to policy manipulation. I nonetheless remain rather sanguine about the prospects of further change if only because the cultural climate appears to be increasingly receptive to this trend.

One set of policies that has been mentioned here involves creating larger incentives to contribute to children and disincentives to withhold support. Experimental programs may provide indications of the results to be expected from the judicious use of the carrot and stick. We probably should not expect too much from policy interventions, if only because we are not prepared to build either a very large carrot or stick. The crux of the problem is that men looking at marriage today may sense that it offers them a less good deal than it once did. This is the inevitable result of reducing male privileges, female deference to men, and a range of services that were customarily provided as part of the conjugal bargain. The loss of these privileges has persuaded some men to opt out of family life altogether.

Those who have not done so now expect more emotional gratification from marriage; more than ever before, intimacy has become the glue of family life. Recently, men have begun to realize a second source of benefits from family life—the gratifications of parenthood and the satisfactions of close ties with their children. These men have become the "new fathers" who are more emotionally invested in parenthood. It is too early to tell whether this new form of fatherhood will enhance stability in family life. Are these more involved fathers more committed to family life, more willing to endure marital discontents in order to remain with their children, and more prepared to sacrifice their own emotional needs in the interests of their offspring? I am not so certain, but time will tell. In the meantime, it may be necessary to devise all the means we can muster to produce more nurturant males, in the hope that they will help to strengthen our present imperfect and tenuous forms of marriage and parenthood.

Bibliography

Benson, Leonard. 1968. *Fatherhood: A Sociological Perspective*. New York: Random House.

Bernard, Jessie. 1981. "The Good Provider Role: Its Rise and Fall." *American Psychologist* 36: no. 1:1-12.

Bloom-Feshbach, J. 1981. "Historical Perspectives on the Father's Role." In *The Role of the Father in Child Development*, 2nd ed., edited by Michael E. Lamb. New York: John Wiley & Sons.

Cherlin, Andrew J. 1981. *Marriage, Divorce, Remarriage*. Cambridge, Mass.: Harvard University Press.

Demos, John. 1986. *Past, Present and Personal: The Family and The Life Course in American History*. New York: Oxford University Press.

Eggebeen, David, and Peter Uhlenberg. 1985. "Changes in the Organization of Mens' Lives: 1960-1980." *Family Relations* 34, no. 2:251-57.

Ehrenreich, Barbara. 1983. *The Hearts of Men: American Dreams and the Flight from Commitment*. New York: Anchor Press.

Filene, Peter G. 1986. *Him/Her/Self: Sex Roles in Modern America*. Baltimore: The Johns Hopkins Press.

Frieden, Betty. 1963. *The Feminine Mystique.* W. W. Norton and Company, Inc.
Furstenberg, Frank F., Jr. 1966. "Industrialization and the American Family: A Look Backward." *American Sociological Review* 31:326-37.
Furstenberg, Frank F., Jr. 1987. "The New Extended Family: Experiences in Stepfamilies." In *Remarriage and Step-parenting Today,* edited by Kay Pasley and Marilyn Ihinger-Tallman: 42-61. New York: Guilford Press.
Furstenberg, Frank F., Jr., Christine Winquist Nord, James L. Peterson, and Nicholas Zill. 1983. "The Life Course of Children of Divorce: Marital Disruption and Parental Contact." *American Sociological* Review 48, no. 10:656-68.
Furstenberg, Frank F., Jr., and Graham B. Spanier. 1984. *Recycling the Family: Remarriage After Divorce.* Beverly Hills: Sage Publications.
Goode, William J. 1982. "Why Men Resist." In *Family in Transition,* edited by Arlene S. Skolnick and Jerome H. Skolnick: 201-18. Boston: Little, Brown and Company.
Greven, Phillip. 1970. *Four Generations: Population, Land and Family in Colonial Andover, Massachusetts.* Ithaca, NY: Cornell University Press.
Hoffman, Lois Wladis. 1983. "Increasing Fathering: Effects on the Mother." In *Fatherhood and Family Policy,* edited by Michael E. Lamb and Abraham Sagi, 167-90. Hillsdale, NJ: Lawrence Erlbaum Associates.
Juster, Thomas F., and Frank B. Stafford. 1985. *Time, Goods and Well-Being.* Ann Arbor: Institute for Survey Research.
Komarovsky, Mirra. 1940. *The Unemployed Man and His Family.* New York: Dryden Press.
Lamb, Michael E., ed. 1982. *Nontraditional Families: Parenting and Child Development.* Hillsdale, NJ: Lawrence Erlbaum Associates.
Lamb, Michael E., ed. 1987. *The Father's Role: Applied Perspectives.* New York: John Wiley & Sons.
Lamb, Michael E. ed. 1987. *The Father's Role: Cross Cultural Perspectives.* Hillsdale, NJ: Lawrence Erlbaum Associates.
Lasch, Christopher. 1977. *Haven in a Heartless World: The Family Besieged.* New York: Basic Books.
Lewis, Robert A. 1986. "Men's Changing Roles in Marriage and the Family." In *Men's Changing Roles in the Family,* edited by Robert A. Lewis and Marvin B. Sussman. New York: Haworth Press.
Lewis, Robert A., and Marvin B. Sussman, eds. 1986. *Men's Changing Roles in the Family.* New York: Haworth Press.
Morgan, S. Philip, Diane Lye, and Gretchen Condran. Forthcoming. "Sons, Daughters and Divorce: The Effect of Children's Sex on Their Parent's Risk of Marital Disruption." *American Journal of Sociology.*
O'Connell, Martin, and Carolyn C. Rogers. 1984. "Out-of-Wedlock Births, Premarital Pregnancies, and Their Effect on Family Formation and Dissolution." *Family Planning Perspectives* 16, no. 4:157-62.
Parke, Ross D., and Barbara R. Tinsley. 1984. "Fatherhood: Historical and Contemporary Perspectives." In *Life Span Developmental Psychology: Historical and Cohort Effects,* edited by K.A. McCluskey and H.W. Reese. New York: Academic Press.
Pleck, Joseph. 1985. *Working Wives Working Husbands.* Beverly Hills: Sage Publications.
Presser, H.B., and V. Cain. 1983. "Shift Work Among Dual-Earner Couples With Children." *Science* 219:876-79.
Rossi, Alice S. 1985. "Gender and Parenthood." In *Gender and the Life Course,* edited by Alice S. Rossi. New York: Aldine Publishing Company.
Rotundo, E. Anthony. 1985. "American Fatherhood: A Historical Perspective." *American Behavioral Scientist,* 29, no. 1:7-25.
Russell, Graeme. 1986. "Primary Caretaking and Role Sharing Fathers." In *The Father's Role: Applied Perspectives,* edited by Michael E. Lamb: 29-57. New York: John Wiley & Sons.

Shorter, Edward. 1975. *The Making of the Modern Family*. New York: Basic Books.

Stein, Peter J. 1984. "Men in Families." *Marriage and Family Review* 7, no. 3:143-62.

Stone, Lawrence. 1979. *The Family, Sex and Marriage In England 1500-1800*. New York: Harper & Row.

Thornton, Arland, and Deborah Freedman. 1983. "The Changing American Family." *Population Bulletin* 38, no. 4:2-44.

Tocqueville, Alexis de. 1954. *Democracy in America*, 2 vols. New York: Vintage Books.

Vinovskis, Maris A. P., and Lindsay Chase-Lansdale. 1987. "Should We Discourage Teenage Marriage?" *Public Interest* 87:23-37.

The 1985 Virginia Slims American Women's Opinion Poll. A Study conducted by the Roper Organization, Inc.

Weitzman, Lenore J. 1985. *The Divorce Revolution: The Unexpected Social and Economic Consequences for Women and Children in America*. New York: Free Press.

Wilson, William Julius, and Kathryn M. Neckerman. 1985. "Poverty and Family Structure: The Widening Gap between Evidence and Public Policy Issues." In *Fighting Poverty: What Works and What Doesn't*, edited by Sheldon H. Danziger and Daniel H. Weinberg: 232-59. Cambridge, Mass.: Harvard University Press.

Chapter Six

THE LINKS BETWEEN GOVERNMENT POLICY AND FAMILY STRUCTURE: WHAT MATTERS AND WHAT DOESN'T

Mary Jo Bane
Paul A. Jargowsky

Nary a political speech gets made these days without invoking the family. Nearly everyone believes that government should either do more to help families or do less to hurt them. These legitimate concerns arise from the disturbing increases in poverty among children and the profound changes in family structure that have occurred in the past several decades, most notably the increase in the percentage of children living in households headed by women. The obvious relationship between poverty and family structure has led to calls for government policies that prevent poverty through strengthening families, as well as policies that attempt to alleviate disadvantage among children. Given the intense interest in strengthening families and the likely legislative action to that end, we need to understand how government policies have affected families directly or indirectly, intentionally or unintentionally.

Many scholars and politicians argue explicitly that government policy affects family structure. The "law of unintended consequences" is frequently cited to explain what happened to marriage rates and fertility. For example, many conservatives point to welfare as the cause of the increase in female-headed families and the decline of marriage, at least among blacks.

An implicit assumption about the efficacy of government policy in changing family structure also undergirds many proposals by liberals. Concerned with the alarming rate of poverty among children, especially those in single-parent families, liberals advocate actions such as subsidizing child care, providing medical care to working poor families, mandating maternal and paternal leave, and instituting children's allowances. They argue that these measures would strengthen and support two-parent families and lessen the pressures and stresses that lead to the formation of poor single parent families.

Before heeding either the conservatives' calls for a reduced role in family issues or the liberals' calls for a more supportive government role, policymakers need a better understanding of what the impact of government policies has been. In this chapter, we seek to sort out the effects on family structure, if any, of government policies in five areas often mentioned as candidates for policy action: family law, welfare, prevention of teen pregnancy, family supports, and economic policy. We summarize the policy arguments that are made and then review the evidence on the relationship between these policies and family structure.

Our review of the evidence made us skeptical about the efficacy of government policy with regard to preventing family disruption or encouraging the formation of stable families. (This is not to say that government policy cannot be effective in achieving other goals, such as reducing poverty among children or increasing access to health care.) Policies like welfare, childcare, tax credits, and so on are not important determinants of trends in marriage, fertility, or the formation of single-parent families. Even economic policy appears to have only weak effects, at least in the short run. The most important causes of changes in family structure lie outside the realm of policy, perhaps in the profound changes in social attitudes about what constitutes acceptable behavior.

As a result, we argue that direct, intended effects of government policies on family structure are less plausible than we had hoped, and that indirect, unintended effects of government policies are less problematic than we feared. We take seriously, however, the notion that government can contribute to an environment that is generally supportive of families and children. Government can make a difference in children's lives, even if it is not capable of changing the circumstances of their birth. Furthermore, government can attempt to play a leadership role in the evolution of social attitudes, although this effort has no guarantee of success and may raise troubling issues in a pluralistic society.

WHAT IS THE PROBLEM?

Before looking at policy responses to the family "problem," we need some better sense of what the problem is. We see three formulations in current debate:

□ Large proportions of children are poor and disadvantaged. With a poverty rate of about 20 percent, children are the worst off age group in the population, and worse off than they were two decades ago. Poverty and disadvantage among children are bound to lead to lost opportunities among adults.

□ Large and increasing proportions of children are spending at least part of their childhood in single-parent families. Single-parent status is strongly associated with poverty and disadvantage. Moreover, a single parent must handle both the caretaker and provider roles and thus has less time for each than two parents do. Other things being equal, children can benefit from the care and support of two parents.

□ Many adults are failing to form and stay in families: not marrying, not having children, or leaving marriages. This situation may reflect a deterioration of one of the most basic and important institutions in our society.[1]

There is a fair amount of disagreement within society about whether each of these formulations, in fact, expresses a real problem. People agree that poverty and disadvantage among children are problems, but there is less agreement about whether single parenthood is a problem per se. There is even greater controversy about whether the nation should be concerned with the decrease in the formation of traditional families. Historically, marriage and fertility behavior have not been a concern of public policy in this country, largely because of strong feelings about personal privacy. Many European nations, in contrast, have direct government policies whose stated purposes are to influence marriage and birth rates.

In recent years, however, proposals for a "national family policy" have been raised with increasing frequency in this country. Many conservatives argue that government ought to weigh in on the side of traditional family values, although many people, including many conservatives, believe that this is territory that should be tread upon lightly. Liberals propose family support policies as a congenial means of packaging antipoverty programs.

We venture into this debate for several reasons. First, marriage and fertility decisions lie behind the dramatic increase in the proportion of children in single-parent families, as we shall shortly show. Second, we believe that low levels of marriage and family formation may indicate a generally unsupportive climate for families and children in the society. Third, politicians, policymakers, and the public make a multitude of assumptions about what the intended or unintended effects of such policies have been or could be. For all those reasons, a review of the evidence is needed, regardless of how one feels about the legitimacy of government policies in this area.

MARRIAGE, FERTILITY, AND THE LIVING ARRANGEMENTS OF CHILDREN

Much policy discussion concerns the effects of government policies on the living situations of children. Government policy affects children's lives through its effects on the behavior of adults. It is important to understand, therefore, how trends in the marriage and fertility behavior of adults interact to produce changes in the living situations of children. The trends in family breakup and unmarried motherhood directly influence the status of children, as do the underlying trends in marriage and fertility rates generally. We turn now to an analysis of these trends.

Living Arrangements of Children

Family situations of children have changed dramatically since 1970. Among white children, one in five did not live in a two-parent family in 1985, more than double the 1970 rate; among black children the proportion rose from 41 percent in 1970 to 60 percent in 1985.[2] Most of the children who do not live with both their parents live in households headed by their mothers. But this is only part of the story. Because families change, some children in two-parent families in 1985 may have been or may eventually end up in a single-parent family for some period of time. Perhaps half of all white children and more than three-quarters of black children will spend at least some of their childhood in a single-parent household.[3]

The change is astonishing both for its size and for the speed with which it has happened. Our goal is to understand whether government policies contributed to the change and whether government policy might be part of a solution. First, however, we detour to discuss marriage and the family decisions of adults.

Trends Among Adults

The trends in children's living arrangements result from the behavior and decisions of adults. The increase in the proportion of children with single parents could occur if the number of children with single parents went up or if the number of children in two-parent families went down. Since 1970, both changes have occurred and both are contributing to the large increase in the proportion of children in single-parent families. Both changes need explanation.

Two factors determine the number of children in single-parent families: the number of single parents and the number of children per single parent. The number of women who are single mothers (defined here using data from the Current Population Survey conducted by the U.S. Bureau of the Census as women divorced, separated, widowed, or never married at the time of the survey who reported children ever born) has gone up substantially for both whites and blacks (table 6.1).

Yet, like the figures for mothers generally, the number of children per single mother fell quite substantially. The increase in single parents outpaced the decrease in the number of children per single parent, so the number of such children went up. The increase in the number of single parents itself has two components: the total number of women of childbearing age and the proportion that becomes single parents. Both have gone up.[4] More women, more of them single parents, having fewer children each.

Turning now to the number of children in two-parent families, the number of women of childbearing age has increased, but the proportion who are married has declined substantially. The number of children per married mother has also dropped substantially, resulting in a large decrease in the number of children in two-parent families.

The increase in single-parent children and the decrease in two-parent children in 1970–80 led to the dramatic shift in the proportion of children in single-parent families. Interestingly, however, the driving force behind the increase has not been the increase in the number of single-parent children, but the declining fertility of married women.

To see this, we need to control for population growth by dividing the number of children in each category by the total number of women of childbearing age.[5] This procedure standardizes the number of children by the number of potential mothers and allows us to separate real changes in the behavior of potential mothers from changes in their number. *The number of children in single-parent families per woman stayed constant* from 1970 to 1985. While the number of such children has grown, the rate of growth has been roughly the same as population growth. In contrast, the number of children in two-parent families per woman has declined precipitously. Figures 6.1 and 6.2 show these trends for whites and blacks respectively.

To summarize, the trends among adults that led to the stunning increase in the proportion of children in single-parent families are:

□ A marked decrease in fertility for all women, including single parents;

Table 6.1 SELECTED TRENDS IN FERTILITY

	White 1970	White 1985	Percentage change	Black 1970	Black 1985	Percentage change
Children ever born (thousand)	58,821	56,359	−4	10,079	10,691	+6
To currently married mothers	53,030	45,094	−15	6,314	4,658	−26
To single mothers	5,791	11,265	+95	3,765	6,032	+60
To never-married mothers	634	1,340	+111	965	2,711	+181
To divorced, separated, or widowed mothers	5,157	9,925	+92	2,810	3,321	+18
Percentage of children[a]	100.0	100.0	n.a.	100.0	100.0	n.a.
To currently married mothers	90.2	80.0	n.a.	62.6	43.6	n.a.
To single mothers	9.8	20.0	n.a.	37.4	56.4	n.a.
To never married mothers	1.1	2.4	n.a.	9.6	25.4	n.a.
To divorced, separated or widowed mothers	8.8	17.6	n.a.	27.9	31.1	n.a.
Women ages 18–44 (thousand)	31,831	42,782	+34	4,173	6,523	+56
With children	21,407	25,943	+21	3,070	4,583	+49
Currently married	19,208	20,585	+7	1,816	1,786	−2
Single parent	2,199	5,358	+144	1,254	2,797	+123
Never married	331	923	+179	449	1,459	+225
Divorced, separated, or widowed	1,868	4,435	+137	805	1,338	+66
Percentage of women ages 18–44	100.0	100.0	n.a.	100.0	100.0	n.a.
With children	67.3	60.6	n.a.	73.6	70.3	n.a.
Currently married	60.3	48.1	n.a.	43.5	27.4	n.a.
Single-parent	6.9	12.6	n.a.	30.1	44.9	n.a.
Never married	1.0	2.2	n.a.	10.8	22.4	n.a.
Divorced, separated, or widowed	5.9	10.4	n.a.	19.3	20.5	n.a.
Children ever born per mother						
All mothers	2.75	2.17	−21	3.28	2.33	−29
Currently married mothers	2.76	2.19	−21	3.48	2.61	−25
Single-parent mothers	2.62	2.10	−20	3.00	2.16	−28
Never-married mothers	1.91	1.45	−24	2.15	1.86	−13
Divorced, separated, or widowed mothers	2.76	2.24	−19	3.48	2.48	−29

Source: Calculated from data in Current Population Reports, Series P-20, nos. 212, 308 and 406, "Marital Status and Family Status: March 1970"; "Fertility of American Women: June 1976"; and Fertility of American Women: June 1985." The 1976 publication reports 1970 data. For 1970, the calculations assume that the number of children ever born is the same for currently married as for divorced, separated, and widowed women, an assumption which seems consistent with reported data for other years.

a. The percentage of children ever born by the marital status of the mother, reported here, differs slightly from the current living arrangements of children by marital status, reported in the text and in the appendix.

Figure 6.1 CHILDREN PER WHITE WOMAN

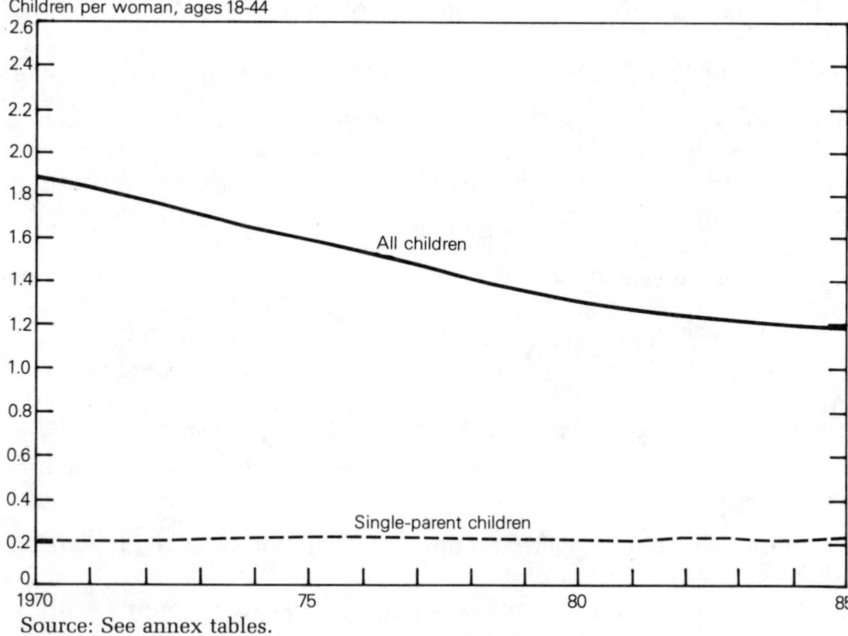

Source: See annex tables.

Note: All children and single-parent children.

Figure 6.2 CHILDREN PER BLACK WOMAN

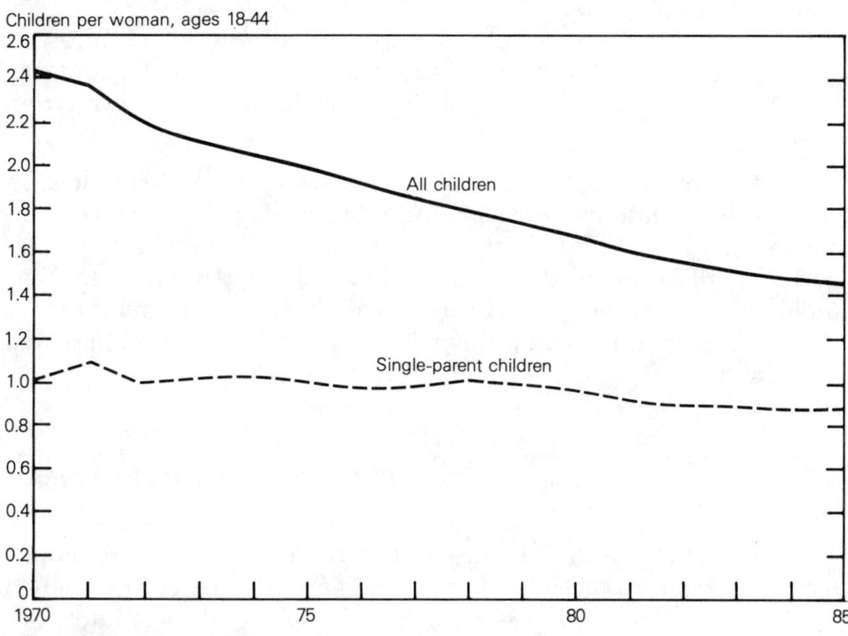

Source: See annex tables.

Note: All children and single-parent children.

□ An increase in the number of women who become single parents;
□ On balance, a roughly constant rate of single-parent children per woman.
□ A sharply declining rate of two-parent children per woman.

Thus, to explain the explosion in single-parent children, one needs to understand both the increase in the number of women who become single parents and the decrease in the number of children born to married mothers.

The Problem Revisited

Children in female-headed families are disadvantaged. These families are almost five times as likely to be poor as two-parent families.[6] In addition, children in female-headed families appear to be less likely to finish school and achieve academically.[7] As a result the three formulations of the problem stated at the beginning of this section are interrelated:

□ If you care about poverty among children, you have to be worried about single-parent families.
□ If you care about the *numbers* of children in single-parent families, because of their poverty and other indicators of disadvantage, you ought to be concerned about trends in family breakup and in births to unmarried mothers.
□ If, in addition, you care about the *proportions* of children in single-parent families, you should also be concerned about the decrease in marriage and the decrease in fertility among married women.

We believe that analyses of policies toward families should take all three formulations into account. If the trends in family formation and fertility reflect underlying societal attitudes about children, they may bode ill for the next generation. In arguing for attention to these problems, we are not necessarily claiming that government can or should do something about them. That is a separate topic, to which we now turn.

THE ROLE OF GOVERNMENT

After reviewing the trends on family structure and poverty among families, Senator Daniel P. Moynihan, in *Family and Nation*, called for a government response—for a "family policy" directed not only at alleviating poverty and disadvantage among children in single-parent families, but also at discouraging the formation of such troubled families.[8] The Reagan administration, in its family policy report, called for government support and encouragement of traditional two-parent families—although by policy instruments different from those Moynihan had in mind.[9]

In thinking about what "family policy" might be, we are unfortunately confronted head-on with the question of what such policy should try to accomplish. The trends just described make answering that question quite difficult. Should the government be in the business of actively discouraging out-of-wedlock teen pregnancy? A fair number of people, both liberals and conservatives, would presumably answer yes to the general question, even though they would almost certainly disagree about appropriate means for promoting the goal. But what about encouraging teen marriages: is that an appropriate role for government? Or encouraging marriage among nonteens? Or discouraging divorce? Or encouraging childbearing?

The Reagan administration's answer to these questions is that government ought to support traditional family values and behavior: life-long monogamous marriage; marital fertility, parental care of children and "lovingly packed lunch boxes."[10] Liberals, including ourselves, are somewhat more squeamish. Some take the timid position that government ought not to be in the business of directly encouraging undesirable behavior nor of discouraging traditionally valued choices to marry and have children. We argue for policies that invest in children in all types of families, on the ground that society has a legitimate interest in the future of the next generation.

Liberals are often reluctant to go much beyond those rather innocuous principles in their policy advocacy. In our analysis, however, we ask the more general question of what government policy *can* do: how government policy actions in the past have affected family structure and behavior and what future government actions might be effective in staying or reversing some of the trends. The next section of this chapter deals with direct and indirect government policies that affect families. In the final section we return to the question of what government policy ought to be.

EFFECTS OF GOVERNMENT POLICY ON FAMILY STRUCTURE

In considering the question of the effects of government policies on families, we look at five broad policy areas: laws on divorce, birth control, and abortion; welfare; teen pregnancy prevention programs; family supports, including day care and parental leave; and economic policy. These areas represent the range of policies that people seem to talk about the most, and they are in at least some respects politically controversial. Because substantial changes in current laws on divorce, birth control and abortion are not real options for political reasons, we devote less space to discussing them. The other four policy areas are currently topics of policy discussion and are likely to see serious change in the next decade.

In this section we focus on the effects of each of these government policies on family structure, particularly on marriage, fertility, and family breakup. A complete analysis of policy options would also look at the effects of the policies on the well-being of families and children independent of changes in family structure. In the next section we raise some of these larger questions of costs and potential benefits.

Divorce, Birth Control and Abortion

Since 1960, state laws regulating divorce, birth control, and abortion have been dramatically liberalized, often under mandates from the U.S. Supreme Court. By the late 1970s, nearly all states established "no fault" divorce procedures. In 1965, *Griswold v. Connecticut* ruled that state laws prohibiting the sale of contraceptives to married couples were unconstitutional; that ruling was extended to unmarried persons in 1972. In 1973, *Roe v. Wade* overturned state prohibitions on abortion during the first trimester.

These events, although important in their own right, were arbitrary markers of deeper changes in attitudes and practices. States had been gradually becoming more liberal in their application of old fault-based divorce laws even before they went to no-fault. Few states by 1965 actually prohibited (or enforced their prohibitions on) contraceptive sales. Changes in laws regulating birth control accompanied more important changes in technology, specifically, the availability of birth control pills. Many states had liberalized their abortion laws before 1973.

Whatever the direction of causality, however, dramatic changes in behavior occurred simultaneously with the legal changes. Divorce increased with the liberalization of divorce laws, in many cases because of the substitution of formal divorce for informal separation or desertion, in other cases because of a shift in the location of divorce from one place (like Nevada or Mexico) to another, but almost certainly because marital breakup was truly increasing. At least some of the fertility decline of the 1960s must be due to the increased availability of birth control.[11] And abortion clearly played a large part in keeping teen births relatively constant while teen pregnancies rose.[12]

What would have happened if the laws had not changed? In the cases of divorce and birth control, we believe that the legal changes mostly followed fundamental changes in attitudes and practices. As Max Rheinstein put it at the time, "the change in social climate is finding expression in a new rise in the rates of divorce, indicating a rise in marriage breakdown, as well as in a set of laws and legislative drafts."[13] Had the laws on birth control not been changed, they probably would have been enforced with about the same vigor that characterizes state laws prohibiting adultery and homosexuality. Indeed, family size has also declined for Catholics, for whom the "laws" concerning birth control have not changed.

About abortion, we are less sure. When abortion was illegal, it was not counted, and so it is impossible to plot a real trend over time. Nonetheless, it seems likely that much of the documented increase in abortions after Roe was real. Legalization of abortion substantially reduced its risks and costs, especially compared with the risks and costs of the alternatives. The change in the law had an important effect on abortions and birthrates.[14]

An equally interesting question is the extent to which changes in the law in these areas led or contributed to the general changes in attitudes toward sex and marriage that characterized the 1960s and 1970s. Similarly, one can ask whether the rhetoric of the President Reagan and other political leaders in support of traditional family values contributed to a change in the other direction in the 1980s. We have neither data nor insights on the issue, but leave it as an open question. In policy terms, however, we believe that attempts to reverse current laws would almost surely fail, because such action does not seem to be broadly supported by public opinion. Seven years of effort by conservatives, with the blessing if not the active participation of the Reagan administration, brought about little change even at the height of Reagan's popularity.[15] We turn, therefore, to those policy suggestions that are more likely to become law.

Welfare and the Family

The past few years have seen considerable discussion of the actual or potential effects of the welfare system on family structure. Charles

Murray has made the most powerful presentation of the argument that generous welfare systems have destructive effects on family structure.[16] He argued that welfare makes it possible for fathers to avoid financial responsibility for their children and for mothers to support themselves independent of marriage. Welfare rewards child-bearing outside marriage and family breakup. It also rewards, in the form of higher benefits, having additional children while unmarried. Support for this argument, in Murray's view, comes from the fact that a number of indicators of family structure deteriorated during the 1970s, the same period when spending on social welfare programs expanded dramatically. He concluded that abolishing the welfare system would be the most effective policy for strengthening families and reducing poverty.

A number of empirical and logical critiques of Murray's work have appeared, and we cannot review them all here.[17] Several empirical findings seriously challenge Murray's conclusions. One is based on the facts about changes in the welfare system during the 1970s. Murray argued that the welfare system expanded substantially during the same period that family structure was deteriorating. In fact, the real value of welfare benefits expanded only during the first half of the 1970s and then contracted because benefit levels did not keep pace with inflation. Between 1975 and 1985 the real value of the maximum welfare payment in the median state dropped 33 percent.[18] In addition, administrative procedures for qualifying for and receiving welfare loosened during the early 1970s and then tightened considerably as a result of pressure for quality control and error reduction. These administrative changes and benefit reductions resulted in basically stable caseloads in Aid to Families with Dependent Children (AFDC) between 1975 and 1985, despite growth in the number of poor female-headed families. This pattern of an expanding and then contracting welfare system does not correspond to the important trends in family structure during the period, when the proportion of families with children headed by women grew consistently and steadily.

A second challenge to Murray's argument comes from an examination of state-to-state differences in welfare benefit levels and their relationships to family structure. Welfare benefit levels vary considerably among states; in 1980, for example, maximum AFDC benefits for a family of four ranged from $120 a month in Mississippi to more than $500 a month in California. Food stamps reduce the differentials somewhat, but the range is still substantial. If welfare had important effects on family structure, one would expect to see lower rates of family breakup, births to unmarried mothers and female headship in the low-benefit states. The data, however, show no such relationship. In fact, many of the states with the lowest benefits have the highest fraction of children living in female-headed families.[19]

A more sophisticated analysis of state-to-state differences, controlling for a variety of measured and unmeasured characteristics and comparing women likely to receive AFDC with those who were not, was reported by Ellwood and Bane in 1985. They found small effects of AFDC benefit levels on divorce and separation rates, and no discernible effects on rates of births to unmarried mothers. They did, however, find that single mothers in states with higher benefits were more likely than those in low-benefit states to live alone rather than in a parent's household. The combination of these effects led them to conclude that "the number of single mothers would increase by perhaps 5 percent in response to a $100 benefit increase," which would be a huge benefit increase in any state.[20] Some of the increase in single-parent households might be positive for the families concerned, allowing them to escape dangerous or conflict-filled situations. The increase surely does not seem large enough to warrant radical dismembering of the welfare system.

A third challenge to Murray's argument is that, as mentioned, a principal cause of the increase of the proportion of children in female-headed families has been the decrease in the fertility of married women. AFDC surely cannot be held accountable for this behavior by nonrecipients.

This evidence, and other evidence presented by Murray's critics, strikes many people as unconvincing. How, they ask, can the availability of welfare not lead to an increase in single-parent families? Surely, goes this argument, if no welfare benefits were available to single-parent families there would be fewer single-parent families? If there were no welfare, there would not be large numbers of single parents living alone supporting themselves on welfare. There would be, however, large numbers of independent, single-parent households supporting themselves through work and child support, as one sees today among many divorced women. Many single mothers would live with their own parents, and some single parents would send their children to live with other people, as is true today in many southern states with extremely low welfare benefits. We believe that behavior would change dramatically only if changes in welfare caused or were accompanied by dramatic changes in attitudes towards marriage and childbearing. It appears to us that much larger trends than welfare are driving family structure.

Teen Pregnancy Prevention Programs

Teen pregnancy prevention programs are a current favorite of both liberals and conservatives, although there is considerable disagreement about specific program choices. In any consideration of the effects of such programs on family structure, two questions need to be asked:

- If prevention policies were effective, how much difference would the resultant decrease in teen pregnancy make in overall family structure patterns?
- How effective are various programs likely to be in preventing teen pregnancy?

The amount of media and policy attention given to preventing teen pregnancy makes it important to understand the actual contribution that teen pregnancy has made to the growth of single motherhood over the past 15 years, and the extent to which the prevention of teen pregnancy could be expected to affect the incidence of single motherhood. Several questions are of interest: What proportion of single mothers are currently unmarried teens? What proportions of adult single mothers were teens when they had their first children? What do the trends in teen motherhood suggest about single parenthood in the future?

The contribution of current teen parents to single motherhood is actually surprisingly low. In 1985, about 82,000 women under age 20 headed households of themselves and their children, and an additional 236,000 women under age 20 lived with their children in their parents' households. This total of 318,000 accounted for only about *4 percent of all single parents* in 1985.[21]

An additional group of single mothers—estimates range from 25 to 40 percent—were teens when they had their first babies.[22] At first, this group seems to represent a large contribution of teen pregnancy to single motherhood. However, it may be more a reflection of the general marriage and fertility patterns of the 1950s and 1960s. Among women born between 1940 and 1960, between a quarter and a third of all women became mothers in their teens, and two-thirds of them were married. Thus, even if teen mothers were no more likely to become divorced or separated than mothers in general, between a quarter and a third of the single mothers from these cohorts would be expected to have been teen mothers.

The contribution of teen parenthood to single motherhood is likely to fall of its own accord. Figures 6.3 and 6.4 show the trends in married and unmarried teen motherhood. (The data are presented in the annex.) Overall, the trend in the proportion of women who become mothers by age 20 is down for whites and stable for blacks, to a current level of about a fifth of all women. More of them are unmarried, and thus more likely to become single mothers, but another trend suggests that the proportion becoming unmarried teen mothers is also starting to fall. When one looks at the most recent cohort for which data has been reported, women born between 1960 and 1964, the proportion who have become unmarried mothers by age 18 is lower than the proportions for earlier cohorts for both blacks and whites.

In any case, it is not at all clear that preventing every teen birth would have much effect on the number of single parents. It would obviously eliminate the four percent of single parents who are currently teen mothers. Women whose childbearing was delayed would be somewhat less likely than teen parents to end up as never-married, divorced, or separated mothers. The difference, however, would have only a small effect on the number of single-parent families.

None of this is to say that out-of-wedlock teen motherhood is not an important problem or that prevention programs should not be pursued. Such programs are not, however, likely to have important effects on the number of single mothers even if they are successful, and examples of successful programs are not easy to come by.

The National Academy of Sciences recently published a comprehensive review of teen pregnancy prevention programs.[23] The researchers described programs, falling into four categories: programs designed to increase knowledge about and to change attitudes toward teen pregnancy and parenthood, such as sex education and family communications programs; programs that increase access to contraception, such as contraceptive services and school-based clinics; programs to enhance life options, such as role modeling, mentoring, and youth employment programs; and programs that provide abortion services.

The researchers looked for evaluations of the programs, particularly those that examined effects on behavior. In general, they found little reliable research, but a few of its findings are of note. Contraception and abortion services can clearly reduce teen pregnancy and

Figure 6.3 MOTHERS BY AGE 20, WHITE

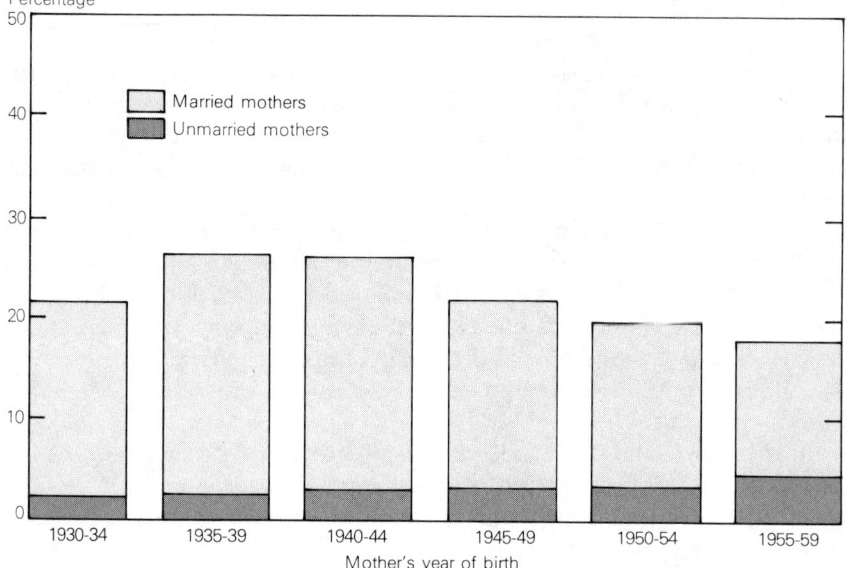

Source: See annex tables.

Figure 6.4 MOTHERS BY AGE 20, BLACK

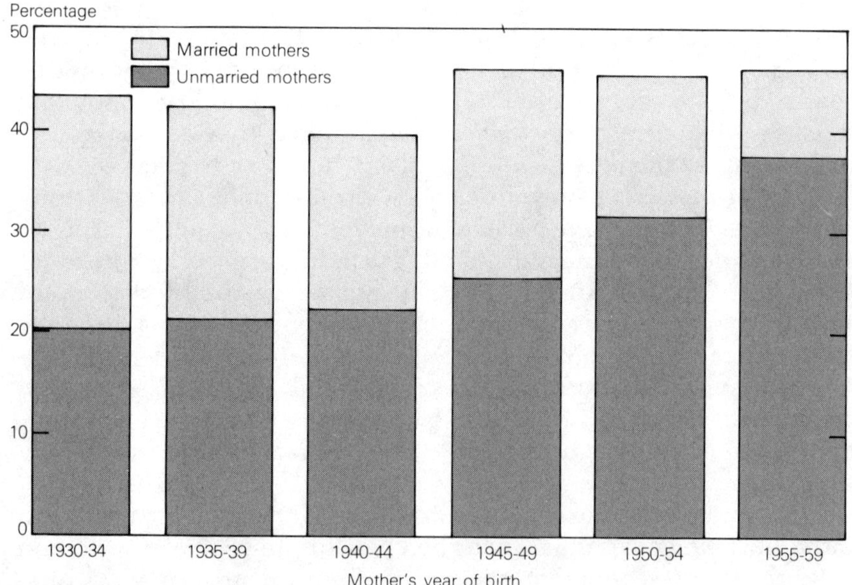

Source: See annex tables.

parenthood, without, according to several studies, increasing sexual activity. One study showed that increasing the family planning services available in given areas reduced pregnancy among 16- to 18-year-old black women. Two projects, one in Saint Paul and one in Baltimore, report positive but small results in reducing teen pregnancy from school-based clinics.

The effects of other types of programs are much less clear. Some programs designed to increase knowledge about pregnancy and parenting appeared to do so, but seemed to have little effect on attitudes or behavior. No evidence exists on the potential effectiveness of mass media campaigns. Little evidence exists from those programs that seek to deter teen pregnancy by enhancing life options of boys and girls. One youth employment program, the Job Corps, appears to have reduced teen parenthood, perhaps because it is a closely controlled residential program. One program aimed at improving self-esteem, the Teen Outreach program in Saint Louis, showed some success in lowering pregnancy rates. Several comprehensive community approaches to teen pregnancy prevention are currently being tried, but no data exist as yet on their success.

The evidence from these programs suggests that some approaches to teen pregnancy prevention can be modestly successful. The best evidence comes, however, from programs that focus on contraception, rather than from those that attempt a more comprehensive approach to life planning. At this point, more experimentation and demonstration are clearly needed, but the evidence to date suggests that one's expectations about program success should be modest. Combined with the data on the actual contribution of teen pregnancy to single motherhood, this suggests that programs aimed at preventing teen pregnancy are unlikely to make a large dent in the problem of the increase in single-parent families.

Family Supports

The most popular "family policy" proposals among liberals are for programs that support families in various ways, thus presumably encouraging family formation and discouraging family breakup. The proposed packages vary but can include parental leave, day care, and children's allowances.

The argument for such policies goes as follows. Raising children is very expensive. Most families need to have two employed adults to support themselves decently. Moreover, women have become increasingly committed to the labor force for noneconomic reasons as well. Dropping out of the labor force for long periods of time has thus become increasingly unattractive. Faced with these dilemmas, some couples decide not to have children at all or to have fewer children than they might once have had. In other families, economic and other stresses might increase the likelihood of family breakup. To make it easier for families to have and raise children under satisfactory conditions, the argument goes, employers and government should provide supports such as child care and parental leave.

European countries have had considerable experience with family policy along these lines. Many of the countries have much more extensive family programs than anything being proposed in the United States. Most of these countries provide medical care for all families; maternity leave both before and after the birth of a baby, usually at least partially compensated; child allowances, sometimes increasing with family size; and tax relief for families with children. Some countries have invested substantial national resources in cash benefits and services for families. At the time of Kamerman and Kahn's six country survey in the late 1970s, for example, the German Democratic Republic provided 100 days of paid parental leave, compensated at 100 percent of salary. Enough child care was provided to serve 50 percent of 0- to 3-year-olds and 85 percent of 3- to 6-year-olds. France had very generous child allowances, averaging about 28 percent of the average female wage. Hungary also provided substantial child allowances and a child care allowance for mothers who stayed home with their children; these two allowances equaled about 105 percent of the average female wage. Sweden provided 270 days of parental leave at 100 percent of salary, and substantial child care.[24]

Many of these programs were explicitly pronatalist in intent and design, responding to the decline in birthrates during the 1930s and losses in population from World War II. They thus provide interesting material for investigating whether family supports, in fact, seem to have any effects on family formation and fertility. The most extensive work has been done on fertility. The evidence is difficult to evaluate, because it is impossible to know what would have happened to fertility in the absence of family policies. Paul Demeny, however, summarized his review of the literature with the statement, "The modal finding is that the effects are nil or negligible."[25] One study of the effects of pronatalist policies in France attributed about 10 percent of the fertility increase during the late 1940s and 1950s to pronatalist policies.[26] This is about the maximum effect that can be found, however, and even this modest finding is subject to alternative interpretations.

Figure 6.5 TOTAL FERTILITY

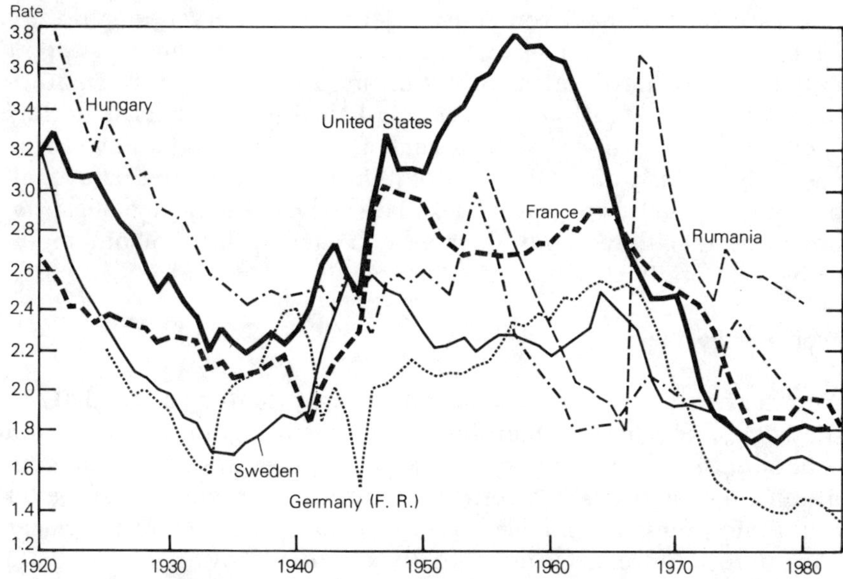

Source: Michael S. Teitlebaum and Jay M. Winter, *The Fear of Population Decline* (Orlando, Fla.: Academic Press, 1985), appendix A.

Perhaps the best evidence of the effects of family policies is the trends in birthrates in several countries with different family policies.[27] Figure 6.5 shows the trends in total fertility rates from 1920 to 1983 for six countries: the United States, France, Sweden, Romania, Hungary and the German Federal Republic. The trends are similar in many important respects. All decline sharply from 1920 to the mid-1930s, then most rise until the early or mid-1960s when they sharply decline. There are differences, too: the United States soars above the others during the baby boom, and Hungary and Romania start declining in the 1950s. By the early 1980s, five of the six countries were below replacement level. Yet the United States had almost no family supports, France had a long history of pronatalist policies, Sweden had extensive management of the labor market, and Germany and Hungary had different packages of family supports. Only Romania is clearly different, as a result of its draconian reversals on abortion, divorce, and birth control. Even that country, however, is moving toward the general trend after a brief interruption.

It is, of course, impossible to know what fertility would have looked like in European countries if their family policies had not been in effect. Most observers, however, interpret the data as Demeny did, as evidence that even substantial policy interventions do not have much impact on fertility. It is possible that family support policies might have larger effects on marriage and family stability than they do on fertility, but it is hard to argue logically why they should. Family support policies such as day care and parental leave may substantially affect the lives of families and children. They may be well justified in terms of these benefits. The evidence suggests, however, that they should not be expected to bring about much change in family structure or behavior.

Economic Policies

Another frequently mentioned set of policy proposals has to do with the economic status of families. The general argument flows from economic theory and demographic data concerning economic conditions and marriage and fertility. Other things being equal, better economic times are thought to be associated with more marriages and more children. "Can we really afford to have a child?" is a question that many couples ask. Thus, government economic policies are plausible candidates for having potentially powerful, though indirect, effects on family behavior.

If this argument is correct, two policy proposals would follow from it.

- □ A high-employment, high-productivity economy would create a more favorable environment for families, and thus would encourage family formation.
- □ Special, focused efforts may be needed to increase opportunities for young men in urban poverty areas with particularly low rates of family formation.

To judge the potential effects of government policy, not all relationships between economics and family structure are of interest. As fascinating as they might be from a research point of view, large-scale changes in economic organization, which might well have profound effects on family structure, are simply not policy alternatives. Nor, for that matter, are economic events on the scale of the Great Depression. If government officials had the power to choose between the Great Depression or the post-World War II boom, they would presumably choose good times regardless of the effect on family structure.

What is relevant from the perspective of policy is some degree of fine tuning of the economy. The level of unemployment, other things being equal, can be nudged in one direction or another by fiscal and monetary policies, as can the level of wages. Government can dampen cycles as they occur, or exacerbate them. Government may also be able to direct economic development efforts to particular groups or locations. In this section, then, we will investigate the effect that cyclical variations in economic activity have on family policy variables, on the presumption that we have at least partial control over such variations and their regional and demographic incidence.

There are several different schools of thought about how economics, and hence economic policy, might affect family structure. We discuss several hypotheses in the subsections that follow and then review the data and discuss the implications for policymakers.

NEW HOME ECONOMICS

One school of thought, associated with Gary Becker[28] and referred to as "the new home economics," argues that decisions to marry and have children can be treated as economic decisions.[29] Marriage is analyzed in the context of a favorable division of labor. Traditionally, women married men with higher earning capacity than themselves, given the prevailing wages for women, and men gained homemaking services that they themselves had little desire to perform and found expensive to pay for. Thus, marriage was a good deal for both men and women in the context of available wages and opportunities. As opportunities for women expanded in the labor market, marriage became less beneficial to women.

Fertility decisions are viewed like the purchase of any commodity. Children are evaluated in terms of the benefits they provide, such as ego enhancement, future income, and old-age security; the benefits are weighed against the costs, including the forgone wages of the caretaking parent, usually the mother. Increases in male income are thought to lead to more children. In contrast, as economic opportunities for women have improved, women have been drawn into the labor force, increasing the costs to them of having and rearing children.[30]

COHORT SIZE CYCLES

Frank S. Levy and Richard C. Michel have shown that economics and demographics have combined to restrict greatly the economic mobility of the baby boom cohorts relative to their parents.[31] Young men in the 1970s could no longer expect to see their earnings increase during the decade of their twenties, eroding the basis for the support of families.

Similarly, Richard Easterlin has argued that a cohort's willingness to marry and procreate will be proportional to the ratio of their perceived lifetime earnings potential and their prior expectations.[32] The parents of the baby boom generation, he argues, were a small cohort that formed low expectations while growing up during the Depression. After World War II, this small generation was in great demand in the economy, and therefore the ratio of their earnings potential to their expectations was very high. In contrast, the children of the baby boom were crowding one another from the start, in maternity wards, in schools, and finally in the labor market. Growing up during the optimistic 1950s and 1960s, they formed high expectations, but their actual earnings were low. The result was falling fertility and marriage rates.

■ *MARRIAGEABLE POOL HYPOTHESIS*

Wilson, Aponte, and Neckerman have argued that extremely high levels of unemployment and, to a lesser extent, high mortality among black males in inner city poor neighborhoods account in part for the very low marriage rates in such areas.[33] According to this hypothesis, women do not view unemployed (and not likely to be employed) males as "marriageable."

This notion is a straightforward application of economic concepts to extreme situations of the ghetto. Chronically unemployed black males with virtually no sources of regular income have little to offer females in inner city neighborhoods, who can at least get low-paying service jobs or AFDC. Thus, one could be skeptical of the economic model of marriage and still believe that, in the extreme conditions of inner-city neighborhoods, the model could have explanatory power.

■ *EMPIRICAL EVIDENCE*

Historical trends of marriage and fertility during the Great Depression and the postwar economic boom support the notion that the state of the economy affects family structure. Women who were ages 30 to 34 in 1940 were of typical marrying and childbearing age during the years of the Depression. In 1940, 80.4 percent of this age group were married. By 1950, when they were 40 to 44 years of age, they had had 2,170 children per 1000 women, a sharp decline from the 2,446 children per 1000 women of the cohort 10 years their senior.

The postwar years showed much higher rates. In 1960, 88.7 percent of 30 to 34 year olds were married. By age 40 to 44, this cohort had 2,952 children per 1000 women. The high rates in 1950 and 1960 reflect a greater tendency to marry during the 1940s and 1950s reflecting, at least in part, the economic boom of the postwar years.

By 1980, only 78.2 percent of 30- to 34-year-old women had married. By 1985 at 35 to 39 years of age, that cohort of women had had only 2,003 children per 1000 women. This situation seems to reflect, at least in part, the economic turbulence of the period.[34]

Yet the general economic conditions over decades are not really policy options among which we can pick and choose. Instead, the argument for a profamily economic policy usually focuses on the business cycle: heating up the economy to produce more jobs at higher wages. To investigate whether we can expect short-run economic policies to have effects, we must see whether short-run fluctuations in the economy are reflected in marriage and fertility patterns.

MALE INCOME AND MARRIAGE RATES

Between 1970 and 1985, real median incomes for males generally fell, for both blacks and whites, after a long period of steady increases. Median income of all males over 14 with income peaked in 1973 for both blacks and whites. For whites, it then declined 20 percent in real terms, reaching its lowest point in 1982; for blacks the decline was 21 percent and the low point came in 1983.[35] Other economic indicators showed a similar pattern.[36]

At the same time that median income was falling, marriage rates and the percentage of men married and living with their spouses also fell. However, two facts are worth noting. First, the pattern does not hold up well before 1973. Indeed, marriage rates declined swiftly in the relatively good economic times of the late 1960s and early 1970s. After 1973, as the economy faltered, marriages continued to decline but at a somewhat slower rate.

The second fact to consider is that year-to-year variations around the general time trend are not closely correlated with economic conditions and marriage rates. The year-to-year variations in marriage rates do not seem to be correlated with the annual variations of the business cycle. Figures 6.6 and 6.7 show the two trends over time for whites and blacks, respectively. Furthermore, the upturn of median incomes in the late 1970s was not accompanied by an upturn in marriage rates, which fell very steeply during that period. The

Figure 6.6 MARRIAGE AND MEDIAN INCOME, WHITE MALES, AGES 25 TO 29

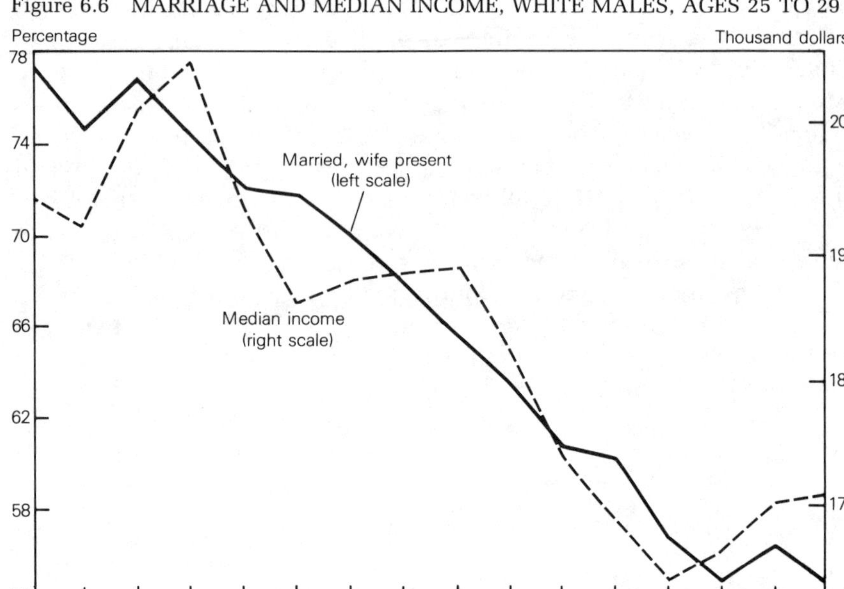

Source: See annex tables.

Figure 6.7 MARRIAGE AND MEDIAN INCOME, BLACK MALES, AGES 25 TO 29

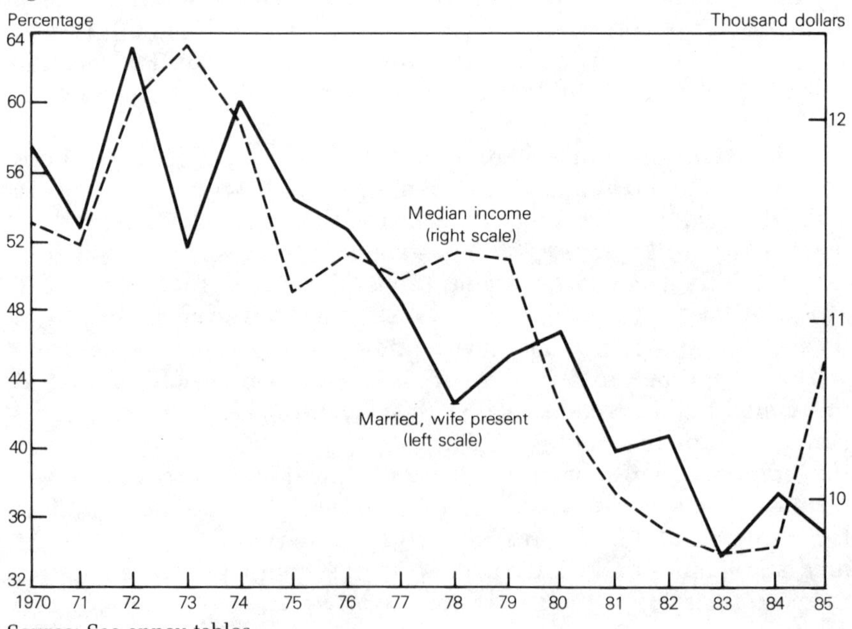

Source: See annex tables.

recent economic upturn also does not seem to be accompanied by an upturn in marriages, although it may be too soon to tell.

MALE INCOME AND FERTILITY RATES

Procyclical fertility, at least until the boom of the 1960s, was combined with plummeting birthrates, and was considered such a "regularity" that it was rarely questioned.[37] As with marriage rates, however, the connection between fertility and economics is much harder to find in more recent years or in annual changes in the economic data. The fertility rates for both whites and blacks fell during the 1970s as median income for men also fell. But the decline of birthrates started well before the decline in median incomes, and the sharpest declines occurred during before 1973, while incomes were still rising. Further more, cyclical variations of business are not at all reflected in the drifting pattern of birthrates after 1973.

These analyses suggest that policy-driven changes in male income will have little or no discernable effect on fertility. But before exploring that further, let us look at the other side of the argument, the economic opportunities for women.

FEMALE INCOME AND FAMILY BEHAVIOR

Several changes have increased the economic opportunities available to women. First, there have been direct government policies, notably, civil rights legislation and affirmative action. In addition, changes in the economy have reduced the number of blue-collar manufacturing jobs, which are predominantly held by men, and increased the number of jobs in service occupations, which are more often held by women.

Economic opportunities for women showed somewhat different trends from those for men during the decades of the 1970s. Women's labor force participation increased substantially and their median income actually increased even after correcting for inflation. For white women with income, median income increased 17 percent in real terms between 1970 and 1985; for blacks, the increase was 10 percent.[38] These increases in female median income were driven both by increases in hours and employment and increases in wages.

The general pattern suggests that increasing opportunities for women were accompanied by decreasing marriage and fertility. Several detailed econometric studies lend further support to the argument. Butz and Ward, for example, argue that "the remarkable postwar growth in employment of women of child-bearing age may have been sufficient to weaken and then reverse the longstanding positive association between business cycles and fertility."[39] Using a model that incorporates women's wages as the opportunity cost of fertility, they are able to predict the sharp declines of the 1960s and the leveling off of the mid-1970s using data from 1948 to 1956, the latter year being one year before the peak of the baby boom. Another study indicates, however, that annual changes in women's earnings appear to have more of an effect on the timing of births than on eventual family size.[40]

Once again, however, the relationship is based on long-term changes in women's labor force behavior and not specifically related to year-to-year swings in the business cycle. Female median income fell a fair amount in the late 1970s while neither marriage nor fertility rose. Sharp recent increases in female income are not reflected in sharply decreasing marriage or fertility rates.

Perhaps more important, the major change in women's labor force behavior was a far more fundamental shift than could have been either caused or prevented by any fiscal or monetary policy. The historic change was driven by, and was a part of, the general change in the attitudes of our society toward women and in the attitudes of women towards the activities from which they could derive satisfaction. It is beyond the ability of economic planners to put the genie back into the bottle. Furthermore, few people would advocate the policy that is the logical implication of the Gary Becker type of models for encouraging marriage and fertility: increasing the differentials between male and female incomes.

Implications for Economic Policy Arguments

In analyzing the effects of economic policies on family structure, we are led to draw a sharp distinction between economic effects in general and the potential effects of economic policy tools. The logic and evidence for economic effects on marriage and fertility rates seem to work best when seen from a distance. We are aware of no evidence that indicates that more modest changes in wages and employment can make any noticeable change in the marriage and fertility trends.

The "jobs in the ghettos" argument may be another story but there does not seem to be much evidence to evaluate the proposal one way or another. Wilson finds small relationships between changes in marriage and changes in employment data by region.[41] Stronger relationships might show up in analyses of city-to-city data, which, as far as we know, have not been done. But for economic policies to substantially affect family structure in inner cities, two things would have to be true. First, improvements in the economic fortunes of young black men in the inner cities would have to contribute to a reduction in single-parent families in the black community. Second, geographically targeted government economic development policies would have to be able to bring about such changes in the fortunes of young black men. There are certainly reasons to doubt both of these propositions. First, as already noted, the rate of family formation has been significantly lower among blacks than among whites since World War II.[42] This situation has persisted with little change through good times and bad, through times of black progress and black setbacks. Second, employment and training programs for hard-core unemployed, even the best of them, show only modest effects on the earnings potential and employment of their clients.[43]

We are inclined to be skeptical about economic policy as a means to reverse unfavorable family structure developments. There are good reasons to pursue higher employment levels and economic development in poor neighborhoods, and we support such initiatives, hold little hope that such policies can contribute significantly to changing trends in the family structure.

THE POLICY DILEMMA

The question we have been addressing thus far is whether government policy has had or could have direct, important effects on family structure: marriage, fertility, divorce, and separation. The answer seems to be no, at least for such policies as welfare and family supports. Even short-term economic policies do not hold much promise for changing trends in family structure. Both conservatives and liberals should find this analysis, if they believe it, troubling. Direct government policy is neither the problem nor the solution, at least in terms of "causing" or "preventing" marital breakup and unmarried parenthood.

This conclusion does not imply that policy for families is of no importance or should not be pursued. Preventing family breakup is only one of several reasonable goals; improving the well being of families and the general environment supporting families also is important.

Government policies have failed to achieve these goals. The overall pattern of changes that we observe suggests a generally unsupportive environment for families and children:

- Although poverty is more prevalent among female-headed families, 3.4 million married-couple or male-headed families were in poverty in 1986. Of these, the householder in 2.1 million families was in the labor force, suggesting that even intact families can suffer economically.[44]
- Declining marriage rates and fertility rates, which since 1971 have been below replacement level, suggest a society that is not organized around or concerned with families and children.
- At the same time, the increasing proportions of women with children who have never married or whose marriages have broken up suggests a climate in which it is difficult to hold families together.

Policy discussion has generally focused only on the problems of female-headed households and households on public assistance, tending to ignore the problems of intact families and working poor families. Yet, as we argued earlier, the rise in the proportion of children in female-headed families has at least as much to do with declining fertility of married women as with the proportion of mothers who go it alone. If government policy is going to contribute to an environment that supports families and values children, it must deal with the problems of both types of families.

Our hunch is that the real force behind family change has been a profound change in people's attitudes about marriage and children. The traditional moral imperative to "increase and multiply" has lost its force as both men and women have looked for satisfaction in other areas of life. Technology has enabled women to control fertility, and often difficult economic conditions have made it seem more important to do so. Living arrangements and sexual orientations that would have been unthinkable a generation ago have been accepted as part of the freedom and diversity that characterize contemporary America. If it is true that profound changes in social attitudes, interacting perhaps with general economic conditions, have shaped family behavior, it is not surprising that discrete policy decisions have had little impact.

Our findings do not, however, lead us to advocate a policy of "benign neglect" toward trends in family structure. Rather, we think the goal of public policy in this area should be to shape a social and economic climate that values children and supports family life. Public policy should in our opinion attempt to reflect and reinforce those values and structures in American society that care for and invest in children. As part of this goal, policymakers might pay particular attention to the problems of children in poverty. Such attention might bring about small shifts in attitudes and behavior and might, at the very least, improve the conditions for some of the most disadvantaged families and children.

What might be the elements of such policy? Leadership and rhetoric are part: celebration by public and political leaders of American families and their children. (This is likely to be more effective if it is praise for ordinary families rather than hand-wringing about families in difficulty.) Another part is almost certainly the creation and maintenance of an economic climate in which families can earn adequate income through work. Other possibilities include programs and policies that invest in children, based on the societal interest in nurturing and educating the next generation: education, including preschool education; health care for children; child support enforcement; child care and parental leave; and welfare reforms focused on self-sufficiency and investment in children. Proposals in all these areas have been more or less seriously discussed; they represent an attempt to increase the public response to the problems of families and children.

Policy Trade-offs

Unfortunately, not every policy that has good family goals is necessarily a good idea. In examining policies that purport to support families, one should ask about several issues:

□ Does the program contribute to the well being of families and children, especially disadvantaged children?
□ What impact does the program have on the perceived value of children and family life? What, if anything, does it contribute to the evolution of social attitudes?
□ How are these effects balanced against other, "unintended" effects of the program on other population groups, the economy, and so on?
□ How are these effects balanced against alternative uses of the resources that would be required?

This kind of policy analysis requires detailed specification of proposals; it is not a trivial exercise. All we can do in this chapter is look in a rather cursory way at some of the proposals that can be described as supports for families and raise some of the questions that need to be asked. Two examples are parental leave—for example, a proposal requiring employers to provide paid parental leave—and child care—for example, providing government subsidized child care to low-income families and making it available on a sliding fee scale to other families. As will become apparent the answers to the questions we raise depend in many cases on specific program details; some program designs are much more congruent than others with overall goals. We cannot consider program variants in any detail, but will simply try to indicate general considerations.

One question that needs to be asked about family support programs such as parental leave and child care is whether they would contribute, financially and symbolically, to a supportive environment for families and children. Do they appropriately convey the concern of the society for the well-being of children and their families? What message do they send? There may be two. One is of general support for families and children; the other is of special attention to working families, those with a single parent who works or those with two employed parents.

The dual nature of the message raises an interesting issue. The minority of families with two full-year, full-time workers tends to be better off than families with a single earner. Moreover, some American families do not believe that full-time work by mothers of young children is appropriate, although the proportion of mothers who work full time has certainly been increasing rapidly and attitudes toward mothers' employment have been changing. How strongly should government policy support one kind of family over others, and is it appropriate in a pluralistic society to throw the weight and money of government behind certain work patterns? These conflicting views must be dealt with as program details are worked out, and the issue will probably be resolved in the political arena.

A second issue concerns whom the programs are most likely to help and whom, if anyone, they hurt. Both parental leave and child care programs involve substantial subsidies to the people who participate in them. Not all families with children, however, will be eligible for or choose to use the programs. The question is, therefore, who will participate in the programs and benefit from the subsidies, and who will pay for them. Part of the answer to this question comes from the work patterns of families; as noted earlier, employed single parents and families in which both parents are employed are most likely to benefit. This is obviously true of parental leave policies, which would be likely to be of most benefit to full-time working parents in well-established careers and industries.

Who would benefit from child care subsidies depends partly on whether subsidies were limited to families in which the parents worked a certain number of hours. Family preferences about child care arrangements also are relevant. Many families work split shifts; others use informal care. Of employed mothers whose youngest child was less than five years old, 31 percent had child care provided in their own home; 16 percent had care provided in another home by a relative; 22 percent had care in another home by a nonrelative; and 14 percent placed their children in a group care center.[45] Some studies suggest that these choices are based on preferences as well as on cost: many families appear to prefer to keep children out of formal group care, at least when they are younger than nursery-school age.[46]

Day care centers, as opposed to care by relatives, "family day care," or other informal arrangements, are used more often by higher-income families.[47] This means that a program that subsidized only formal, licensed care might not meet the needs of many families. This problem could be solved by providing the subsidies to informal as well as formal care, perhaps even to care by relatives or parents themselves. This solution, however, raises questions about quality of care and perhaps conflicts with the child development goals that many people hold for child care programs. All these questions need to be dealt with in making program choices.

A third set of questions is about the effects of parental leave and child care programs on families and children. There is general scholarly agreement about the beneficial effects of preschool programs on children's development—a finding that was anticipated by dramatic increases in the number of middle-class families sending their 3- and 4-year-olds to nursery school. There is some debate about the effects of other types of day care, especially on younger children, although the bulk of the research appears to support the conclusion that day care is not harmful.[48] Given the lack of firm conclusions in child development research and given the varying preferences of families for their children, it is hard to argue for limiting subsidies to a fixed package of parental leave for a certain period of time plus day care of a given type. It seems more prudent to design policies that offer families a fair amount of choice about child care, perhaps including the ability to trade off day care and parental leave. This compromise would not, however, satisfy people who "know" that some programs are best for children.

A fourth set of questions is on indirect effects. Would requiring employers to provide parental leave disproportionately hurt certain kinds of employers, for example, small businesses? Are employers likely to start discriminating against parents? There will be some increases in the costs of doing business to the extent that the costs of parental leave and child care are put on employers. This situation might affect some industries disproportionately and in the long run might raise American production costs vis-à-vis foreign costs. There might, however, be some compensating productivity increases in the form of decreased turnover, absenteeism, or stress on the job. Possible indirect effects should be taken into account when programs are designed.

A final and important question concerns alternative uses of resources that would be devoted to child care or parental leave. Subsidized day care involves substantial costs, whatever the policy design. The program could, and presumably would, be set up in such a way that most of the subsidies would go to low- or middle-income families. It is therefore important to ask about trade-offs between spending money on day care for these families and spending it on other services, cash transfers, or tax reductions. It is interesting to note, for example, that formal day care for a welfare family with two children could easily cost $5,000 a year, whereas yearly AFDC benefits for a family of three in many states are lower than that amount. Subsidized day care may have substantial long-term benefits in helping families achieve or maintain financial self-sufficiency; nursery-school-like settings may represent important investments in children. Nonetheless, these trade-offs need to be weighed in assessing policies.

Policy Choices

Even a cursory analysis of family policies suggests the complexity of designing programs that would improve the general environment for families and enhance the specific well being of poor children. But although the design issues may be complicated, the general principles are not beyond reach. We are not particularly confident that any set of government policies can turn around trends in family structure. We believe, however, that government policies can make it easier to form and support families, can reinforce the society's care and concern for children and the families that raise them, and can alleviate some of the ills of disadvantaged families.

TRENDS IN FAMILY STRUCTURE AND GOVERNMENT POLICY

Trends in family structure in the United States and in many other countries have been changing dramatically. Adults now have many fewer children, both in and out of wedlock. A greater proportion of families with children are now headed by only one parent, so that more of our children are raised in a household with only one wage-earner. Small and inadequate child support payments from the absent parent have combined with the low earning power of the custodial parents, mostly women, to increase poverty among children. Many analysts are rightly concerned that increasing poverty among children may contribute to greater social problems and a less productive labor force in the years ahead.

We have investigated the role that government policies have had or could have on changes in family structure. There are two main reasons for being concerned with government's role. First, a number of conservative analysts have alleged that government policies have caused or at least contributed to the changes. Second, both conservatives and liberals at this point are urging that government react to the changes in family structure by revising current policies or enacting new policies, although they have very different policy changes in mind.

To determine what role government policies have had, and thus what role they could have, in altering basic trends in marriage and fertility, we have investigated several different policy areas: divorce, birth control, and abortion; welfare; teen pregnancy prevention; family supports; and short-term economic policies. In each area, we found reason to believe that government policies did not contribute substantially to the relevant family structure trends. More important, we found little reason to believe that changes in existing policies or new policies could reverse the declines in marriage and fertility.

Our position, then, is that no government policies that are feasible within the American political context could appreciably change American family structure. In particular, no government policy will reverse the increase in the proportion of children in female-headed families. Thus we favor attacking the problem of poverty among children directly, through policies that support the families in which poor children live. Second, we support policies that send appropriate signals about society's concern for children. In other words, we believe that an important consideration for evaluating social policies is whether they will contribute to enhancing the status and dignity of families having and raising children. If government policies are going to have any impact at all on family structure, it will be through an indirect process of providing a supportive environment for bearing and raising children within families.

We cannot demonstrate that such an effect would occur, but in any case we believe it is appropriate for government to show concern for the next generation. By fighting poverty among children and supporting families, government will be making important long-term investments in our nation's future. These investments must be carefully evaluated in terms of their direct effects, symbolic value, and indirect effects, but we must be careful not to ignore the long-term benefits of such policies because they are intangible or hard to value. Shaping an economic and social climate that values and rewards families and their children will not be easy or cheap, and it is likely to generate controversy, but we believe it is one of the most important tasks facing the nation in the next decade.

Notes

1. Among the books that articulate these versions of the problem are Marian Wright Edelman, *Families in Peril* (Cambridge, Mass.: Harvard University Press, 1986); Daniel Patrick Moynihan, *Family and Nation* (New York: Harcourt Brace Jovanovich, 1986); and Ben Wattenberg, *The Birth Dearth* (New York: Pharos Books, 1987).

2. U.S. Bureau of the Census, *Current Population Reports*, "Marital Status and Living Arrangements" (March 1985 and March 1970), table 4.

3. Sandra Hofferth, "Updating Children's Life Course," *Journal of Marriage and Family* 47 (1985): 93–116.

4. Among whites, the proportion almost doubled, with the biggest growth coming from marital disruption. By 1985, about 12.6 percent of white women ages 18 to 44 were single mothers. Among blacks in the same age group, the proportion of women who were single mothers increased by about 50 percent, to 44.9 percent of black women. Among blacks, the largest growth occurred among never-married mothers.

5. This idea comes from David Ellwood, who looked at total births to unmarried mothers standardized by total women in chapter 3 of *Poor Support: Poverty and the American Family* (New York: Basic Books, 1988).

6. U.S. Bureau of the Census, *Current Population Reports*, "Money Income and Poverty Status of Families and Persons in the United States: 1985," Washington, D.C., 1986.

7. For a review of some of this literature and an excellent general discussion of single-parent families, see Irwin Garfinkel and Sara S. McLanahan *Single Mothers and their Children* (Washington D.C.: Urban Institute Press, 1986).

8. Moynihan, *Family and Nation.*

9. Gary L. Bauer, *The Family: Preserving America's Future,* Report of the Working Group on the Family (Washington, DC: U.S. Department of Education, Office of the Undersecretary, November 1986).

10. Ibid.

11. In the 1960s fertility fell to levels common before World War II, before the wider availability of birth control or the invention of the Pill.

12. Studies on the relationship between abortion and teen pregnancy are reviewed in National Research Council, *Risking the Future* (Washington D.C.: National Academy Press, 1987).

13. *Marriage Stability, Divorce, and the Law* (Chicago: University of Chicago Press, 1972), 311.

14. An interesting natural experiment on the effects of reversing these policies—that is dramatically tightening laws on abortion, contraception, and divorce—occurred in Romania in the late 1960s. The result was a huge increase in the birthrate the year after the laws were changed, followed by a decline in subsequent years, but to a slightly higher level of births than had characterized the immediate prereform period. These data are reported inseveral sources, including C. Alison McIntosh, *Population Policy in Western Europe* (Armonk N.Y.: M.E. Sharpe, Inc., 1983).

15. Indeed, it was Robert Bork's position on the right-to-privacy decision in *Griswold v. Connecticut* that began to erode support among Republican senators for his nomination to the Supreme Court.

16. *Losing Ground* (New York: Basic Books, 1984).

17. See, for example, Christopher Jencks, "How Poor Are the Poor?" *New York Review of Books* (May 9, 1985), 41; Institute for Research on Poverty, *Losing Ground: A Critique,* Special Report No. 38, August 1985, with several articles; and David T. Ellwood and Lawrence Summers, "Is Welfare the Answer or the Problem? in Sheldon H. Danziger and Daniel H. Weinberg, eds., *Fighting Poverty: What Works and What Doesn't* (Cambridge, Mass.: Harvard University Press, 1986).

18. This figure and other facts about the welfare system come from an excellent compilation, U.S. Congress, House Ways and Means Committee, *Background Material on Programs Under the Jurisdiction of the Committee on Ways and Means* (Washington, D.C., 1987).

19. Ellwood and Bane, in a 1984 summary of their work on the relationship of AFDC benefits and family structure, write that even controlling for "a host of state characteristics, from income and education levels, to racial composition, to the religious composition of the state . . . in virtually every straightforward cross-sectional regression . . . the coefficient on welfare had the wrong sign." David T. Ellwood and Mary Jo Bane, "Family Structure and Living Arrangements Research: Summary of Findings," prepared for the U.S. Department of Health and Human Services, March 1984.

20. David T. Ellwood and Mary Jo Bane, "The Impact of AFDC on Family Structure and Living Arrangements," in Ronald G. Ehrenberg, ed., *Research in Labor Economics* 7 (Greenwich, Conn.: JAI Press, 1985). New estimates by Laurie Bassi are larger, but not large enough to justify draconian budget cuts in the pursuit of reducing single parentage. Laurie J. Bassi, *Family Structure and Poverty Among Women and Children: What Accounts for the Change?* Unpublished paper, Georgetown University, June 1987.

21. Calculated from *Current Population Reports*, P-20, no. 410, "Marital Status and Living Arrangements: March 1985," Washington, D.C., 1976. If this seems counterintuitive, remember that there were about 250,000 births to unmarried teens annually in the early 1980s. The vast majority of these were to 18- and 19-year-olds; thus the average length of time an unmarried teen parent stays in that status could easily be less than two years.

22. David Ellwood reports an estimate of 25 to 30 percent in his forthcoming book. The larger number comes from estimates of the proportions of women on welfare who had their first children as teens. See National Research Council *Risking the Future* (Washington, D.C.: National Academy Press, 1987).

23. NRC, *Risking the Future*.

24. The policies of five European countries plus the United States are described in detail in Sheila B. Kamerman and Alfred J. Kahn, *Child Care, Family Benefits and Working Parents* (New York: Columbia University Press, 1981). McIntosh, *Population Policy in Western Europe*, also describes these policies.

25. Paul Demeny, "Pronatalist Policies in Low Fertility Countries: Patterns, Performance and Prospects," *Population and Development Review* (supplement to vol. 12, 1986), 350.

26. Gerard Calot and Jacqueline Hecht, "The Control of Fertility Trends," in Council of Europe, *Population Decline in Europe* (London: Edward Arnold, 1978), cited in Demeny, "Pronatalist Policies."

27. Our data are drawn from Michael S. Teitelbaum and Jay M. Winter, *The Fear of Population Decline* (Orlando, Fla.: Academic Press, 1985), appendix A.

28. See Gary S. Becker, *A Treatise on the Family* (Cambridge, Mass.: Harvard University Press, 1981), especially chs. 2 and 5.

29. Treating such decisions as economic decisions does not rule out such factors as love. In a 1974 article, Becker writes:

At an abstract level, love and other emotional attachments, such as sexual activity or frequent close contact with a particular person, can be considered particular nonmarketable household commodities. . . . That is, if an important set of commodities produced by households results from "love," the sorting of mates that maximizes total commodity output over all marriages is partly determined by the sorting that maximizes the output of these commodities.

"A Theory of Marriage," in Theodore W. Schultz, ed., *Economics of the Family* (Chicago: University of Chicago Press, 1974), 327.

30. See, for example, Gary S. Becker, Elizabeth M. Landes, and Robert T. Michael, "An Economic Analysis of Marital Instability," *Journal of Political Economy* 85, no. 6 (1977); and Becker, *A Treatise on the Family*.

31. "An Economic Bust for the Baby Boom," *Challenge* (March/April 1986): 33–39.

32. Richard A. Easterlin, *Birth and Fortune: The Impact of Numbers on Personal Welfare* (New York: Basic Books, 1980).

33. William Julius Wilson, *The Truly Disadvantaged* (Chicago: University of Chicago Press, 1987), chapter 3 (with Kathryn Neckerman), "Poverty and Family Structure," and chapter 4 (with Robert Aponte and Kathryn Neckerman), "Joblessness versus Welfare Effects."

34. Marriage data are from *Historical Statistics of the United States*, vol. I, Series A160–170, pp. 20–21. Fertility data are from published reports of the 1940 and 1950 censuses and from the 1980 and 1985 *Current Population Reports* fertility series.

35. Council of Economic Advisers, *Economic Report of the President*, 1987, Washington, D.C., table B-29.

36. Unemployment was higher in both peaks and valleys of successive business cycles. We have chosen to focus on median income for men with income, because the data are readily available and incorporate both changes in earnings and changes in hours and employment.

37. William P. Butz and Michael P. Ward, "The Emergence of Countercyclical U.S. Fertility," in *American Economic Review* 69, no. 3 (June 1979), 318.

38. CEA *Economic Report of the President*, 1987.

39. Butz and Ward, "Countercyclical U.S. Fertility," p. 321.

40. Belton M. Fleisher and George F. Rhodes, Jr., "Fertility, Women's Wage Rates, and Labor Supply," *American Economic Review* 69, no. 1, 21.

41. William Julius Wilson, *The Truly Disadvantaged: The Inner City, the Underclass, and Public Policy* (Chicago: University of Chicago Press, 1987), ch. 3.

42. Andrew J. Cherlin, *Marriage, Divorce, Remarriage* (Cambridge, Mass.: Harvard Univeristy Press, 1981), 95.

43. Judith Gueron, *Work Initiatives for Welfare Recipients* (New York: Manpower Demonstration Research Corporation, 1986). See also Daniel Friedlander and David Long, *A Study of Performance Measures and Subgroup Impacts in Three Welfare Programs* (New York: Manpower Demonstration Research Corporation, 1987).

44. U.S. Census, *Money Income and Poverty: 1985*, table 19.

45. U.S. Bureau of the Census, Current Population Reports, *Who's Minding the Kids?* Household Economic Studies, Series P-70, no.9.

46. Laura Lein, *Families Without Villians* (Lexington, Mass.: Lexington Books, 1984).

47. Employed women with family incomes of less than $15,000 had children in nursery schools or day care centers 12 percent of the time; employed women with family incomes over $25,000 used such care 17 percent of the time. U.S. Bureau of the Census, *Current Population Reports*, "Child Care Arrangements of Working Mothers: June 1982," Special Studies Series P-23, no. 129, table 2.

48. A recent review of the literature finds that few recent studies show negative effects. See Stella Chess and Alexander Thomas, *Know Your Child: An Authoritative Guide for Today's Parents* (New York: Basic Books, 1987), pp. 360–63.

Table 6A.1 TOTAL CHILDREN AND CHILDREN NOT LIVING WITH BOTH PARENTS

	Number of women ages 18 to 44		Children not living with both parents				Total number of children per woman		Number of children not living with both parents per woman	
			Number		Percentage					
Year	White	Black	White	Black	White	Black	White	Black	White	Black
1970	31,784	4,113	6,502	4,169	10.9	41.8	1.8	2.42	0.20	1.017
1971	32,306	4,233	7,173	4,623	12.1	45.9	1.8	2.38	0.22	1.094
1972	32,975	4,402	7,052	4,382	12.1	45.7	1.7	2.18	0.21	1.007
1973	33,518	4,525	7,248	4,619	12.6	48.5	1.7	2.10	0.22	1.021
1974	34,183	4,654	7,527	4,781	13.3	50.2	1.6	2.05	0.22	1.035
1975	34,869	4,780	8,085	4,790	14.6	50.6	1.5	1.98	0.23	1.009
1976	35,600	4,933	8,087	4,773	14.9	50.4	1.5	1.92	0.23	0.973
1977	35,822	5,091	8,105	4,990	15.2	53.2	1.4	1.84	0.23	0.989
1978	37,142	5,236	8,522	5,300	16.2	56.4	1.4	1.79	0.23	1.011
1979	37,935	5,396	8,543	5,314	16.5	57.2	1.3	1.72	0.23	0.986
1980	38,788	5,562	8,804	5,373	17.3	57.8	1.3	1.67	0.23	0.971
1981	40,192	5,905	9,127	5,384	17.7	57.3	1.2	1.59	0.23	0.918
1982	41,007	6,075	9,801	5,399	19.2	57.6	1.2	1.54	0.24	0.895
1983	41,497	6,228	9,642	5,559	19.0	59.3	1.2	1.51	0.23	0.893
1984	42,215	6,404	9,611	5,530	19.0	59.0	1.2	1.46	0.23	0.860
1985	42,678	6,494	10,146	5,738	20.0	60.5	1.1	1.46	0.24	0.889

Source: Current Population Survey, *Marital Status and Living Arrangements*, Series P-20, March 1970 through March 1985.

Table 6A.2 MOTHERS BY AGE 18 AND AGE 20 (WHITE) (percentage)

Women born	1930–34	1935–39	1940–44	1945–49	1950–54	1955–59	1960–64
Mother by age 20	21.4	26.2	26.0	21.6	19.6	17.9	n.a.
Unmarried mother by age 20	2.2	2.4	2.9	3.2	3.5	4.6	n.a.
Married mother by age 20	19.2	23.8	23.1	18.4	16.1	13.3	n.a.
Mother by age 18	6.9	7.4	7.7	6.7	6.9	7.1	6.4
Unmarried mother by age 18	0.8	1.1	1.3	1.4	1.9	2.3	2.8
Married mother by age 18	6.1	6.3	6.4	5.3	5.0	4.8	3.6
Children born	**1947–52**	**1952–57**	**1957–62**	**1962–67**	**1967–72**	**1972–77**	**1977–82**
Percentage of first births to unmarried mother							
Age 15–17	12.0	15.1	16.7	20.2	28.0	32.8	43.1
Age 18–19	9.7	6.7	8.9	12.1	12.0	20.9	27.8

Source: Data on women are from Current Population Reports June Survey, June 1983. Percentage of births to unmarried women are from *Statistical Abstract: 1985*, table 96. Distribution of births calculated from *Statistical Abstract*, tables 82 and 94.

Table 6A.3 MOTHERS BY AGE 18 AND AGE 20 (BLACK) (percentage)

Women born	1930–34	1935–39	1940–44	1945–49	1950–54	1955–59	1960–64
Mother by age 20	43.2	42.3	39.4	45.9	45.4	46.0	n.a.
Unmarried mother by age 20	20.3	21.1	22.3	25.4	31.5	37.5	n.a.
Married mother by age 20	22.9	21.1	17.1	20.5	13.9	8.5	n.a.
Mother by age 18	20.8	23.4	19.4	20.7	24.0	26.4	16.9
Unmarried mother by age 18	11.4	13.3	13.1	14.6	19.2	23.6	15.8
Married mother by age 18	9.4	10.1	6.3	6.1	4.8	2.8	1.1
Children born	1947–52	1952–57	1957–62	1962–67	1967–72	1972–77	1977–82
Percentage of first births to unmarried mothers							
Age 15–17	54.9	57.0	67.6	70.6	80.1	89.3	93.4
Age 18–19	39.7	41.7	45.9	42.7	57.3	70.9	79.0

Source: See table 6A.2

Table 6A.4 DISTRIBUTION OF BIRTHS

	1960			1985		
	Number of births (thousand)	Percentage of all births	Births per 1,000 women age 18–44	Number of births (thousand)	Percentage of all births	Births per 1,000 women age 18–44
Births to						
Unmarried teens under age 20	91.7	2.2	2.54	267.8	7.4	4.97
Married teens under age 20	502.3	11.8	13.92	269.2	7.4	5.00
Unmarried, Non-teens	132.6	3.1	3.67	418.8	11.5	7.78
Married, Nonteens	3,531.4	82.9	97.86	2,673.2	73.7	49.65
Total births	4,258	100.0	118.00	3,629	100.0	67.40
Number of women	36,085	n.a.	n.a.	53,843	n.a.	n.a.

Source: See table 6A.2.

Table 6A.5 BASIC FAMILY STRUCTURE AND INCOME TRENDS
MARITAL STATUS: MARRIED, SPOUSE PRESENT

	Men					
	Whites			Blacks		
	Age group			Age group		
Year	20–24	25–29	30–34	20–24	25–29	30–34
1970	42.6	77.5	85.6	35.3	57.7	75.3
1971	42.8	74.6	82.1	26.2	52.8	69.2
1972	41.2	76.8	83.0	29.0	63.2	63.4
1973	40.9	74.4	85.1	29.8	51.8	70.2
1974	40.5	72.0	83.3	29.2	60.0	69.8
1975	37.8	71.8	82.7	30.5	54.4	62.7
1976	34.4	70.0	80.2	27.7	52.7	63.8
1977	33.6	67.9	80.0	23.0	48.4	64.3
1978	31.7	65.6	78.1	19.4	42.5	62.5
1979	30.4	63.5	75.2	18.4	45.3	56.6
1980	29.5	60.7	74.4	17.2	46.7	54.8
1981	28.4	60.3	72.5	17.1	39.8	53.4
1982	26.6	56.8	71.2	15.7	40.7	56.9
1983	25.5	54.9	70.6	11.3	33.8	53.5
1984	23.9	56.5	69.3	8.6	37.4	44.4
1985	22.8	54.9	68.6	11.2	35.2	42.8

	Women					
	Whites			Blacks		
	Age group			Age group		
Year	20–24	25–29	30–34	20–24	25–29	30–34
1970	58.0	82.5	86.5	42.6	59.7	61.3
1971	57.7	81.1	85.9	37.6	51.3	56.6
1972	58.2	79.8	85.4	37.8	53.1	54.7
1973	56.8	80.7	84.2	34.5	50.0	51.4
1974	55.5	77.7	83.3	36.2	48.9	55.3
1975	54.1	77.3	82.0	29.3	48.2	52.5
1976	51.3	75.8	81.6	30.3	44.6	51.7
1977	49.9	73.6	80.7	26.7	47.4	52.3
1978	47.6	71.9	78.5	20.9	41.2	48.5
1979	46.3	70.9	77.9	23.2	38.4	46.4
1980	45.0	68.8	76.2	23.5	38.5	45.1
1981	43.6	67.7	74.8	22.2	38.0	43.7
1982	41.7	65.6	73.7	22.3	39.7	44.8
1983	40.5	64.9	74.7	16.4	36.9	41.8
1984	39.5	64.9	72.2	16.8	32.2	44.4
1985	37.6	64.8	71.8	17.1	30.5	40.5

Source: Current Population Reports, *Marital Status and Living Arrangements*, Series P-20, table 1 (relevant years).

MEDIAN INCOME, ALL PERSONS WITH INCOME (1985 dollars)

Year	Whites		Blacks	
	Male	Female	Male	Female
1970	19,423	6,278	11,472	5,715
1971	19,223	6,502	11,353	5,698
1972	20,093	6,727	12,101	6,285
1973	20,463	6,834	12,377	6,168
1974	19,315	6,800	11,967	6,139
1975	18,589	6,836	11,113	6,210
1976	18,778	6,814	11,306	6,421
1977	18,823	7,103	11,170	6,133
1978	18,885	6,789	11,313	6,113
1979	18,237	6,511	11,289	5,925
1980	17,400	6,458	10,456	5,979
1981	16,910	6,528	10,055	5,799
1982	16,437	6,650	9,850	5,866
1983	16,654	7,037	9,739	6,013
1984	17,055	7,197	9,785	6,384
1985	17,111	7,357	10,768	6,277

Source: Council of Economic Advisers, *Economic Report of the President* (Washington, D.C., 1987), table B-29.

BIRTHS PER 1,000 WOMEN

Year	Ages 18 to 44			All races, by age group			
	All	Whites	Blacks	15–19	20–24	25–29	30–34
1960	118	113.2	153.5	89.1	258.1	197.4	112.7
1965	96.6	91.4	133.2	70.5	195.3	161.6	94.4
1970	87.9	84.1	115.4	68.3	167.8	145.1	73.3
1971	81.8	77.5	109.5	64.7	150.6	134.8	67.6
1972	73.4	69.2	100.3	62.0	131.0	118.7	60.2
1973	69.2	65.3	94.3	59.7	120.7	113.6	56.1
1974	68.4	64.7	90.8	58.1	119.0	113.3	54.4
1975	66.0	62.5	87.9	55.6	113.0	108.2	52.3
1976	65.8	62.2	87.2	53.5	112.1	108.8	54.5
1977	66.8	63.2	88.1	52.8	112.9	111.0	56.4
1978	65.5	61.7	86.7	51.5	109.9	108.5	57.8
1979	67.2	63.4	88.3	52.3	112.8	114.4	60.3
1980	68.4	64.7	88.1	53.0	115.1	112.9	61.9
1981	67.4	63.9	85.4	52.7	111.8	112.0	61.4
1982	67.3	63.9	84.1	52.9	111.3	111.0	64.2
1983	65.8	62.4	81.7	51.7	108.3	108.7	64.6
1984	65.4	62.2	81.4	50.9	107.3	108.3	66.5

Source: Current Population Reports, *Fertility of American Women*, Series P-20, table 4 (relevant years).

About the Authors

Mary Jo Bane is Professor of Public Policy and Director of the Center for Health and Human Resources Policy at the John F. Kennedy School of Government, Harvard University. Her publications include *Here to Stay: American Families in the Twentieth Century* (1976) and *The State and the Poor in the 1980's* (1984).

Andrew J. Cherlin is Professor of Sociology at The Johns Hopkins University. He has published extensively on the topic of the contemporary American family, including *Marriage, Divorce, Remarriage* (1981) and "The Family," in *Challenge to Leadership*, edited by Isabel V. Sawhill (1988).

Gretchen Condran, a demographer, is a research associate of the Population Study Center at the University of Pennsylvania. She is currently writing a book on the sources of mortality decline in 19th century Philadelphia, and is involved in a project to derive new model age patterns of mortality for the elderly.

Cynthia Fuchs Epstein is Professor of Sociology at the Graduate Center of the City University of New York and a Resident Scholar at the Russell Sage Foundation. Her publications include *Women in Law* (1981; paperback edition, 1983). She has just completed a book entitled *Deception Distinctions: Sex, Gender and the Social Order* (forthcoming).

Frank Furstenberg is Professor of Sociology and Research Associate in the Population Studies Center, University of Pennsylvania. His publications include *The New American Grandparent* with Andrew J. Cherlin (1986), and *Adolescence in Late Life* with J. Brooks-Gunn and S. Philip Morgan (1987).

Paul A. Jargowsky, a public policy analyst, coordinates several research projects for the Center for Health and Human Resources Policy at the John F. Kennedy School of Government, Harvard University. His publications include "A Democratic Framework for Poverty Policy," in Robert A. Levin, ed., *Democratic Blueprints: 40 National Leaders Chart America's Future*, with Mary Jo Bane (1988) and "Urban Poverty Areas: Basic Questions Concerning Growth, Prevalence and Dynamics," in Michael G.H. McGeary and Laurence E. Lynn, Jr., eds., *Urban Change and Poverty* (1988).

Carolyn C. Rogers, a demographer, is currently a research associate with Child Trends, a non-profit research organization in Washington, D.C. Formerly with the U.S. Bureau of the Census, she designed questionnaires and prepared reports on fertility, birth expectations, and child care for the June supplement to the Current Population Survey.

Nicholas Zill, a social psychologist, is Executive Director of Child Trends. He has written research papers on the effects of marital conflict and divorce on children, on children in stepfamilies, and on trends in the education of the handicapped.